CW01151543

Consumer Culture
Selected Essays

Consumer Culture
Selected Essays

Edited by Gjoko Muratovski

intellect Bristol, UK / Chicago, USA

First published in the UK in 2016 by
Intellect, The Mill, Parnall Road, Fishponds, Bristol, BS16 3JG, UK

First published in the USA in 2016 by
Intellect, The University of Chicago Press, 1427 E. 60th Street, Chicago, IL 60637, USA

Copyright © 2016 Intellect Ltd

All rights reserved. No part of this publication may be reproduced, stored in a retrieval system, or transmitted, in any form or by any means, electronic, mechanical, photocopying, recording, or otherwise, without written permission.

A catalogue record for this book is available from the British Library.

Cover designer: Gjoko Muratovski
Copy-editor: MPS Technologies
Production managers: Steve Harries and Mike Grimshaw
Typesetting: John Teehan

ISBN 978-1-78320-546-2
ePDF ISBN 978-1-78320-547-9
ePub ISBN 978-1-78320-548-6

Printed and bound by Short Run Press Ltd, UK

Contents

	Consumer Culture: An Introduction Gjoko Muratovski	1
Chapter 1	Icons of Popular Culture: Religious Dimensions of Branding Gjoko Muratovski	9
Chapter 2	Business, National Identities and International Politics: The Role of Built Environments and Architectural Propaganda in Nation Branding Gjoko Muratovski	41
Chapter 3	Race, Advertisements and YouTube: Identity and Nationality Kathleen Connellan	75
Chapter 4	The Use of Gold Rush Nostalgia on Wine Labels: Brief History of New Zealand's Central Otago Wine Region Lloyd Carpenter	99
Chapter 5	*Mad Men* and Women: Construction and Management of Advertising Executives in Popular Culture Anne Peirson Smith	119
Chapter 6	The Big Earn: A Study of Criminal Business Enterprises in Popular Culture Carolyn Beasley	139
Chapter 7	Brand IKEA in a Global Cultural Economy: A Case Study Susie Khamis	157

Chapter 8	The 'Good' Corporation: The Uneasy Relationship Between Reputation and Responsibility Robert Crocker	173
Chapter 9	Acceleration in Consumerism, Technology and Sustainability Robert Crocker	195
	Notes on Contributors	215

Introduction

Consumer Culture: An Introduction

Gjoko Muratovski

Introduction

Whether we like it or not, we live in a world that is driven by consumer economics. While people often tend to see economics as something that falls only within the domain of big business and governments, many fail to notice how consumer economics influences every facet of our lives. Our culture, attitudes and behavioural characteristics are, in one way or another, defined by the way we consume.

Consumer culture theory (CCT) is a field of study that has been particularly focused on developing new theoretical knowledge on all issues related to consumption and marketplace behaviours. One of the key figures in this field, Eric Arnould, describes consumer culture as '[…] the central construct, conceived as a social arrangement in which the relations between lived culture and social resources, between meaningful ways of life and the symbolic and material resources on which they depend, are mediated through markets' (Arnould, 2006: 605). This type of research addresses the sociocultural, experiential, symbolic and ideological aspects of consumption, and is inspired by an emerging theory that addresses the complex dynamics between consumer identity projects, marketplace structures, marketplace ideologies, emergent socio-historic patterning of consumption and popular culture (Arnould, 2006: 605).

CCT research presents a continual reminder that consumption is a historically shaped mode of sociocultural practice that can be found within dynamic marketplaces. This type of research, as Arnould and Thomson (2005: 875–876) argue, also highlights the notion that the 'real world' that we often take for granted is neither unified, monolithic, nor transparently rational. In doing so, CCT research shows that our lives are constructed around multiple 'realities' linked to fantasies, invocative desires, aesthetics and identity play, and that we use consumption to experience things that differ dramatically from our everyday lives (Arnould and Thomson, 2005: 876). What is more, this way of looking at consumption is even changing the way economics is being taught at universities. For example, academics increasingly use various popular culture references in their teaching in an attempt to help students understand a range of business concepts that drive our economy (Suddath, 2013; Williams, 2013).

In this book, *Consumer Culture: Selected Essays*, I introduce you to nine studies that examine various aspects of consumer culture. All of these studies are markedly different to each other in terms of the topics they examine and in the way that the authors have approached the issues that are being examined. Rather than trying to define a set of limitations of how CCT should be studied and presented, I have chosen to celebrate the difference that exists within this field. Anything else would have been a futile task, as this is a rich and diverse field that defies strict methodological conventions (for a review of the field of CCT, see Askegaard and Scott, 2013).

None of the chapters try to define what CCT is, as that is not the focus of this book. Rather, *Consumer Culture: Selected Essays* will contribute to this field by providing a range of studies on how economics and business cultures define the very fabric of our society by influencing the ways we live our lives. By approaching these issues from new and previously unexplored perspectives, the authors in this book have examined a myriad of ways in which business affects society. The book presents the works of seven authors, including myself: Gjoko Muratovski, Kathleen Connellan, Lloyd Carpenter, Anne Peirson-Smith, Carolyn Beasley, Susie Khamis and Robert Crocker.

Summary of Contents

In 'Icons of Popular Culture: Religious Dimensions of Branding', I examine branding not as a marketing concept, but as a belief system that is integral to popular culture. In this study, I have explored how five iconic brands – Apple, Coca-Cola, McDonalds, Disney, Harley-Davidson and Nike – have assumed religious dimensions. By adopting elements of religious propaganda, these brands have replaced a consumer culture driven by wants and needs with one of desire and worship. In doing so, the brands have created alluring narratives that have transcended the material values of their products. In return, they have managed to surround themselves not with consumers, but with loyal followers. This process of cultural transformation has triggered the emergence of what has now been referred to as 'consumer religion'.

In 'Business, National Identities and International Politics: The Role of Built Environments and Architectural Propaganda in Nation Branding', I have looked at how 'new' nations exhibit consumerist ideologies in order to establish themselves and achieve their national and international objectives. Countries (like corporations) have their own images and reputations. This perception has often been used as a foundation of a new form of brand building – nation branding. However, this study holds the position that regardless of some similarities, there is a fundamental difference in the branding of products, corporations and places – in this case, cities and nations. Then again, unlike their commercial counterparts, nation brands are not only driven by economic benefits but also by cultural and sociopolitical reasons. Through a historical overview and selected case studies – United Arab Emirates, Turkmenistan and Macedonia – the study blends issues of corporate branding and national identities, and examines the role of built environments and iconic architecture in developing nation brands.

In 'Race, Advertisements and YouTube: Identity and Nationality', Kathleen Connellan looks at racial stereotyping in advertising on YouTube. According to Connellan, while racial and ethnic signifiers operate across several commercial platforms in popular culture, advertising on YouTube offers a media space that is fluid and accessible. The reading of Internet advertising in this study reveals that it is intricately related to the subject and power. Consequently, this study looks at the devices utilised to position the subject in advertisements on YouTube through the Foucauldian lens of power relations. Connellan uses critical race methodology to discover how racial signifiers operate in YouTube advertisements. The approach is therefore a theoretical one that engages with the phenomenon of YouTube and looks at the discursive nature of its messages and narratives, which, in the selected examples, are intrinsically embedded in capitalist aspirations of progress and economic status. Examples are drawn from South Africa and Australia to examine representations of identity in post-apartheid, multicultural and migrant societies.

In 'The Use of Gold Rush Nostalgia on Wine Labels: Brief History of New Zealand's Central Otago Wine Region', Lloyd Carpenter reflects on the Central Otago gold rush theme on wine labels from the wine-making region of New Zealand. Before it became known for its wines, Central Otago was transformed by gold. While gold miners sought riches, some early pioneers experimented with grape cultivation. When the gold was gone, wine was forgotten and the area developed farming and tourism, but in the early 1980s it transformed again. Vintners realised that classic 'terroir' conditions of Burgundy, Champagne and Bavaria were emulated in Central Otago's dusty countryside. In the mid-2000s, faced with a plethora of high-quality wines, some winemakers looked to the history of the region in order to differentiate themselves. This chapter examines how and why the Central Otago 'goldfields' vineyards exploit nostalgia to market their wine by creating a romantic, mythic past.

In '*Mad Men* and Women: Construction and Management of Advertising Executives in Popular Culture', Anne Peirson-Smith examines how creative industry executives are constructed in the hugely popular television series *Mad Men*. Peirson-Smith studies the mediated constructions of fictional executives working in the advertising and creative industries. In doing so, she analyses the various visual and linguistic discourses that frame the fictional world of advertising, the cultural workplaces and spaces and the people who inhabit them and play out imagined realities. Themes such as gender, ethnicity and power relations are also addressed in the process of understanding why these narratives have meaning, and hold the interest of the viewer.

In 'The Big Earn: A Study of Criminal Business Enterprises in Popular Culture', Carolyn Beasley examines the fictional criminal as a branded entrepreneur. Inspired by international writers such as Richard Stark and Elmore Leonard, and successful television series such as *The Sopranos* and *Breaking Bad*, Beasley explores how affable gangsters, professional burglars and menacing Mr Bigs' *modus operandi* function as a brand recognisable to other criminals and to the wider public.

In 'Brand IKEA in a Global Cultural Economy: A Case Study', Susie Khamis defines the world's largest furniture and furnishings retailer as an icon of contemporary global capitalism. Known primarily for its price-friendly and easy to assemble products, IKEA benefits from the growth of urban, apartment living and a penchant for the minimalist Swedish aesthetic. This study considers how IKEA sustains its brand image across increasingly diverse markets, particularly in regions that are culturally dissimilar to its main sales base – Western Europe. While IKEA's model of operation has proven to be very successful, Khamis explores how IKEA articulates its brand to specific consumer groups in ways that spotlight the brand's core values. Since IKEA does not adapt its product range for different markets, local marketing campaigns are telling insights into how IKEA's consumers differ, even though IKEA's product range does not. This, in turn, underlines the importance of strategic marketing – in this study, television commercials – as one way that global brands maintain their appeal trans-nationally without product differentiation. Khamis also highlights the cultural logic of branding, whereby narrative and mood are used to distinguish otherwise generic, mass-produced commodities.

In 'The "Good" Corporation: The Uneasy Relationship Between Reputation and Responsibility', Robert Crocker provides a critical reflection on the modern-day corporation. Here, he examines how corporations increasingly try to portray themselves as socially responsible organisations, and what happens when they fail to deliver on their promises. Like modern branding, corporate public relations (PR) was first professionalised in 1920s America out of a need for credible positive narratives that could speak to the values, beliefs and expectations of Americans, and turn large and previously rapacious conglomerates into corporate 'good citizens' with a positive role to play in building a 'better future'. Advertising, all forms of design and large staged events, such as Expos and World Fairs, were marshalled to serve the ends of these campaigns. Widely adopted after World War II by leading European corporate giants, this style of image-making has continued to shape the marketing and branding strategies of many large enterprises today. As Crocker argues, the concept and metrics of corporate social and environmental responsibility were originally developed by leading consumer rights groups and environmental NGOs eager to hold this kind of corporate image-making to account. Corporate social responsibility (CSR) and 'sustainability reporting' have in turn become important vehicles for corporate marketing to present 'evidence' for a more credible 'cultural' narrative of corporate good citizenship. However, this study argues that 'sustainability reporting' has become an increasingly challenging field for many companies struggling to control the narrative of their own image, and can expose them to cynicism and anger when they seem to fail the standards set by their published commitments.

In the final chapter, 'Acceleration in Consumerism, Technology and Sustainability', Robert Crocker examines where society is going in terms of technology and sustainability. The networked computer has progressively colonised, transformed and accelerated older established technological systems in transportation, communication and manufacture over the last 30 years. As Crocker reflects, in today's global economy the increasing mobility of people, goods and information enabled by this technology has led to an acceleration and expansion of consumerism, giving rise to what has been termed appropriately, 'hyper-consumption'. Reflecting upon the concept of 'social acceleration' and on recent technologies and scientific advances, Crocker argues that there is little in the way of good news for resource-use reduction and sustainability. Rather than attaining a progressive 'dematerialisation' that was once predicted to slow or replace the 'box economy', the material economy is being expanded and accelerated by the virtual economy. By referring to the 3D printer in a case study, Crocker points out that it becomes apparent that this supposedly 'cleaner' and more democratic technology cannot 'solve' our existing ecological problems, and may in fact make these worse – for the 3D printer, despite optimistic talk of this 'disruptive' technology, will predictably become one more source of a growing army of cheap 'stuff' in the home, in its turn adding to resource depletion, overconsumption and waste. Rejecting the equally optimistic notion that greater sustainability can be achieved through the democratisation and localisation enabled by this innovation, the chapter concludes by arguing that industrial 'un-sustainability' is not so easily undone. Rather, it is systemic and grounded in today's hyper-consumption, whose psychosocial or cultural basis cannot be substantially changed by material innovation alone. This understanding, as Crocker points out, is crucial to solving the global environmental crisis, and should inspire both businesses and designers to move towards a more securely founded sustainability.

Conclusion

Economics and popular culture are intricately linked. They often influence each other – sometimes in obvious ways, and at other times in an inconspicuous and somewhat unlikely manner. This relationship is not necessarily universal. It can vary across time (in historical terms) and space (in geographical terms). In today's globally connected society, people are increasingly sharing common business cultures. By studying global and local issues, national and international business practices, and by considering historical and contemporary views, the authors in this book have examined the role that economics plays in society. The aim of this book is to inspire other scholars to carry out further studies in this area and we hope that readers will expand on the scholarship herein. This collection of scholarly studies brings together varied yet related perspectives on the relationship between businesses and everyday culture. By considering how commercial narratives are embedded in popular culture, we hope to increase awareness of the role of emotion and persuasion in all aspects of our lives – from consumption and politics to personal wealth and the environment.

Enjoy reading.

The Editor

References

Arnould, E., 2006. Consumer culture theory: retrospect and prospect. *European Advances in Consumer Research*, 7:1, pp.605–607.

Arnould, E. and Thomson, C., 2005. Consumer culture theory (CCT): twenty years of research. *Journal of Consumer Research*, 31:4, pp.868–882.

Askegaard, S. and Scott, L., 2013. Consumer culture theory: the ironies of history. *Marketing Theory*, 13:2, pp.139–147.

Suddath, C., 2013. State Penn professor uses pop culture to teach economics. *Bloomberg Businessweek*, [online] 14 February. Available at: http://www.businessweek.com/articles/2013-02-13/penn-state-professor-uses-pop-culture-to-teach-economics. Accessed 22 June 2014.

Williams, L., 2013. Professors embrace pop culture to teach economics'. *USA Today*, [online] 21 April. Available at: http://www.usatoday.com/story/money/business/2013/04/21/professors-embrace-pop-culture-to-teach/2099897/. Accessed 22 June 2014.

Chapter 1

Icons of Popular Culture: Religious Dimensions of Branding

Gjoko Muratovski

Abstract

By standing for something greater than their products, leading brands aspire to establish their own 'corporate religions'. Apple, Coca-Cola, McDonalds, Disney, Harley-Davidson, and Nike operate more like religious cults than commercial enterprises, converting their consumers into devoted believers and loyal followers. These brands have managed to replace a culture of needs with a culture of desire and worship. In this process of cultural transformation, the world of branding has taken refuge in the world of sacred and assumed almost religious dimensions. Brands have become modern-day totems – commercial idols around which a meaningful existence is formed. This, in return, has triggered the emergence of what has now been referred to as 'consumer religion'. Unlike most people think, branding is not only a marketing concept, but also a system of belief that is integral to our culture.

Keywords

branding, religion, totems, icons, Apple, Coca-Cola, McDonalds, Disney, Harley-Davidson, Nike

Introduction

Regardless of its popularity, 'branding' is a term that resists clear definition. Etymologically, the term comes from the word 'burn', and as such, this term has been used in the context of marking one's property with a heated iron (Pavitt, 2000: 19). While from a contemporary perspective it seems that branding has originated from the practice of trademarking, it can be argued that it was the other way around. A review of the literature suggests that branding evolved from the process of marking property and ownership, or from the process of identifying the origin and content of goods. However, if we try to look beyond its contemporary application, we will see that branding existed long before it was used in a commercial context. If we examine what branding stands for in a broader sociocultural context rather than commercial, then we can see that branding has a much longer history, and that the term itself is incorrect.

Despite the fact that trademarks were effectively used since the Middle Ages, and crude examples of trademarking can be found even before that, branding as a commercial concept emerged in the middle of the nineteenth century. This was a time when technology, combined with literacy and rising standards of living, created the first mass market. The idea behind this was simple: a producer would take a household product – a commodity, no different from any other made by someone else – and would give it distinctive characteristics through imaginative use of name, design, packaging, and advertising. Rather than simply marking the product in terms of origin or ownership, the producer would create a brand from this product by giving the product an identity and special features. In this way, the product would appear unique and different from its competitors (Moor, 2007: 15–18).

This technique proved to be highly successful. Branding increased the sales of products, or enabled producers to charge a premium for the same product over its generic competitors. This meant that when products became associated with powerful, complex, highly charged, and immediate symbolism, a strong and lasting effect on the consumers was inevitable. This seemingly new concept also demonstrated that ordinary, often irrelevant objects could become powerful emotive symbols, affecting how people that used them wanted to be seen by others. In time, branding managed to replace a culture based on needs with a culture driven by desires (Muratovski, 2010: 32). It was no longer a matter of rational thoughts arising out of sheer necessity, functionality, and practicality that moved people into changing their purchasing patterns – it was the irrational, emotional impulses that created new engagements between the masses and the products (Curtis, 2002). The apparent power that branding had over public opinion and collective behaviour did not go unnoticed. This idea was so strong that its applications have gone beyond consumer products and commercial establishments. It was not long before this concept was expanded and became widely adopted by political organisations, social movements, and by governments. For many organisations, regardless of their nature, status, and origin, branding became the orthodox way towards identity formation and promotion (Olins, 1990). However, the original form of branding appeared long before organised trading and commercial trademarks even existed. From a sociocultural perspective, branding can be traced all the way to the early days of human history when people cohabited in tribes and worshiped idols.

When early humans were faced with dramatic natural phenomena, as a way of coping with the new and the unknown, they began to create stories, myths, and legends in an attempt to explain the things that they could not understand. In doing so, they used themselves as a reference and imagined that all physical entities in nature are gifted with similar powers, including speech, desire, and thought. From such perspective, the wind and the river could speak and obviously travel; trees could articulate; and lower animals were perceived as equals. This way of observing the surrounding world has given rise to some of the earliest forms of religion: animism and naturism – the attribution of human features, a soul, or supernatural powers to animals, plants, objects, and natural phenomena; and totemism – a practice of marking out tribal relationship with certain animals or natural objects, and their veneration (for classical studies on this topic, see Hume, 1757: 10; Durkheim, 1912: 86–88; Freud, 1919: 128; Spence, 1921: 17).

A tribe would often have its own distinctive totem, or a series of totems, that they would identify with and worship. As such, the totems also acted as a form of differentiation among various tribes and tribal members (Freud, 1919: 4). Further, the tribal members would make some kind of objects and emblems that would bare the image of the totem, and even tattoo these emblems on their bodies. Further, they would carry the totem with them in a hope that the special characteristics of their 'tribal god' will be transferred to them (Freud, 1919: 174).

This idea is so strongly embedded in our subconsciousness that it persists even today. Contrary to the common belief that totemism ceased to exist as a system of belief, as a model it was never really abandoned. One example of this is heraldry – a system by which symbols such as national emblems, coats of arms, and armorial elements bearing animals, plants, and objects are devised, described, and regulated (Pastoureau, 1997). Such symbols have been in continuous use since medieval Europe. Today, they are used to a lesser extent, and perhaps not in the way they were originally envisioned. Heraldry still demarks European as well as Asian, African, Pacific, and South-American postcolonial 'aristocracies' of power, and is still applied, both in commercial branding and in the strongly renascent practice of establishing family history. Totems can still be found in the form of emblems of various townships, schools, universities, and far beyond this. The names and emblems of many sports teams complete with uniforms, memorabilia, club colours, emblems, supporter banners, mascots, and merchandised souvenirs are evident examples that we have never really abandoned totemism. Examples of this practice are numerous and can be frequently found around the world and in a range of sports – from the NBA to AFL and Rugby Union (e.g. NBA teams with totemic brand features: Atlanta Hawks, Chicago Bulls, Charlotte Bobcats, Dallas Mavericks, Memphis Grizzlies, New Orleans Hornets, etc.). In addition to this, we still give human names to cyclones, storms, and typhoons. We still call planets by the names of long forgotten gods. We continue to assign female gender roles to ships and yachts, and cars often bear trademarked names or emblems that depict animals. One thing is clear: we still live in a time when people idolise objects and concepts that are associated with natural and supernatural elements (Muratovski, 2010: 203).

What we can deduct from this empirical observation is that branding, in its purest form, has religious rather than commercial origins. That is why a more appropriate term to define brands would be 'totems' – sacred objects and emblems that particular communities identify with (Muratovski, 2013a). This idea, however, is not based on a new theory. The uneasy relationship between religion and branded goods has often been the topic of study for scholars coming from a range of disciplines, such as business, marketing, consumer behaviour, and communications (for example, see Belk, Walledorf, and Sherry, 1989; Schouten and McAlexander, 1995; Moraru, 2013). The similarities between branding and religion have also been noted and examined by theologian scholars such as David Chidester (1996, 2005), Tricia Sheffield (2006), and Vincent J. Miller (2009).

The key link that brings these seemingly disparate concepts – branding and religion – together is the notion of belief. Just as religion, the consumer culture in which we live in today is also formed around a set of beliefs. The key element of the 'consumer religion' is the belief that happiness can be achieved by a possession of branded goods (see Miller, 2009: 1; and also Jhally, 1998). For example, many people 'believe' that driving a particular brand of cars, wearing certain fashion labels, or using a particular type of mobile phone over another is a good thing, and that this is something worth pursuing. Such attitudes can be seen across all social groups and subcultures around the world.

Some businesses understand this type of behaviour better than others. In an attempt to fabricate a 'simulacrum of credibility', certain corporations have developed quasi-religious indoctrinations as sources of inspiration. They have established their own systems of belief by producing 'credos of values' in an effort to motivate and engage their employees and their clients. In doing so, they have been successful in uniting their constituencies with their own visions, myths, and symbols (de Certeau, 1984: 180). By standing for something greater than their products, these businesses have established their own 'corporate religions' (Kunde, 2000) and began to operate more like 'religious cults' than commercial enterprises (Atkin, 2004), converting their consumers into 'devoted believers' and 'loyal followers' (Lindstrom, 2008). Apple, Coca-Cola, McDonalds, Disney, Harley-Davidson, and Nike are some of the brands that employ such principles. These brands have stepped into a place where the power of the narrative has replaced the product, and the idea of the brand has become everything (see also Ritzer, 1993; Bryman, 1999, 2003).

Apple Inc.

There are very few commercial brands that can inspire the same level of commitment and dedication from its customers as Apple can. Whenever Apple opens a new store or launches a new product, it draws crowds in the thousands. Even for insignificant events, such as the opening day of their fifth store in Manhattan, Apple fans formed a waiting line of nearly one kilometre long. Over 2500 people were waiting in the line, including one retiree from California who already attended 30 store openings nationwide (Tibken, 2011). For the Apple fans, a new store opening is such an important occasion that some of them took advantage of the setting to propose marriages (Evans, 2006). This type of behaviour associated with new store openings is not only characteristic to the United States. The opening of their first store in Tokyo drew never before seen crowds with the waiting line exceeding eight city blocks (Mogg, 2011). The number of people that visit Apple's stores in a single quarter exceeds 60 million, which is more than the number of people who visit Walt Disney's four biggest theme parks in a year (Tibken, 2011).

This kind of consumer devotion, typically exhibited by religious followers, has prompted the media to refer to Apple as a 'new religion' that offers 'divine instruments' worth the effort of a 'pilgrimage' (Heussner, 2010; Rosenwald, 2011). With this in mind, it is not a surprise that some have even described Apple's founder, Steve Jobs, as a 'technological messiah' (Jones, 2011), and the 'high priest' of Apple (Rosenwald, 2011). According to the *New Statesman,* Jobs blurred the line between salesmanship and evangelism; like a 'religious revivalist', he was selling not just consumer commodities, but also a 'vision of life' – their article states. His preacher-like appearance and quasi-religious product launches – as the commentary continues – were part of the 'magic' that allowed the 'devotees' to ignore that the products themselves were often 'overpriced and underpowered' (Jones, 2011). In what is essentially an article on the 'church of Jobs' and the 'cult of Apple', the following paragraph from the *New Statesman* sums up Jobs's life story:

> The Book of Jobs would, no doubt, begin with the company's birth in the humble location of Jobs's garage in 1976. The founder's expulsion from Eden – his removal from the company in the mid-1980s – was followed by a long period of exile (the Pixar years). In Jobs's case, the second coming – his return to Apple in 1997 – preceded the miracle of resurrection that he managed to perform, taking the company from near-bankruptcy to global dominance in the space of a decade. There's even an antichrist in this gospel, in the shape of Bill Gates. For many years, there was just a small band of loyal followers holding off the darkness of Microsoft. But Apple's final triumph was assured. And while he has now logged off for the last time, Jobs has left behind him a multitude of followers to preach the word unto whatever Windows-using heathens might still be out there. (Jones, 2011, para.3)

The religious aura that surrounds Apple inspired a team of BBC journalists to investigate why Apple fans exhibit such devotion. After consulting neuroscientists who conducted MRI scan tests on selected individuals, they have uncovered that Apple imagery activates the same parts of the brain in brand-loyal Apple 'fanatics' that religious imagery does in devoted followers of a religion. They have also confirmed that once a brand achieves this effect, there is no turning back for the devotees as they are becoming hooked to the brand's products and corporate culture (Riley and Boome, 2011).[1] Ironically, this comes at odds with advertising campaigns that were meant to portray Apple as a company that stands against conformity and corporate brainwashing and delivers technological liberation, individual creativity, and freedom of expression. These values were vividly presented in their Orwellian commercial *1984* (1984) directed by Ridley Scott, and later reinforced through their *Think Different* (1997–2002) campaign.

The Coca-Cola Company

Coca-Cola is a product that no one needs, but everyone wants. The drink that contains 99% sugar and water was invented in 1886 and sold for just 5 cents per glass in the first 70 years. Today, Coca-Cola is a US$74 billion brand and is marketed in more than 200 countries (Bhasin, 2011). Nevertheless, Coca-Cola was not an instant success. John Pemberton, the drink's inventor, in the first year sold just nine glasses of the drink a day (The Coca-Cola Company, 2011). As a part of his sales pitch, Pemberton referred to Coca-Cola as "the greatest blessing to the human family, Nature's (God's) best gift in medicine" (cited in Chidester, 1996: 749, parentheses added by Chidester).

Coca-Cola's success was achieved by what appears to be a religious zeal and great deal of perseverance that the company demonstrated since its inception. From the beginning, Coca-Cola company managers, advertisers, bottlers, and distributors displayed distinctively religious moods and motivations around their product. This can be seen by a range of public statements made by Coca-Cola executives over a course of many years. According to the religious studies scholar, David Chidester (1996), Asa Candler, the Atlanta entrepreneur who started the Coca-Cola empire, was described by his son as a person that regarded the drink with an almost 'mystical faith'. Robert Woodruff, who became president of the company in 1923, demonstrated a devotion to Coca-Cola that many thought it resembled 'idolatry'. Harrison Jones, the leading Coca-Cola bottler of the 1920s, often referred to the drink as 'holy water' and treated the iconic bottle as a 'sacred object'. Archie Lee, Coca-Cola's advertising executive in the 1920s, believed that Coca-Cola is a 'new religion', more important than the one promoted by the doctrines of the Church. Delony Sledge, the advertising executive in the early 1950s, agreed with this. He proclaimed: 'Our work is religion, not business' (cited in Chidester, 1996: 749–750). Even four decades later, the same religious-like devotion remained. As Coca-Cola's CEO Roberto Goizueto proudly proclaimed: 'In every country in the world, Cola dominates. We feel that we have to plant our flag everywhere, even before the Christians arrive. […] Cola's destiny is to inherit the earth' (cited in Angelico, 1998).

The powerful advertising machine of The Coca-Cola Company even managed to replace the religious meaning of Christmas with the 'spirit of Coke'. Today, Santa Claus is so widely accepted that many would be surprised to learn that the character was virtually non-existent until it had its debut in a Coca-Cola ad placed in *The Saturday Evening Post* in 1931. In a somewhat different shape and form, Coca-Cola first introduced Santa Claus (Saint Nicholas) or 'Father Christmas' in the 1920s, when they began a major campaign to promote their summer time refreshment soft drink during the winter season. Until 1931, the Santa Claus promotional campaign remained minimal. Then, Coca-Cola commissioned the artist Haddon Sundblom to create a new version of Santa Claus. Sundblom created Santa's definite, 'traditional' look, which was repeated year after year in his paintings till 1964. The same look continues to be used even today, although different artists are now commissioned to deliver the visuals. In the course of more than 80 years, Coca-Cola's Santa Claus became such a powerful image that it reached almost every corner of the world. Today, the look of Santa is so firmly embedded in the public mind that we have ceased to think of him as a commercial character designed to sell soft drinks in winter, and we have learned to love him for what he represents – a friendly figure that reminds people of the joy of celebrating Christmas with family and friends (Moraru, 2013).[2]

According to Madalina Moraru (2013: 28), living the consumer experience during Christmas reveals a 'paradoxical' relationship between religion and marketing. By featuring the image of a religious figure (Santa Claus/Saint Nicolas) in their marketing and advertising campaigns, Coca-Cola has managed to alter the religious meaning of Christmas. As Moraru (2013: 28) points out, Coca-Cola has become a 'ritualised brand' – at least during Christmas – and with their global influence they managed to change the culture surrounding this period. This does not necessarily mean that the sacredness has disappeared from Christmas. Through 'contagious social consumerism' people have developed new customs, but the sacred element that encourages religious behaviour towards objects and celebrations still remains. The main difference is that many people now view Coca-Cola, rather than the Church, as the 'host' of Christmas (Moraru, 2013: 28).

Reflecting on the success that Coca-Cola had over the years, one of their executives made a bold statement that Coca-Cola has entered the lives of more people than any other ideology, including the Christian religion (cited in Chidester, 1996: 750). Considering that Coca-Cola is now recognised by 94 per cent of the world's population and is the second-most understood term in the world, after 'Okay' (Bhasin, 2011), it appears that the company has succeeded in its mission.

The McDonald's Corporation

Richard James 'Dick' and Maurice James 'Mac' McDonald, two brothers from Manchester, New Hampshire, opened a barbecue restaurant called 'McDonald's' in 1940 in Southern California. After some adjustments to the business concept and the commencement of a franchise, the business was further modified in 1955 and expanded by their business partner Ray Kroc. Kroc later bought out the business interests of the McDonald's brothers and went on to establish what we know today as The McDonald's Corporation. What has come to be a fast-food phenomenon of the American suburbs and medium-sized towns of the 1940s is now a vast multinational corporation with more than 34,000 restaurants that serve over 69 million customers daily in 119 countries (The McDonald's Corporation, 2012).

The brand has infiltrated popular culture globally as one of the strongest symbols of American culture. Nevertheless, their strongest consumer base still remains in the United States. A survey of American schoolchildren found that 96 per cent could identify the company's trade character, Ronald McDonald. The only fictional character with a higher degree of recognition was Coca-Cola's Santa Claus (Ritzer, 2010: 11). This comes as no surprise if we consider that McDonald's franchises are so widely spread in America that it is impossible to get farther than 107 miles (172 km) from one of their restaurants (Ritzer, 2010: 2). In addition to their standard restaurants, today McDonald's fast food can also be found in hotels, railway stations, airports, on in-flight meals, in high schools, hospitals, and even in the military. They can also be found at the Guantanamo Bay US Naval Base in Cuba and at the Pentagon (see Ritzer, 2010: 10), which only confirms that McDonald's is the fast-food restaurant 'superpower'. This resonates with the statement made by one of McDonald's chairmen, Michael Quinlan, in the 1990s: "Our goal: to totally dominate the quick service restaurant industry worldwide. […] I want McDonald's to be more than a leader. I want McDonald's to dominate" (cited in Papiernik, 1994: 28–30).

The impact of McDonald's on people's everyday lives is hard to overstate. For many people, McDonald's restaurants have become 'cathedrals of consumption' (Ritzer, 1993) – 'sacred institutions' (Kottak, 1983) to which people will come from long distances, not for mere lunch, but for an experience of 'celestial joy' brought to them by 'the missionaries of the fast-food chain' (Keller, 1990). Their visual presence is so strong and far-reaching that according to the author of *The New York Times* bestselling book *Fast Food Nation: The Dark Side of the All-American Meal* (2001), the Golden Arches are now more widely recognised than the Christian cross (Schlosser, 2012: 282).

The ongoing global success of The McDonald's Corporation can in part be attributed to adaptability to local cultures. The methods that McDonald's uses for spreading its fast-food empire around the world are quite similar to the 'colonising' methods that were introduced by the Catholic Church in the seventeenth century (see Jowett and O'Donnell, 2006: 2).[3]

Just as the Catholic Church, McDonald's are very successful in the cultural adaptation in the countries where it opens its franchises. For example, while all of the Catholic Churches operate in a same way and use the same iconography, we can see subtle differences in how the religious practices have been culturally adapted in their 'franchises' across the world. For example, the narrative structure of the Gospels (a story about sacrifice and rebirth) connects with a primordial myth system found among many other sacrifice-based systems around the world. The figures of Christian scripture and tradition often appropriate the pantheon of pagan deities, using a 'manufactured' resemblance – as in the case of the pregnant Virgin of Guadalupe of Mexico that replaced a pregnant Aztec female deity; or as in the case of the Catholic cross in Ireland, which is positioned within a circle that represents the Celtic sun god (O'Shaughnessy, 2004: 91). This type of cultural adaptability is a feature characteristic of many religions. Many religious belief systems have gained inspiration from myths and legends found in the cultures where they were established. As they began to expand, they became open to the idea of making contact with stories found elsewhere and integrating them within their own ethos. McDonald's are using the same principles in their business strategy. While their main menu is basically the same all over the world and offers a distinctively 'American' food (e.g. hamburgers, fries, Coke, and milkshakes), their non-American restaurants also feature lines of locally themed meals, adapting themselves to the diverse tastes of their non-American customers. Despite their rigid rules when it comes to the uniformity of the brand and the predictability of the food and the service, McDonald's are willing to be flexible and to adapt to other cultures, as long as people eat their meals under the Golden Arches. If this means using Indian spices in India, or French cheese in France, so be it (see Bryman, 2003: 158).[4]

In addition to being flexible when it comes to adapting to other cultures, the biggest strength of both the Church and McDonald's is that they are consistently 'themed' throughout all of their franchises. This monolithic type of corporate identity ensures instant familiarity and recognition. Both institutions are very consistent in terms of corporate decoration, modes of service delivery, staff clothing, and various architectural cues that are pervasive features of their establishments. This 'reflexive theming', as Bryman (2003: 156) calls it, is internally generated and then continuously reproduced, ensuring that the core idea of the establishment is not diluted by external factors. In addition to this, accent is always given on the promotion of universal values, such as family values. McDonald's, for example, routinely depicts itself as a clean, family-friendly environment (Bryman, 2003: 157). The emotional labour that is expected from McDonald's employees is also a part of the corporate identity of the establishment. The company urges its employees to be pleasant, cheerful, smiling, and courteous to the customers, even when the customers are rude and offensive (Bryman, 2003: 160). Anyone that has been approached by Mormon missionaries or Hare Krishnas recruiters would have experienced the same attitude. What is more, they too wear distinctive uniforms when they represent their organisations; the Mormons even wear name badges – just like their McDonald's counterparts.

The Walt Disney Company

Walt Disney was a man who made unique contributions to family entertainment and media enterprises. Beginning in the 1920s, Disney used early film technology to make animated film shorts, which he followed with more sophisticated feature-length films. Later on, he creatively used television programming to promote his last and greatest success – the Disneyland theme parks. Disney's theme parks have become such cultural phenomenon that some have went as far as to describe them as 'middle-class holy cities' worth the effort of a 'pilgrimage' (King, 1983).

Today, The Walt Disney Company owns eleven theme parks on three continents and employs over 90,000 people. The company also owns and operates media networks, parks and resorts, studio entertainment, consumer products, and interactive media, to name a few (The Walt Disney Company, 2012). It seems that Disney is relentless when it comes to pursuing consumer markets; from cartoons and comics books to home décor, bridal gowns, and thematic cruise liners, their brand is omnipresent. They even have their own, real-life town based in Florida, called Celebration. With its picture-perfect streets lined with homes fronted by porches, picket fences, and manicured lawns, Celebration is, by design, a vision of American nostalgia – an idyllic community – developed by the creative minds in Disney.

While Celebration is designed to recall the image of 'small-town' America, and the idealism and safety that people associate with that image, according to Kathleen M. Hogan (1998), this is a community that is controlled by a strictly enforced set of rules and regulations, but not in a totalitarian fashion. Rather, as Hogan (1998) argues, Celebration emerges from two prevalent strains in American thought: the search for a utopian life and the romance of the past. This town is structured around a set of principles to which every resident must subscribe. By using idealised architectural forms that Americans associate with 'the best and most pure' aspects of American life, The Walt Disney Company has attempted to create a utopian community that is ruled by a single vision. This community is envisioned to act as an example for the rest of society – 'a city upon a hill', in which the residents live a more meaningful existence.

Nevertheless, the very idea of creating a utopian community based on systems of belief and governed by corporate leaders is arguably religious in origin (i.e. the myth of Eden). Historically speaking, there are many examples of utopian communities in America – some of them dating as early as 1683 (see NPS 2011; Yale University Library, 2012). Many have failed, very few have persevered, and some have ended tragically – such is the case of the 'People's Temple' cult and their infamous Jonestown settlement where the cult members performed a controversial mass suicide after being guided to do so by their spiritual leader, Jim Jones. However, as Hogan (1998) points out, unlike other utopian communities established by religious cults or communal sects, Celebration's uniqueness does not derive from some kind of special relationship with God, or from a revolutionary conception of human relationships. Instead, the township is based on the idea of the ideal American 'small-town' community, as imagined by The Walt Disney Company. Celebration is based on the concept of nostalgia for the 'days gone by' – a time when things were better, life was easier, and people were happier; a time when families had values and neighbours mowed their lawns regularly.

These sentimental longings are based on an idealised version of pre-war America – as seen on TV, and not on an actual, historical past. What Disney is selling here is a 'dream come true' – as their marketing slogan colourfully puts it (Jhally, 2003). Nevertheless, the town of Celebration is a living concept town, with its own school and city council, where the ideal has become a reality. Just like a Disney amusement park or a resort, Celebration is spotless. There is no litter or overgrown lawns, and the garages, trash, and recycling receptacles are hidden in narrow alleys that run behind individual houses so that they cannot be seen from the road. Even the style of the houses is regulated. There are only six types of houses that people can choose from: Classical, Colonial Revival, French, Coastal, Mediterranean, and Victorian, with Victorian style being the most popular. The whole town planning is also designed to steer people's behaviour in a particular way. For example, the yards are small, even for the large houses, so that neighbours are nearby and interaction is ensured. Also, by limiting the size of their yards, the residents are 'encouraged' to engage in communal activities by using the many parks and common areas in the town (Hogan, 1998).

Regardless of the secular ideas on which Celebration is built, the mechanics behind it are conspicuously religious and cult-like. For example, opposite the Town Hall is the Preview Center – the tallest building in town. This is the building where residents and visitors can learn about the Celebration's philosophy and the five important principles behind it:

Health, Education, Technology, Community, and Place. The church-like building, with a tower at the front, can be seen from almost anywhere within Celebration. In this case, the Preview Center functions as the town's 'cathedral' where Disney's 'religion' is being taught. The Town Hall, normally an institution characterised by rigorous self-governance and democratic principles, functions as the Town Manager's office – an unelected position that is filled by an appointee from Celebration's governing board, which is run by Disney. Even the public school functions by different rules. The school follows a self-developed curriculum that does not conform to the typical American model, and the teachers are trained in this 'unique' method in a teaching academy established in Celebration by Disney. The school has been a point of a raging controversy since it opened and several families have either moved out of Celebration or have sent their children to private schools elsewhere (see Hogan, 1998). Since then, other schools and new programs approved by the Florida Department of Education have also been introduced in Celebration (see The Celebration Company, 2011).

When homeowners move into Celebration, they sign a document called the 'Declaration of Covenants'. This is an interesting choice of words. While Disney could have called this document a contract or an agreement, they have chosen a term that has a theological connotation – covenant is more commonly used to describe an agreement that brings about a relationship of commitment between God and his people. As Hogan (1998) rightfully points out, this title for a homeowner's agreement echoes the language of the covenant that religious communities like the Shakers use to describe their shared values, and is further evidence of the 'special' status that Celebration assigns itself. The notion of 'belief' is also reinforced here. For example, under *Part One: Introduction to the Community* in their declaration, the following quote by Anatole France is used as an opening: "To accomplish great things, we must not only act, but also dream; not only plan, but also believe" (The Celebration Company, 2003: 3). The declaration lists the rules by which residents must abide. Some of them are quite peculiar, but expected – considering the image that the town tries to project. For example, the declaration dictates the length of time that a person can display political signs during an election period, it limits the number of signs to one, and dictates the size of the sign as well. The declaration also stipulates that cars cannot be parked in the driveway for more than 24 consecutive hours. Instead, they must be stowed in the garage so that they cannot be seen from the street. There is also a policy that prohibits more than two people to occupy a single bedroom. Furthermore, if the Celebration Board, which consists of unelected officials, receives complaints from other homeowners about a resident's pet, they can remove the pet from the community without the owner's permission. Furthermore, in what resembles an inquisition-style institution set up to combat or suppress heresy, the Celebration's Company Joint Committee handles enforcement of the covenants and they carry an inspection of the town twice a year. In the declaration, there is a quote by Henry Adams that reminds the residents why this is necessary: "Chaos is the law of nature; order is the dream of men" (The Celebration Company, 2003: 16).

Like other American utopian experiments, as Hogan (1998) argues, Celebration represents a group of individuals organised in a society around a single, strongly held set of ideas. Everyone there is supposed to have the same set of ideals and goals, and a single concept of how life should be lived. This kind of life comes at a cost. In order for utopian communities to function as they are planned, they have to some extent separate themselves from society to practice their beliefs. These beliefs are voiced by a 'dynamic and persuasive leader' (in this case The Walt Disney Company), and the residents must accept these beliefs if they want to be a part of this community. As with all utopian settlements, the physical environment of Celebration is regarded as an integral part of their system of belief and has been designed to support that system (Hogan, 1998). Here, Disney has created a 'brand nirvana' and has given thousands of families an opportunity to live their life inside a 'dream' – their brand. The key to Disney's success with Celebration is that there are virtually no other marketing messages inside the town competing for attention (Klein, 2000: 154–156). No other brand except the brand of Celebration is allowed to engage in corporate communications with the town residents inside the town limits. Naomi Klein, describes this as '[…] perfect, synergised, cross-promoted marketing moment' (cited in Jhally, 2003). For people to voluntarily agree to have their lives governed by a brand, and to pay to live inside the brand, is the highest level of accomplishment that a corporate brand can ever achieve (Muratovski, 2013b: 52–53).

Another example of Disney's use of quasi-religious elements as a part of their corporate branding can be seen in their highly inspiring campaign *I am a Princess* (2012). The video is meant to empower young girls by assuring them that they are all 'Princesses' in their own way in the real world. In a highly positive and emotional way, the video presents young girls coming from diverse backgrounds and placed in various situations and roles; sometimes assuming leadership roles and being physically active, and at other times being educated, kind, and compassionate. As the video progresses, the girls start to be juxtaposed with various Disney princesses. At the beginning of the video, in a prayer-like fashion the voice of a young girl begins reciting what it means to be a (Disney) Princess:

I am a Princess.
I am brave sometimes, I am scared sometimes.
Sometimes I am brave even when I am scared.
I believe in loyalty and trust.
I believe loyalty is built on trust.
I try to be kind, I try to be generous.
I am kind even when others are not so generous.
I am a Princess.
I think standing up for myself is important.
I think standing up for others is more important, but standing with others is most
    important.
I am a Princess.

I believe compassion makes me strong.
Kindness is power.
And family is the tightest bond of all.
I have heard I am beautiful, I know I am strong.
I am a Princess.
Long may I reign.

Virtues and moral sentiments, such as those present here, are often integral elements that can be found in prayers. Prayers are a common feature of all religions and they come in many forms. Some prayers are highly ritualised and follow a strict sequence of actions, while others are more spontaneous. Certain prayers are individual and are done privately, and others are collective and are done in the presence of fellow believers. Some people pray to seek guidance in life and others pray for the purpose of fulfilling or respecting the requirements of their religion – as a form of observance. In a way, what prayer is to a religion is what rational thought is to a philosophy; it is the very expression of the ideology behind the belief. Though most prayers appear to be driven by personal beliefs, these beliefs are to a great extent a social construct. In most cases, it is the society that creates and regulates the type of the social and religious rites and liturgies that are expressed in people's beliefs. Therefore, if a religion wants to be accepted by the society, first it needs to develop an understanding of the values in which the society already believes in (Encyclopaedia Britannica, 2012). Through a consistent representation of socially recognisable values, Disney has managed to create an ideology that is universally appealing. Fantastic storytelling, charismatic characters, and familiar and repetitive settings bring this ideology to life in everything that Disney does. Themes such as nostalgia, escape and fantasy, romance and happiness, innocence, individualism, sexual stereotypes, and the reinvention of folk tales are key elements of the Disney 'universe' (see Bryman, 1999: 28). The prevalence of these themes can be seen both in Celebration and in their corporate communication strategies as presented in ads such as *I am a Princess* (2012), and beyond.

On another note, it is also worth mentioning that Disney sells its persuasive storytelling expertise to other interested parties. In the period during the WWII, the US government commissioned The Walt Disney Company to produce 32 short propaganda films to help them sell the War to the American public. The Navy was the first, and other branches of the government, including the Army, Air Force, Department of Agriculture, and Treasury Department, followed Disney's creative approach to generating educational films, propaganda materials, and even insignias (Stillich, 2009). Another of their clients is the Mormon Church, for whom Disney produced a film called *The Other Side of Heaven* (2001), starring Christopher Gorham and Anne Hathaway. The film tells the story about a Mormon missionary in the Tongan islands in the 1950s and his adventurous experiences. Based on a personal encounter with Mormon missionaries in Europe, I have seen how they use this film as a part of their recruitment campaigns. As a part of their 'sales pitch',

Mormon missionaries invite prospective new members to join them for a friendly, casual gathering and a free screening of a 'Disney' movie. What I have found particularly interesting was that they were not willing to specify the title of the movie, or what was the movie about, when asked about it; they would just reiterate the fact that it was a film made by Disney. In doing so, they were clearly trying to capitalise on the positive image that Disney has around the world, by aligning themselves with the values for which Disney supposedly stands for. The film was directed by Mitch Davis and produced by Gerald Molen – both of them Mormons.

Harley-Davidson Motor Company

According to Douglas Atkin, the author of *The Culting of Brands* (2004), cults are groups or movements that can exhibit a great devotion or dedication to some person, idea, or thing, and they are fuelled by innovative ideologies. Cult members demonstrate an acute sense of belonging and provide voluntary advocacy on behalf of the cult (Atkin, 2004: xxii). Cults in return are dedicated to their members and make them feel special and individual. They celebrate the things that make their members different from everyone else. They say: 'You are different, we're different too.' The way cults attract members is by accepting that being different is good. This often means targeting people who feel alienated from the mainstream. As Atkin points out, Harley-Davidson Motor Company operates in the same manner, and even embraces this concept in their brand guidelines document: "Harley Truth #1: Harley is not for everyone" (Atkin, 2004: 18–19).

In this case, the motorbike acts as a totem for those who see themselves as part of the Harley tribe. Their worship for the motorbike and what this machine represents can also be seen in their dress, their appearance, and their values. The Harley-Davidson motorcycle is what marks them out from other groups. To them, the motorcycle is not merely a means of transport, but a symbol that stands for a certain kind of working-class masculinity and freedom (Lury, 1996: 17–24). Regardless of whether Harley riders like to see themselves as 'gang members', 'urban cowboys', or 'weekend warriors' when they are riding, they all choose to share the same type of distinctive clothing that acts as a symbolic code and makes them feel as being one with the motorcycle. As a kind of a uniform, their leather boots, fingerless gloves, sleeveless denim jackets, or studded and ornamented leather jackets create a 'fearsome look'. The clothing in this case is not meant to protect the rider from the elements, or to make the ride more enjoyable, as one would expect. Instead, the loose clothing blows in the wind and reduces the rider's speed, but in return it allows the rider to feel the excitement of travelling. This, paired up with their often-aggressive style of riding, only amplifies the wildness, noise, surprise, and intimidation that the motorcycle is meant to project, especially since the motorcycles themselves are designed to accentuate these features. This includes chromium-plated parts that give the bikes an exaggerated look of 'fierce power', such as the high 'cattle-horn' handlebars, exposed engines, and noisy exhausts. While the high handlebars force the rider to sit upright, which can result in a highly uncomfortable riding experience and further reduce the speed, they also give the rider a 'frightening appearance'. This 'ensemble' of symbolic elements gives a formidable expression of identity to the culture that Harley-Davidson Motor Company represents (Lury, 1996: 17). Therefore, it can be argued that the relationship that Harley riders have with their motorcycles is not functional or instrumental, but a symbolic one that allows them to display a particular set of values.

This set of values is clearly exemplified in the Harley-Davidson ad *Live By It* (2006). Filmed in black and white (probably to reinforce the sense of timelessness), the ad shows endless highways and American landscapes dominated by Harley riders of all walks of life. The ad begins with one lone Harley rider who slowly becomes accompanied by more and more Harley riders going the same way. They are all different, yet they all have the same attitude. They do not talk between themselves in the ad, but it seems that they all understand each other. Soon they form a large community of Harley riders, and all of them ride together. In the final scene, suddenly they are all gone, and the lone Harley rider rides off into the sunset. The message is clear: even when you are alone, you are still a part of the Harley community – or tribe.

This ad affirms the religious ritual of the congregational gathering for the purpose of reinforcing the social solidarity of a community. Also, this ad portrays Harley-Davidson as a 'church' in terms that the brand has the power to meet people's personal needs and to reinforce social integration (see Chidester, 1996: 748). From what it can be seen by the narration that accompanies the video, Harley-Davidson are clearly aware of the religious dimensions they possess as a brand. What begins as a single voice soon becomes a recitation of multiple voices, male and female, all chanting the Harley 'prayer' in unison:

We believe in going our own way, no matter which way the rest of the world is going.
We believe in bucking the system that's built to smash individuals like bugs on a windshield.
Some of us believe in the Man upstairs.
All of us believe in sticking it to the Man down here.
We believe in a sky, and we don't believe in a sunroof.
We believe in freedom.
We believe in dust, thimbleweeds, buffalo, mountain ranges, and riding off into the sunset.
We believe in saddlebags and we believe that cowboys had it right.
We believe in refusing to knuckle under to anyone.
We believe in wearing black because it doesn't show any dirt, or weakness.
We believe that the world is going soft, and that we are not going along with it.
We believe in motorcycle rally that lasts a week.
We believe in roadside attractions, gas stations, hot dogs, and finding out what's over the next hill.

We believe in runway engines, pistons the size of garbage cans, fuel tanks designed
    in 1936, freight train-sized headlights, chrome and custom paint.
We believe in flames and the skulls.
We believe life is what you make it, and we make it one helluva ride.
We believe that the machine you sit on can tell the world exactly where do you stand.
We don't care what everyone else believes.
Amen.

The advertisement ends with the Harley-Davidson logo and the slogan 'Live by it'. In this way, Harley riders' relation to each other is mediated through a particular understanding of the motorcycle as a totem to which they belong and with which they identify.

Interestingly, the most authentic Harley riders represent only a fraction of the Harley customers. The 'bad boy' image that a Harley projects has been first projected by an article ran by *Life* magazine on 21 July 1947, describing a motorcycle rally in Hollister, California, as a riot that terrorised the small town. The photograph that accompanied the story showed a drunken man sitting on a motorcycle surrounded by empty beer bottles. But, as Harley-Davidson point out on their website, the photo was later revealed to have been staged and the motorcycle rally in Hollister was actually a peaceful event. Nevertheless, the image of 'drunken, out-of-control motorcycle gangs' started to form in the public's imagination (Harley-Davidson Museum, 2013). The rebel image was further reinforced in the public mind by motorcycle clubs such as the Hell's Angels (founded in 1948) and movies such as *The Wild One* (1953) and *Easy Rider* (1969). With time, iconic images of black leather riders and chopped Harley's on the open road have become the epitome of the modern-day rebel in American popular culture (Atkin, 2004: 22).

The Harley-Davidson culture can be seen as a 'sanctuary' where the initiated can experience temporary 'self-transformation' (Schouten and McAlexander, 1995: 50). As a brand, Harley appeals to individuals who do not quite feel at home in the traditional society. These individuals believe that they are 'bad boys' or 'rebels' even though they are very far from being members of a motorcycle gang. Typical Harley riders love the freedom of the road and the company of others who also feel 'trapped' in the suburbia, in their jobs, and by their families (Atkin, 2004: 21). The dominant value in the ethos of the Harley-Davidson community is personal freedom. According to John W. Schouten and James H. McAlexander (1995: 51), there are two kinds of personal freedoms that are particularly important here: liberation (i.e. freedom from) and licence (i.e. freedom to). This personal freedom is embodied by two systems of totemic symbols: (a) the eagle – represented in the Harley logo, and (b) the horse – signified in the motorcycle itself as a metaphor (Harley-as-horse). The spread-winged eagle stands as a symbol of liberation and broadly represents flight and American political freedom, but also predation and power (the latter appealing to different core values such as machismo). The 'Harley-as-horse' metaphor, which is common in biker art, poetry, and fiction, exemplifies personal freedom associated with the western folk hero – a frontiersman whose freedom is based on lack of attachments, or to his medieval and post-apocalyptic versions: the 'black knight' and the 'road warrior' (Schouten and McAlexander, 1995: 51–52). The Harley is seen as the antithesis of confinement, whatever this confinement might be (e.g. cars, offices, schedules, authority, work, family, or relationships). This rebellion from the reality of daily life is further reinforced with symbols such as tattoos, long hair, bushy beards, and associated biker clothing and accessories (Schouten and McAlexander, 1995: 52).

To be discontent with your ordinary life, even though there is no real reason for that, feels like breaking a social taboo; and it is precisely this that makes these individuals feel like rebels in their own right. For them, purchasing a Harley is a form of escapism from the drudgery of their everyday lives. The cult of Harley-Davidson embraces them and tells them that it is all right to feel like you do not belong out there, and that it is all right to be different. For these individuals, being a part of this culture gives them an emotional satisfaction that they cannot find elsewhere (Atkin, 2004: 21). Then again, while the myth of the Harley and its supporting symbolism is one of total freedom, it is ironic that Harley enthusiasts commonly choose to join formal organisations that imply on them rigid new structures, new codes of conduct, new pressures to conform, and new sources of authority (Schouten and McAlexander, 1995: 52).

As most cults (and tribes, for that matter), Harley-Davidson Motor Company too has its own distinctive markings, argot, and iconography. Tattoos, leather, bandannas, beards, ripped jeans, and emblems are all part of the 'uniform' that Harley riders wear to recognise each other and to distinguish themselves from the rest of the society. To exemplify the significance of this, Atkin (2004) reflects on the experience of one young and enthusiastic Harley-Davidson employee by the name of Tom who he interviewed for the purpose of his study. During one Harley rally, Tom had been riding his bike, wearing his leather outfit, and fraternising with the Harley membership. In the evening, Tom decided to continue with the social interaction, and went to one of the members-only bars to have a drink. However, he made a 'critical' mistake and changed his biker clothes with khaki pants and a polo shirt. When he walked into the bar, Tom felt as if the whole place suddenly went silent. The bartender refused to serve him a drink and commented that the whole bar suspects that he was 'a cop or something'. In their conversation, Tom described this as the most uncomfortable experience he ever had. Among the 300 hostile patrons there, he even spotted some Hells Angels he helped earlier that day when they had trouble with their motorbikes (Atkin, 2004: 27–28). In another interview, one Harley rider explained that what they wear is 'essentially a "fuck off" to the outside world' (Atkin, 2004: 29).

Member identification does not end with uniformed clothing alone. An introduction of a jargon in the language can also provide a sense of solidarity to members and exclusion to outsiders. To bikers, for example, people who drive cars are 'cagers'; a dog that runs down the street and tries to take a bike down is called a 'yard shark'; someone who has ridden a thousand miles in 24 hours is called an 'iron butt'; and 'pipes and slippers' are bikers who should be respected because of their age (Atkin, 2004: 30).

As with any cult or religion, the Harley-Davidson iconography also plays a significant part in separating them from the others. Their 'Bar and Shield' emblem, for example, is the Harley-Davidson's coat of arms – a 'knight's battle shield' that further connotes the status of being a mythic warrior on the road (Atkin, 2004: 29). The importance of the Harley-Davidson's iconography for the company can also be seen in the introductory statement in their internal document, *Harley-Davidson Visual Identity and Trademark Guidelines* (2001):

Harley-Davidson logos and trademarks symbolize more than just the quality and heritage of our products. They stand for something important enough that people tattoo them on their skin. It's something that can't easily be expressed with words, but is felt in the soul. For many, 'Harley-Davidson' isn't a name or a brand. It's a way of life.

Although it may be more difficult to capture the Harley-Davidson experience on paper, all members of the H-D family – corporate employees, distributors, dealers, licensees, suppliers, and marketing partners alike – must use words and symbols to communicate with each other and our customers. Our 'visual identity' encompasses all of the ways our brand is communicated graphically – from logos and trademarks to color and typeface. It gives us a direct line to people's emotions, instantly triggering all the thoughts and feelings people associate with Harley-Davidson. So all elements of our visual identity must reflect the strength and tradition that Harley-Davidson represents. All the time.

(Harley-Davidson Marketing Communications, 2001)

By comparing Harley-Davidson to a religious cult, such as the Hare Krishna movement for example, we can see similar patterns in members' behaviour and the corporate culture. As devoted Harley riders have a set of values they pursue and code of behaviour they follow, so do Krishnas, in their own way. Hare Krishnas do not drink alcohol, or eat meat, fish, or eggs. They follow strict rules of behaviour and perform rituals in their worship of the divine. They wear distinctive clothing, carry chanting beads, and believe that spirituality should be a priority in their lives. Krishnas give up all their possessions and severe links with their former lives. Many of them live in Krishna temples and adopt an ascetic and monastic life. They take on new names and vow to abstain from any gambling or illicit sexual behaviour. They chant the Hare Krishna mantra sixteen times a day, and every morning members apply markings to the forehead and nose as a sign that the body is a temple of the supreme lord. Male members shave their heads, except for a small tuft of hair at the back that symbolises their surrender to Krishna. This movement has never been fully accepted in the western world and the strangeness of its doctrine has often caused the Krishnas to be viewed with suspicion by the establishment. Then again, it seems that Krishnas uses the seclusion from the society to empower themselves. They have a well-defined sense of group identity and it is their choice to be separated from the rest. In an interview with a long-standing Hare Krishnas member, Atkin (2004:

19–20) learned that the cult has a very strong sense of 'us' and 'them'; they see themselves as being 'good' and that everyone else is 'bad'. This Krishnas member was not feeling angry towards the establishment for not understanding them, but was feeling sorry for everyone because they were all going to hell except them.

Nike Inc.

As a part of their television series, *Branded: The Power of Brand Names* (1996), BBC profiled Nike and analysed the company's commercial and cultural success. In the documentary, BBC uses a range of religious connotations to describe the company. They referred to Nike's headquarters in Oregon as a 'shrine' and a 'cathedral' to sporting excellence where each building has its own 'patron saint' (an athlete superstar), and 'icons' (images of athletes) adorn every wall. They described Nike's Olympic advertising campaigns as a 'crusade', and Nike's employees as 'disciples' driven by 'religious fervour'. The company was also described as a 'cult – but a good one'. In the documentary, Nike's Chairman and CEO Phil Knight describes Nike as 'more than just a business. [...] [Nike] is a mission' (cited in Swain, 1996). This documentary has prompted me to investigate these statements further, and as a result I conducted an interview with Quan Payne, the Global Art Director for Nike and Director for Digital Sports Initiative of Nike+ (2011–2013):

> Gjoko Muratovski: Based on your experience working for Nike, how would you comment on these statements [from the BBC documentary]?
>
> Quan Payne: I think that to many fans around the world sport is their religion. They live and breathe sport and the passion for their teams. Nike has been able to capture the essence of this passion within the consumer and use it to their advantage. I would not currently say that the idea of religion is part of their current positioning but rather elevating their athletes to the modern version of religious deities: superheroes.
>
> Gjoko Muratovski: Do you agree with BBC that Nike functions as a quasi-religious institution?
>
> Quan Payne: Personally no, but to many who love the brand and have passion for what it does, yes.
>
> Gjoko Muratovski: Can you tell me about the working culture there?
>
> Quan Payne: The internal culture doesn't lend itself to any religious connotations. It functions as any multibillion-dollar company has to. The culture at Nike is one

of constant evolution which stems from the base notion of always striving to do something better.

Gjoko Muratovski: Is it different from other places where you used to work?

Quan Payne: Not significantly. Every large business has slightly different working cultures. Most of the brands that I have worked with have had a lot of brand equity within the markets that they compete so they have similar views.

Gjoko Muratovski: What is the ideology behind the advertising campaigns?

Quan Payne: That Nike can elevate the natural performance of individuals with the pinnacle driving toward the modern superhero.
(Payne, 2013, personal communication)

Payne's comments, to a certain extent, confirm the BBC's statements – even though Payne finds them somewhat exaggerated. However, he mentions the role of the superhero as a central idea around which Nike's brand message is formed. A superhero – or a demigod, such as Hercules, in classical mythology – is a hero that possesses superhuman or extraordinary powers.

For a company that derives its name from the Goddess of Victory (Nike), the glorification of superheroes, or 'demigods', as a part of their brand strategy is quite suitable. Of all the myths, that of the hero is the most common and best known in the world.[5] This myth can be found in the classical mythology of Greece and Rome, in the Middle Ages, in the Far East, among many tribes, in most religions – and even in modern life where heroes and superheroes make frequent appearances in comic books, Hollywood and Bollywood blockbusters, Asian martial arts films, as well as in various computer games and animations. The myth of the hero has an obvious dramatic appeal to individuals, and a less obvious, but nevertheless important, social significance for the communities where the myth originates. Historically, this universal pattern has appeared even among groups or individuals that have had no cultural contact with each other at the time of or since such myths have been developed (Muratovski, 2010: 220).

Even though hero myths can vary substantially in details, the closer one examines them, the more one is able to see that structurally they are very similar. According to Joseph L. Henderson (1964: 101), the archetype of the hero myth can be broken into six basic segments: (1) the tale of the hero's miraculous, but humble birth; (2) the hero's early proof of superhuman strength or supernatural abilities; (3) the hero's rapid rise to prominence or power; (4) the hero's triumphant struggle with the forces of evil; (5) the hero's fallibility in regard to the sin of pride – the quality Aristotle described as *hubris*; and (6) the hero's fall through betrayal or through a 'heroic' sacrifice that ends in his death.[6] The sixth segment, for example, rarely appears in the Hollywood hero tales who generally tend to have happy endings; but this segment is often a prominent feature in classical myths, folk tales, and in real life.

Another important characteristic is that the early weakness of the hero is balanced by the appearance of strong 'tutelary' figure(s) or guardian(s). These enable the hero to perform superhuman tasks that cannot be accomplished unaided. When presented in a story, these godlike figures – as Henderson (1964: 101–103) puts it – act as symbolic representatives of the psyche. They are the larger and more comprehensive identity that supplies the strength that the personal ego lacks: in Freudian terms, they are superego. Their special role suggests that the essential function of the heroic myth is the development of the individual's ego-consciousness – one's awareness of his or her own strengths and weaknesses – in a manner that equips the individual for the challenging tasks with which life confronts them. In real life, and in the case of the athletes, the tutelary figures that Henderson refers to are roles often performed by parents who have provided a great deal of support in their early formative years, or the coaches that have trained them. Once the individual passes the test (achieves sporting victories, for example) and enters the 'mature phase of life', the hero myth loses its relevance. The achievement of that maturity is usually represented with the hero's symbolic death – or in this case, a retirement due to age or injury, or withdrawal due to a public scandal.

This narrative can often be seen with some of the athletes that Nike is associated with, and in a number of cases, all six segments have unfolded in real life too. Examples include athletes such as the Olympic-medal winner Oscar Pistorius aka 'Blade Runner' – double-amputee South African runner who was charged with murdering his girlfriend; Lance Armstrong, a cancer survivor and seven consecutive times winner of the Tour de France before he was suspended for life for doping offences; or Tiger Woods, a former child prodigy and golf world champion who has fallen out of grace after being caught on cheating his wife.

The French sociologist, Jacques Ellul (1973: 172), believes that the hero myth, or the cult of the hero, is a necessary addition to society. In a mass society, individuals often lose control of the expression of their own desires and submit to external impulses towards the security of group affiliation. People's personal inclinations and tastes give way to participation in the collective; and the collective will always be best idealised, patterned, and represented by the hero – the 'one' we believe can embody the enthusiastic will of the many – or at least can provide a support for it. As discussed above, the creation of the hero cult is often seen in connection with champion athletes, but we can see this with movie stars and music idols as well.

According to Ellul (1973: 173), in highly regulated mass societies, the individuals are unable to express their desires through personal thought or action, and instead they project onto the hero all they ever wanted to be. Then, the achievements of the hero become achievements of the admirers, and the admirers begin to admire themselves by identifying with the hero. By doing so, they live vicariously – through an intermediary. They think, feel, and act through their hero, and once again become 'children', ceasing to defend their own interests, as they know that their hero 'loves' them and looks after them.[7] The hero becomes not only a model and a paternal/maternal figure (see Dinnerstein, 1999), but also a powerful and mythical realisation of all that the individual cannot be (in the case of the suppressed female, see de Beauvoir, 1972). The psychological need for a hero is cyclical and arises again and again – whenever and for whatever reason the ego needs strengthening. In other words, when the conscious mind needs assistance in some task that it cannot accomplish on its own, it draws on sources of strength that lie only in the unconscious mind (Henderson, 1964: 114).

According to Carl Jung (1964: 68), the universal hero myth typically refers to a powerful man or 'god-man' (*sic.*) who fights evil in the form of various monsters, demons, or villains, and who liberates his people from destruction and death.[8] In most cases, regardless of the origins of the story, the 'hero' is the focus of the narration. The worship of the hero is frequently accompanied by sacred texts, ceremonies, dances, hymns, prayers, and sacrifices, which grip the audience with spiritual emotions and exalt the individual to identification with the hero. In such situations, true believers become liberated from their personal impotence and misery – as Jung puts it – and they also feel endowed (at least temporarily) with some superhuman qualities, just like their hero. If we take into account the Olympic Games, or any other sporting event for that matter, we can see that the cult of the hero is still present even today.

The Need to Belong

Human beings are 'incurably religious'. This epigrammatic and to some extent facetious statement highlights the most impressive feature of all religions: their ability to transcend space, time, and form – and this continues even today (Encyclopaedia Britannica, 1994: 530). For example, if we take into account the use of religious metaphors by commercial brands as presented in this study, then we can see that the world of branding has taken refuge in the world of sacred and assumed 'religious dimensions' (see Sheffield, 2006). In addition to this, brands also promote tribal behaviour. In a consumer society, people are not simply encouraged to purchase products in order to become a part of the group the products represent, but they must feel that they already naturally belong to that group and therefore they purchase the product. This neo-tribal aspiration is based around what Judith Williamson (1978: 47) describes as a 'commercial totemism'. Marty Neumeier (2006: 151), in his study on branding, agrees with this construct: 'As globalism removes barriers, people erect new ones. They create tribes – intimate worlds they can understand and participate in. Brand names are tribal gods, each ruling a different space within the tribe'.

Our need to belong and to feel as a part of a community can be a powerful motivational force. We often feel very strong need to be integrated into the community, to have a setting, and to experience ideological and affective communication. This causes people to search for something that will fill their inner void. In the absence of true self-fulfilment, we replace this by pursuing some kind of entertainment instead, such as browsing and posting on social networks, reading a book, going to the cinema, shopping, and so on. But these are only temporary remedies. In the search for a deeper and more fulfilling experience, people become ready to listen to all kind of propaganda – whether that might be political marketing, religious indoctrination, or as this study argues, brand advertising. As this state of 'emptiness' can lead to severe personality disorders, communication that encompasses various facets of human relations creates highly desired emotional appeals. In return, a promise of integration can appear as an incomparable remedy (Ellul, 1973: 148–149).[9]

The way people perceive happiness in life is often based around their relationship with other people (Kasser, 2002). For example, a series of surveys conducted in the United States in the mid-1940s examined the link between material wealth and subjective happiness and concluded that social values significantly outweigh material values in terms of importance. According to this study what we want in life is a sense of autonomy and control, good self-esteem, warm family relationships, tension-free leisure time, close and intimate friends, romance and love (Jhally, 1998). This, however, is not to say that material goods were not seen as important. They were still associated with a good quality of life, but what the research showed is that once people achieve a certain level of comfort, objects cease to make people happy (Jhally, 1998; Putnam, 2000: 332–333). A more recent study reaffirmed this position: 'while material goods play a significant role in modern life, increasing levels of material wealth do not lead to corresponding increases in happiness' (Thorpe, 2010: 8). Nevertheless, brand advertising is trying to convince us to think otherwise. Here I am not referring to the daily commercials that focus on selling trademarked fast-moving consumer goods (FMCG), but to the creative advertising designed with emotional manipulation in mind. This is the type of advertising that offers us something that we desire or need on a personal level, and replaces this with a product. In this case the product is not the real offer, but a substitute for something that is of social value to us (Jhally, 1998).

Brands see the real opportunity in the moments when we do not feel happy or satisfied with the quality of our lives. With brand advertising blurring the line between emotional, material, and spiritual satisfaction, we often reach out to shopping to satisfy our unfulfilled desires or to compensate our social needs (Thorpe, 2010: 9). Unfortunately, the 'shopping therapy' results are short-lived, and we soon start to crave for our next consumer 'fix'. While consumption makes us materially richer, it leaves us emotionally sadder; and the cycle continues again (Ehrenfeld, 2008: 36).

Conclusion

Some of the leading brands often tend to share similar characteristics with religious cults or extreme political movements, in a sense that they exhibit a great devotion or dedication to some person, idea, or thing, and they are fuelled by innovative ideologies. Dedicated brand followers, cult members, and extremists share these dogmatic beliefs and tend to demonstrate an acute sense of belonging and provide voluntary advocacy on behalf of the brand, the cult, or the movement. According to Atkin (2000: 20), everyone can become, or has been a 'victim' (*sic*.) to a religious following, political movement, or a seductive brand at some point in their life. At times when individuals feel socially alienated and need some kind of emotional support, but cannot find this support within their own environment, they are at the risk of becoming a 'raw food' for religious and political organisations, or cult-like brands (Atkin, 2000: 20; see also Mikul, 2010).

In a modern society many people often tend to feel different and disassociated from everyone else, even though they may not be unique or unusual in any particular way. At times such as this, when these people do not feel that they 'fit' in their existing environment, they go on a quest to find their place in society. People often want to express their 'true' identity, but they are not always sure what this identity is – and like many others, they tend to look for references in popular culture. This makes them highly susceptible to persuasive messages by iconic brands that dominate the media landscape. Different brands welcome different people in their communities and by that they provide a sense of belonging, social inclusion, and direction in life. When people find a brand that gives them the social and emotional support that they need, but cannot find elsewhere, they begin to form a 'tribe' around this brand, and follow it with a blind faith. The need to believe and to seek meaning in life is a common human characteristic that is both philosophical and religious in nature. Many people believe that owning branded objects will make their lives better, help them identify who they are, or give them a sense of belonging. That is why some scholars (see Kowinski, 1983; Jhally, 1989; Twitchell, 1999) argue that consumerism is the furthest reaching 'religion' of today.

References

Angelico, I., 1998. *The cola conquest: a trilogy*. [video] Montreal: DLI Productions.

Atkin, D., 2004. *The culting of brands: when customers become true believers*. New York: Penguin.

Belk, R. W., Walledorf, M. and Sherry, J. F. Jr., 1989. The sacred and the profane in consumer behaviour: theodicy on the odyssey. *Journal of Consumer Research*, 16:1, pp.1–38.

Bettelheim, B., 1977. *The uses of enchantment: the meaning and importance of fairy tales*. New York: Vintage.

Bhasin, K., 2011. 15 Facts about Coca-Cola that will blow your mind. *Business Insider*, 9 June, http://www.businessinsider.com/facts-about-coca-cola-2011-6?op=1. Accessed 27 November 2012.

Bryman, A., 1999. The Disneylization of society. *Sociological Review*, 47:1, pp.25–47.

Bryman, A., 2003. McDonald's as a Disneyzied institution. *American Behavioral Scientist*, 47:2, pp.154–167.

Cambell, J., 1949. *The hero with a thousand faces*. New York: Pantheon Books.

Chidester, D., 1996. The church of baseball, the fetish of Coca-Cola, and the potlatch of Rock 'n' Roll: theoretical models for the study of religion in American popular culture. *Journal of the American Academy of Religion*, 64:4, pp.743–765.

Chidester, D., 2005. *Authentic fakes: religion and American popular culture*. Berkeley: University of California Press.

Curtis, A., 2002. *The century of the self*. [video] London: BBC Four.

Day, K., 2012. Fengshui: a cultural band-aid for the 21st century? In: *Unbounded: an interior design colloquium*. Melbourne, Australia, 15 November 2012. Melbourne: Swinburne University of Technology.

de Beauvoir, S., 1972. *The second sex*. London: Penguin.

de Certeau, M., 1984. *The practice of everyday life*. Berkeley: University of California Press.

Dinnerstein, D., 1999. *The mermaid and the Minotaur: sexual arrangements and human malaise*. New York: Other Press.

Durkheim, E., 1912. *The elementary forms of religious life*. Reprint 1995. New York: The Free Press.

Egri, L., 1972. *The art of dramatic writing: its basis in the creative interpretation of the human motives*. New York: Touchstone.

Ehrenfeld, J. R., 2008. *Sustainability by design: a subversive strategy for transforming our consumer culture*. New Haven: Yale University Press.

Ellul, J., 1973. *Propaganda: the formation of men's attitudes*. New York: Vintage Books.

Encyclopaedia Britannica, 1994. s.v. 'Systems of Religious and Spiritual Belief'. *Encyclopaedia Britannica: Macroapedia*, 15th Edition. London: Encyclopaedia Britannica (UK). pp.530-577.

Encyclopaedia Britannica, 2012. s.v. 'Prayer'. *Encyclopaedia Britannica: Academic Edition*. [online] London: Encyclopaedia Britannica (UK)., http://www.britannica.com/EBchecked/topic/474128/prayer. Accessed 10 December 2012.

Evans, J., 2006. New York Apple store lovers tell proposal story. *MacWorld*, 31 May, http://www.macworld.com/article/1051096/proposal.html. Accessed 27 November 2012.

Field, S., 2003. *The definitive guide to screenwriting*. New York: Random House.

Freud, S., 1919. *Totem and taboo: resemblances between the psychic lives of savages and neurotics*. London: George Routledge & Sons, Ltd.

Harley-Davidson Marketing Communications, 2001. *Harley-Davidson visual identity and trademark guidelines*. Milwaukee: Harley-Davidson Motor Company.

Harley-Davidson Museum, 2013. *H-D history: July 21, 1947*, http://www.harley-davidson.com/en_US/Content/Pages/HD_Museum/explore/hd-history.html. Accessed 24 July 2013.

Henderson, J. L., 1964. Ancient myths and modern man. In: C. G. Jung, ed. *Man and his symbols*. London: Aldus Books. pp.95–156.

Heussner, K. M., 2010. Looking for a new religion? Apple gives dose of the divine. *ABC News*, 5 August, http://abcnews.go.com/Technology/religion-apple-dose-divine/story?id=11300758. Accessed 29 July 2013.

Hogan, K. M., 1998. Celebration, Florida. *University of Virginia*. [online] Available at: http://xroads.virginia.edu/~ma98/hogan/celebration/main.html. Accessed 9 December 2012.

Hume, D., 1757. *The natural history of Religion. Reprint* 1889. London: A. and H. Bradlaugh Bonner.

Jhally, S., 1989. Advertising as religion: the dialectic of technology and magic. In: I. Angus and S. Jhally, eds. *Cultural politics in contemporary America*. New York: Routledge. pp.217–229.

Jhally, S., 1998. *Advertising and the end of the world*. [video] Northampton: Media Education Foundation.

Jhally, S., 2003. *No logo*. [video] Northampton: Media Education Foundation.

Jones, N., 2011. Steve Jobs: technological messiah. *New Statesman*, 7 October, http://www.newstatesman.com/blogs/nelson-jones/2011/10/steve-jobs-apple-religious. Accessed 27 November 2012.

Jowett, G. and O'Donnell, V., 2006. *Propaganda and persuasion*. Thousand Oaks: Sage Publications.

Jung, C. G., 1964. Approaching the unconscious. In: C. G. Jung, ed. *Man and his symbols*. London: Aldus Books. pp.1–94.

Kasser, T., 2002. *The high price of materialism*. Cambridge: MIT Press.

Keller, B., 1990. Of famous arches, beeg meks and rubles. *New York Times Magazine*, 28 January, http://www.nytimes.com/1990/01/28/world/of-famous-arches-beeg-meks-and-rubles.html?pagewanted=all&src=pm. Accessed 29 July 2013.

King, J. M., 1983. Empires of popular culture: McDonald's and Disney. In: M. Fishwick, ed. *Ronald revisited: the world of Ronald McDonald*. Bowling Green: Bowling Green University Press. pp.106–119.

Klein, N., 2000. *No logo*. New York: Flamingo.

Kottak, C., 1983. Rituals at McDonald's. In: M. Fishwick, ed. *Ronald revisited: the world of Ronald McDonald*. Bowling Green: Bowling Green University Press. pp.53–58.

Kowinski, W. S., 1985. *The malling of America: an inside look at the great consumer paradise*. New York: William Morrow & Co.

Kunde, J., 2000. *Corporate religion: building a strong company through personality and corporate soul*. London: Prentice Hall.

Lury, C. 1996. *Consumer Culture*. New Brunswick, NJ: Rutgers University Press.

Lindstrom, M., 2008. *Buy-ology: truth and lies about why we buy*. New York: Doubleday.

Mikul, C., 2010. *The cult files: true stories from the extreme edges of religious belief*. New York: Metro Books.

Miller, J. V., 2009. *Consuming religion: Christian faith and practice in a consumer society*. New York: Continuum.

Mogg, T., 2011. Eight-block line forms outside Apple store in Tokyo for iPhone 4S. *Digital Trends*, 13 October, http://www.digitaltrends.com/apple/eight-block-line-forms-outside-apple-store-in-tokyo-for-iphone-4s/. Accessed 27 November 2012.

Moor, L., 2007. *The rise of brands*. Oxford: Berg.

Moraru, M., 2013. Sacred and profane view of Christmas in advertising. *Journalism si Comunicare*, 8:4, pp.26–38.

Muratovski, G., 2010. *Design research: corporate communication strategies – from religious propaganda to strategic brand management*. Ph.D. University of South Australia.

Muratovski, G., 2013a. Totem: the religious dimensions of branding. In: *Popular Culture Association/American Culture Association Annual Conference*. Washington DC, 28 March 2013. Washington DC: PCA/ACA.

Muratovski, G., 2013b. Urban branding: the politics of architecture. *Design Principles and Practices: An International Journal – Annual Review*, 6:1, pp.45–58.

Neumeier, M., 2006. *The brand gap: how to bridge the distance between business strategy and design – a white board overview*. New York: Peachpit.

NPS, 2011. Utopias in America. *National Park Service: US Department of the Interior*. http://www.nps.gov/nr/travel/amana/utopia.htm. Accessed 9 December 2012.

Olins, W., 1990. *Corporate identity: making business strategy visible through design*. London: Thames and Hudson.

O'Shaughnessy, N. J., 2004. *Politics and propaganda: weapons of mass destruction*. Manchester: Manchester University Press.

Papiernik, L. R., 1994. Mac Attack?. *Financial World*, 12 April, pp.28–30.

Pastoureau, M., 1997. *Heraldry: its origins and meaning*. London: Thames and Hudson.

Pavitt, J., 2000. In goods we trust. In: J. Pavitt, ed. *Brand New*. London: V&A Publications. pp.19–39.

Putnam, R. D., 2000. *Bowling alone: the collapse and revival of American community*. New York: Simon and Schuster.

Riley, A. and Boome, A., 2011. Superbrands' success fuelled by sex, religion and gossip. *BBC News*, 16 May, http://www.bbc.co.uk/news/business-13416598. Accessed 27 November 2012.

Ritzer, G., 1993. *The McDonaldization of society*. Los Angeles: Pine Forge Press.

Ritzer, G., 2010. *McDonaldization: the reader*. Thousand Oaks: Pine Forge Press.

Rosenwald, M. S., 2011. Apple is a new religion, and Steve Jobs was its high priest. *The Washington Post*, 8 October, http://www.washingtonpost.com/opinion/apple-is-a-new-religion-and-steve-jobs-was-its-high-priest/2011/10/07/gIQAJYIgTL_print.html. Accessed 20 November 2012.

Schlosser, E., 2012. *Fast food nation: the dark side of the all-American meal*. New York: First Mariner Books.

Schouten, J. W. and McAlexander, J. H., 1995. Subculture of consumption: an ethnography of the new bikers. *Journal of Consumer Research*, 22:1, pp.43–61.

Sheffield, T., 2006. *The religious dimensions of advertising.* London: Palgrave Macmillan.

Spence, L., 1921. *Introduction to mythology.* Reprint 1994. London: George G. Harrap & Company Ltd.

Stillich, S., 2009. Donald versus Hitler: Walt Disney and the art of WWII propaganda. *Spiegel Online: International*, October 8, http://www.spiegel.de/international/germany/donald-versus-hitler-walt-disney-and-the-art-of-wwii-propaganda-a-641547.html. Accessed 10 December 2012.

Swain, P., 1996. *Branded: the power of brand names (Nike).* [video] London: BBC.

The Celebration Company, 2003. *Declaration of covenants, conditions, and restrictions for Celebration residential properties.* Celebration: The Celebration Company.

The Celebration Company, 2011. Welcome to Celebration: education. *The Celebration Company*, http://www.celebration.fl.us/town-info/directory/education. Accessed 9 December 2012.

The Coca-Cola Company, 2011. Atlanta beginnings. *The Coca-Cola Company*, http://heritage.coca-cola.com/. Accessed 20 September 2013.

The Coca-Cola Company, 2012. Coke lore: the history of the modern day Santa Claus. *The Coca-Cola Company*, http://www.coca-colacompany.com/stories/coke-lore-santa-claus Accessed 27 November 2012.

The McDonald's Corporation, 2012. Getting to know us. *The McDonald's Corporation*, http://www.aboutmcdonalds.com/mcd/our_company.html/. Accessed 9 December 2012.

The Walt Disney Company, 2012. Company overview. *The Walt Disney Company*, http://thewaltdisneycompany.com/about-disney/company-overview. Accessed 9 December 2012.

Thorpe, A., 2010. Design's role in sustainable consumption. *Design Issues*, 26:2, pp.3–16.

Tibken, S., 2011. Apple opens New York Grand Central store. *The Wall Street Journal*, 9 December, http://online.wsj.com/article/SB10001424052970203413304577088201456063374.html. Accessed 27 November 2012.

Turkle, S., 2011. *Alone together: why we expect more from technology and less from each other.* New York: Basic Books.

Twitchell, J., 1999. *Lead us into temptation: the triumph of American materialism.* New York: Columbia University Press.

Williamson, J., 1978. *Decoding advertisements: ideology and meaning in advertising.* London: Marion Boyars.

Yale University Library, 2012. America and the utopian dream. *Yale University*, http://brbl-archive.library.yale.edu/exhibitions/utopia/utopcom.html. Accessed 9 December 2012.

Notes

1. Martin Lindstrom conducted similar neuroaffective research several years earlier for his project 'Buyology'. He interviewed fourteen religious leaders from around the

world in order to establish the elements of what constitutes a religious belief system and used this knowledge to build a hypothesis that was later tested on brand fans and devoted Christians. He tested a range of brands and the findings correspond with the BBC study; the brains of fans of Apple, Harley-Davidson, or Guinness respond in the same way as the brains of religious followers when exposed to the iconography of their brand preference. Brands that do not fall in the category of highly emotional brands, such as BP or KFC, revealed almost opposite brain response (Lindstrom, 2008).

2. Although Santa Claus is based on the Vatican-authorised figure of Saint Nicholas – protector and benefactor to children – various depictions of the character existed long before the Sundblom interpretation. At the beginning, Santa was not standardised in appearance. His image ranged from big to small and fat to tall. Santa even appeared as an elf and looked a bit spooky. A little known fact is that in a godlike fashion, Sundblom created Santa in his own image: Santa Claus, as we know him, is a self-portrait of Sundblom himself. In the creative process, Sundblom was inspired by Clement Clark Moore's poem 'The night before Christmas', which featured St Nicholas as a kind, jovial man, conveniently dressed in a Coca-Cola's corporate colours – red and white (The Coca-Cola Company, 2012).

3. In 1622, Vatican established the *Sacra Congregatio de Propaganda Fide* (The Sacred Congregation for Propagating the Faith of the Roman Catholic Church) for the purpose of expanding to the 'New World' and for dealing with competitors such as the Protestants.

4. It is worth mentioning that Disney is also using the same principle in their theme parks when they are transported abroad. The Disneyland in Tokyo has been 'Japanised' in terms that the Mystery Tour there has been based on a Japanese ghost house. Similar adjustments were made in the Paris Disneyland, where the alcohol ban also had to be lifted (Bryman, 2003: 164). In Hong Kong, Disneyland was even designed and developed according to the *Fengshui* principles. This would be normally unimaginable, but The Walt Disney Company is acutely aware of the superstition of the Hong Kong market and they have shown a great deal of flexibility here (Day, 2012).

5. One of the most recognised hero myths is the story of Jesus Christ, or 'Christ the Redeemer'. The concept of Jesus belongs to the worldwide pre-Christian theme of the hero and the rescuer, in which traditionally the hero, although overpowered by a 'monster' (a villain of some kind), appears again in a miraculous way and overcomes whichever 'monster' has defeated him. The origin of this basic motif is unknown. However, one apparent certainty is that every generation seems to have known it as a tradition handed down from a preceding time. Jung (1964: 61) argues that we can safely assume that such a theme will have originated at a time when people did not yet know that they possessed a hero myth. According to him, that was an age when humans did not yet consciously reflect on what they were saying. The hero figure should, therefore, be viewed as an archetype that has existed from the earliest times of human history.

6. This theory has been developed by the American mythologist Joseph Campbell. His work on the archetype of the hero, outlining so many of the endless number of hero-variants across any number of cultures, is consciously used to this day within the Hollywood script-writing industry, and beyond, where its formulae are tightened into even-more-highly-structured regimens of how film-scripts and characterisation 'work' (see Campbell, 1949). Further references to this can be found in the works of Syd Field (2003) and Lajos Egri (1972).
7. Bruno Bettelheim (1977), in a landmark study of the ongoing use of European myths and fairy stories in children's culture, interprets the meaning of well-known stories for young children, drawing on case studies to develop what he called an 'explanation of the uses of enchantment'. By analysing the content of such stories and revealing their true meaning, Bettelheim explains how children use them, consciously or unconsciously, to cope with their emotions, whether they are feelings of smallness and helplessness or anxieties that the child feels about strangers and the mysteries of the outside world.
8. Considering that the myth-repertoires collected by the great nineteenth-century mythographers such as the brothers Grimm were collected in ways that suppressed the recording of equivalent female hero-legends, analysts such as Jung and his followers were forced to work over limited and limiting materials. In the present day, however, the hero myth often portrays female characters as well.
9. In small rural environments, community links are stronger and people already feel that they belong to a group. The situation is different in environments such as large cities or highly developed countries. In urban environments, individuals usually live separate from their larger families, their friends are dispersed, and due to the dynamics of their daily lives, they usually do not have the time to join clubs, take part in various social activities, or to be active members of a religious congregation (Ellul, 1973: 148; Putnam, 2000). Ellul (1973: 148) describes these individuals as members of 'fragmented communities' who lack the emotional support that an organised community can provide. This, in return, leads them to feel emotionally empty and devoid of meaning, even though their lives might be fulfilled with numerous daily activities. Another common experience is that in such environments, individuals often feel that even though they are surrounded by people, they are still alone and isolated. To feel lonely while amongst a crowd of people is perhaps the most terrible ordeal of the urban individual. According to Ellul (1973: 9), this is the phenomenon of the 'lonely crowd' – an environment in which a person can share nothing, talk to nobody, and expect nothing from anybody, while still being in the centre of everything. The desire for integration and the social obligation to be a part of a network is a constant element of our human behaviour throughout our existence. Today, we can recognise this desire in the face of the enormous success of social networking sites such as Facebook, LinkedIn, or Twitter (see Turkle, 2011).

Chapter 2

Business, National Identities and International Politics: The Role of Built Environments and Architectural Propaganda in Nation Branding

Gjoko Muratovski

Abstract

Countries, like corporations, increasingly started developing new images and identities for themselves through a range of activities broadly known as 'nation branding'. For some countries, the reasons behind such exercises are commercial in nature, but for others they are sociopolitical. Whatever these reasons are, many countries often resort to projecting their identity and their vision for their future through investments in built environments, ranging from urban design and buildings, to parks, monuments and public art. In line with this, this chapter examines the process of formation of national identities and subsequently their use as a foundation for nation branding, and presents comparative case studies that examine nation-branding exercises undertaken by three distinctive nation-states: United Arab Emirates, Turkmenistan and Macedonia.

Keywords

national identity, nation branding, built environments, architecture, United Arab Emirates, Turkmenistan, Macedonia

Introduction

At the end of the twentieth century and the beginning of the twenty-first century, many countries have assumed a business model of operation and have begun to compete with each other in a corporate manner. Countries, like corporations, have their own images and reputations, and this has been used as a foundation of a new form of brand building. With this, the term 'nation brand' has appeared, together with a nation-brand index that tracks the reputation of particular countries in relation to their activities, promotions and events at home and around the world (Muratovski, 2008). However, the need for the establishment of a strong nation brand is not always commercial; in some cases, the reasons behind this can also be sociopolitical in nature. For example, national 'brand' values are often analogous to national identities. National identities often have an impact on how successful a country is in motivating its own citizens, and attracting tourists, talent, cultural relations, capital, foreign investments and political allies. Therefore, it can be argued that coordinated manifestations of national identity are vital when it comes to nation branding (Muratovski, 2008, 2012).

In this chapter, I will examine (a) the process of formation of national identities, (b) the use of national identities as a foundation for nation branding and (c) I will present comparative case studies that examine nation-branding exercises of three distinctive nation-states.

In the first part of the chapter, I will reflect on the subjectivity of the national identities. In this part, I will refer to theories of 'narrative identity' (Ricoeur, 1991) and 'invented traditions' (Hobsbawm and Ranger, 1983) when addressing issues of national identities formation and change. Furthermore, I will also examine the role of built environments[1] in the formation and manifestation of national identities. Since the expressive power of state-commissioned or state-sanctioned built environments as signifiers of social, economic or political authority during times of prosperity is already acknowledged in the literature (Castoriadis, 1987; Zizek, 1989; Mayo, 1996; Sudjic, 2006; Sklair, 2010; Muratovski, 2012). Here, I will focus on the role of built environments during times of political or economic crisis – an often overlooked area of research (Diamond, 2003; Kaika, 2010; Muratovski, 2013a).

In the second part of the chapter, I will examine the relationship between nation branding and architecture[2] (Kirby and Kent, 2010; Muratovski, 2012, 2013a), architecture and territory (McNeill and Tewdwr-Jones, 2003), architecture and iconicity (Kaika, 2010; Sklair, 2010) and architecture as a catalyst for new experiences and perceptions while being a part of a larger system that brings together economic developments, technological progress and social change (Klingmann, 2007). The discourse on architecture and branding will be related to the problems of place branding (Mayes, 2008; Anholt, 2010; Hankinson, 2010), city branding (Kavaratzis, 2004, 2009; Parkerson and Saunders, 2005; Kavaratzis and Ashworth, 2005; Ashworth and Kavaratzis, 2009) and nation branding (Jaffe and Nebenzahl, 2006).

In the third part, I will examine issues of emerging identities of 'new' nations (Olins, 1990) and I will present examples of the use of state-sanctioned built environments for the achievement of various national, political, economic, social and cultural goals. In doing so, I will reflect on three geographically, culturally and politically distinct examples: United Arab Emirates, Turkmenistan and Macedonia.

This study holds the position that regardless of some similarities, there is a fundamental difference in the branding of products, corporations and places – in this case, cities and nations (see Kavaratzis, 2009). In this I agree with Mihalis Kavaratzis (2004: 58) that '[c]ity branding provides, on the one hand, the basis for developing policy to pursue economic development and, at the same time, it serves as a conduit for city residents to identify with their city'; and with Simon Anholt (2010: 9) that on the international scene, countries are judged by the things they do, and not the things they say. In this regard, city branding will be examined as a foundation on which nation branding is built.

This is a cross-disciplinary study that aims to contribute to the academic discussion on place branding by bringing issues of corporate branding, national identities, architecture and built environments closer together – a relationship that has rarely been examined in such detail in the literature on branding (see Kirby and Kent, 2010). The chapter will not reflect on matters often broadly labelled as 'marketing communications' or 'promotional activities' as they have been covered to a great extent in marketing literature so far. Through a historical overview and selected case studies, I will contribute to the place branding discussion and I will argue that built environments and iconic architecture can play a significant role when it comes to defining sovereign national identities and establishing competitive nation brands.

Part 1: National Identities

We live in a world that is filled with passionately espoused national causes by nations that try to impose their own identities and values on others; by nationalities that have no territory of their own and have to coexist in states that contain more than one nationality; or by various 'neo-nationalist' ideas expressed by newly founded nations (Smith, 1986; Castells, 1997). In the process of rediscovering their 'lost' identities or establishing new ones, some nations look for inspiration in their histories and traditions, and others reach out to new concepts. In either case, these transformations are characterised by shifts towards new forms of experiential stimulation, supported by new or existing cultural narratives (Jensen, 2007: 212). Thus, a new trend has re-emerged: the use of built environments as a way of establishing political authority, reaffirming national identities or promoting nations as cultural, tourist or business destinations. Many emerging nations now use built environments as physical manifestations of their identity and their political aspirations, or as a way of attracting new residents, visitors and investors (Muratovski, 2013a). While from a historical perspective this practice is not new, in the twenty-first century this has been used in a new context.

Subjectivity of the National Identity

One of the most complex issues in social science theory is the process of national identity change and formation. According to Couze Venn (2002), nationalism is a subjective idea that can affect everything from culture and lifestyle to politics. In line with this, Eugene D. Jaffe and Israel D. Nebenzahl (2006: 14) argue that people's beliefs, ideas and impressions create mental images that may or may not be congruent with objectively defined attributes of the nation; the projected idea of 'reality' does not have to exist in order for people to form a mental image of it.

Social scientists, in general, agree that a nation, above anything else, is defined in psychological and emotional terms. According to Anthony D. Smith (1986), there are six basic characteristics that constitute the identity of an ethnicity: (1) a collective name, (2) a common myth of descent, (3) a shared history, (4) a distinctive shared culture, (5) an association with a specific territory and (6) a sense of solidarity. T. K. Oommen (1997) agrees and argues that these characteristics also define a nation. Venn (2002) also suggests that various events, interactions and critical moments in history continually influence identity and the process applies equally to individuals and collectives (nations). According to him, at the end of each process of re-figuration, nations and their people have different and new kinds of stories to tell about themselves, and they are, in a sense, no longer who or what they were before (Venn, 2002: 32–33). This argument is based on Paul Ricoeur's (1991) theory of 'narrative identity'. According to this theory, identities are not definite, but constantly evolving narratives based on a fusion between history and fiction. What is more, Venn (2002) argues that individuals are characterised precisely by the fact that they invent narratives as a form in which various events can be configured, communicated and kept as memories that can be interpreted in different ways. In time, these memories become part of their individual identities (Venn, 2002: 34–35). By the same token, the same analogy can be applied to a nation – collective memory/collective identity.

Many key historical figures, from Alexander the Great and Julius Caesar to Napoleon Bonaparte and Adolf Hitler, have understood only too well that the national identity is not a static phenomenon and that identity can be predefined, managed, designed and communicated in such a way as to serve their immediate political needs. In the process of inventing identities, more important is the invention of the emotionally and symbolically charged signs of 'club membership', rather than dry statutes, constitutions and regulations. In this context, the national flag, the national anthem and the national emblem are the three key elements through which an independent country proclaims its identity and sovereignty. These symbols, significant precisely because of their undefined universality and symbolism, command instantaneous respect and loyalty. If constructed with an emotional appeal in mind, they can in themselves reflect or recreate the entire background, thought and culture of a nation (Hobsbawm, 1983: 11). The same principle can also be seen in state-commissioned or state-sanctioned built environments that act as physical forms of state propaganda (Muratovski, 2013a).

Invented Traditions

Throughout the history, many governments and regimes have created new cultural narratives in an attempt to establish a link between them and some kind of preferred historical past. For example, nothing appears more ancient and linked to an immemorial past than the pageantry surrounding the British monarchy; yet this is a product of the late nineteenth and early twentieth century (Hobsbawm, 1983: 1). Ritualised ceremonies that are shrouded in historical grandeur emerged during the era of nineteenth-century Romantic nationalism, especially between 1870 and 1914. Their purpose was, and to a certain extent still is, to glorify a particular regime, government or a national cause, and to justify their existence by grounding them in history. At the same time, and for the same purpose, other associated trends emerged. This included the erection of national monuments, establishment of museums, collections of folklore and canons of national literature, instalment of national holidays and various 'scientific' classifications of cultures and races. With the use of carefully designed and orchestrated occasions, specific costumes, a rigid order of events, pseudo-antique features and artefacts associated with ancient rituals, such proceedings were intended to symbolise timelessness. In one form or another, 'invented traditions'[3] of this nature have been developed by almost all established nations, and they continue to be introduced by newly emerging nations (Hobsbawm, 1983).

Invented traditions can often be seen in manifestations such as independence days, presidential inaugurations, flag raisings, group singing of anthems, religious or public festivals and funerals of important national figures, military parades as well as various quasi-archaic customs. As such, they are used to inscribe what seems to be a 'preferred' national history in the public consciousness (Edensor, 2002: 72–73). Events of this nature are important because they ground a nation in history by implying continuity with the past, thus symbolising community, legitimising the current state authority and inculcating an aura of tradition (Hobsbawm, 1983). World leaders throughout history, whether intuitively or consciously, have understood that effective identity manifested symbolically in visual or tangible form not only makes the nation recognisable, but it also serves as the first level of communication between the nation and its people (Olins, 1990).

Emerging Identities

Human beings are identity-seeking animals. According to Oommen (1997: 35), when old identities disappear or recede, new ones are invented and constructed. In many cases, the problems of creating a meaningful national identity are almost overwhelming, especially for new countries whose borders have been carved without any regard for historical, tribal, cultural or even geographical factors, but merely as a political compromise between two or more major colonial powers (Muratovski, 2008). When new nations are established, their identity transformations are usually manifested by strong symbolic actions. For example, when Rhodesia became Zimbabwe, the country symbolically reclaimed its cultural heritage. What Robert Mugabe had in common with every other leader of every new regime in every new country was the intuitive understanding of the people's need to belong. Many other new leaders, like Mugabe, also understood that a nation must first be defined in the mind of its people, and only then in legal terms in the eyes of the rest of the world. Therefore, many new nations have often made conscious attempts to develop new or bring back long-forgotten identities in an attempt to create a feeling of distinctiveness, pride and unity – and to show the outside world that their countries are truly sovereign states. Sometimes looking deep into their past, and sometimes trying to create something original, the new leaders of these emerging nations have commemorated their new identities with new names, flags, anthems, emblems, ceremonies and large-scale stage productions representing historical or legendary events, especially local ones. In most cases, the veracity has always been less important than the spectacle itself (Olins, 1990).

Architectural Propaganda

The practice often shows that once new nations establish the basic elements of their identities, they begin to invest heavily in building new national monuments (and often demolishing old ones), introducing new government buildings, erecting large-scale statues and opening new museums, memorials, power stations, factories and dams. The symbolic value of constructing new environments appears to be infinitely more significant than functional or economic utility. However, while the spectators may assume that this is a true testimony of national pride, power or economic success, the reality can often be somewhat different (Olins, 1990; Muratovski, 2008; 2010: 303; 2013b; 2013c).

Conscious attempts by cities and governments to shape their urban identities in order to promote themselves (or perhaps to assert themselves) to specific constituencies are evident throughout history (Muratovski, 2013a). In *The Imaginary Institutions of Society* (1987), Cornelius Castoriadis argues that the use of built environments as a form of propaganda – and architectural design especially – has been essential in sustaining sociopolitical fantasies for the ruling elites throughout history. According to him, iconic architecture produced during times of national restructuring should be seen as part of a wider system of signifiers and symbols necessary for producing new national identities, or reinventing existing identities. Slavoj Zizek (1989) argues that architecture, if symbolically developed, can be used as a tool for educating the society on what to desire, and how to desire it. Maria Kaika (2010: 458) adds that architecture produced within this context contributes to the configuration of the new order and institutes new significations for societies and institutions. Dejan Sudjic (2006: 8) holds a similar opinion. According to him, when built environments are developed in this context they become an 'instrument of statecraft'. Depending on the context, built environments can serve several purposes: they can praise or mythologise the past when used as a form of revivalism; they can 'promise' a better future when used for socio-economic development; or they can pave the way for expanding political authority, regional dominance, cultural superiority or nationalism when used as a demonstration of power (see Mayo, 1996: 81).

For thousands of years, religious institutions and governments have been using architecture as a potent propaganda tool in order to promote their influence and power

(Sklair, 2010). Architectural propaganda of this nature has been communicated through urban design, buildings and a string of monuments.[4] While some of the most prominent examples can be found in the ancient world, most notably in Southeast Europe and Northern Africa, architectural propaganda as a demonstration of governing power or religious authority can also be found in Central and South American countries and in Asia. As Jared Diamond (2003) points out, there are many historical examples of newly established elites who commissioned the construction of extravagant built environments as a way of concealing their lack of real power. In a never-ending cycle, countries and empires have built monuments, temples and buildings of sacred, symbolic or political importance in an attempt to demonstrate their power, claim a right to a territory, commemorate new rulers or establish their presence – often in salute to existing political or religious powers. Some of the earliest examples of this 'theatre of progress' (see Koolhaas, 1994: 13) can be seen in ancient Egypt with the Great Pyramids of Giza.

For example, the largest of the three pyramids was erected by the Cheops dynasty. As Diamond (2003) points out, the extravagance of the Cheops pyramid was nothing more than an illusionary display of power. According to him, Egyptian dynasties that followed the Cheops dynasty were far more powerful, yet they dramatically reduced the scale of their pyramids. Instead, they invested their resources in other ways: launching long-distance trading expeditions, military campaigns of conquest, maintaining big garrisons, constructing fortresses, irrigation works and ship channels – all of which were far beyond the capabilities of Cheops. Therefore, it can be argued that in the case of the Cheops dynasty, the construction of the largest building in the world – and for over 40 centuries, the tallest – was nothing more than a form of architectural propaganda meant to deify the ruling class and hide their absence of real power (Diamond, 2003: 891). Ancient Egypt was not alone in using built environments for propaganda purposes: Mexico, Peru and Japan have similar examples.[5]

Many subsequent empires and governments have also expanded the concept of architectural propaganda, with plans to build or restructure their capital cities as living monuments to their power. In an attempt to glorify the French Empire, Napoleon Bonaparte started the reconstruction of medieval Paris – a process that was later expanded by Napoleon III and Baron Haussmann who wanted to build the 'capital of capitals' (see de Bourrienne, 1832: 218; Pinkney, 1955: 125). Years later, Adolf Hitler, in an attempt to demonstrate the symbolic power of the Third Reich, together with his architect Albert Speer, envisioned (but failed to realise) a megalomaniacal Berlin that was intended to 'dwarf' Paris (Mayo, 1996: 81). At the same time in Italy, Benito Mussolini wished to reconstruct Rome into a vast, orderly and powerful city emulating the Rome of Augustus. The leaders of the Soviet Union had similar plans when they readapted Moscow's Red Square into a grand ceremonial centre best known for the proliferation of the military May Day parades, then followed by the colossal (and unrealised) plan for the building of the Palace of the Soviets in a stupendous, neoclassical style (Cannadine, 1983: 146–147). The United States of America was also a strong adherent to the practice of architectural propaganda. As early as 1791, the president of the United States, George Washington, commissioned the planning of Washington, DC, as the new capital of the United States, for which he appointed the French architect Pierre Charles L'Enfant (Library of Congress, 2010). Washington, DC, was planned to serve as a model for American city planning, and as a symbol of governmental power that would be seen by other nations (National Register of Historic Places, 2001). In Washington, DC, many buildings of national importance including the White House, the United States Capitol and the Lincoln Memorial were built in a neoclassical style inspired by ancient temples of worship – which is a blatant example of the use of religious architectural propaganda for political purposes.[6] Other attempts at American architectural propaganda include built environments such as the Washington Monument, the Jefferson Monument, the Arlington Bridge Memorial and the Vietnam Veterans Memorial. These are only some examples. There are countless parallels to other countries that used the very same form of architectural propaganda for political purposes.

Part 2: Place Branding

As a result of cultural fragmentation and pluralism that often prevails in the fast-paced consumer society of the twenty-first century, many people increasingly experience psychological insecurity that often oscillates between a desire to belong to a community of peers and a need to express their own sense of identity. According to Anna Klingmann (2007), it is precisely within pluralistic societies that signals of identification take on critical importance: 'In a world in which social, economic, and political value systems are defined by continual change and movement, individuals are forced to create their own identities and find ways of signalling their place in the world' (Klingmann, 2007: 56). In a way, the same can be said about cities and nation-states. While individuals often purchase brands as means of identification that can transcend cultural, traditional and local difference, countries resort to commissioning 'brand-name' architects to develop iconic buildings for their cities for the very same purpose (Muratovski, 2012: 196). At this stage, we can draw parallels from the marketing literature in terms of corporate communications, relationship building and the construction of corporate identities. However, it has to be noted that this process calls for a distinctive form of branding – separate from that of product branding or corporate branding.

It can be argued that all cities and every country in the world already possess the basic elements of a brand, and people, albeit unconsciously, already see them as such (see Ashworth and Kavaratzis, 2009: 521). Cities, and countries alike, have existing 'corporate identities'; they have their names, visual identities (most often a coat of arms, a flag and other similar signs), symbols (landmarks and monuments), brand images (a perception about them that is embedded in people's minds) and so on. From a marketing perspective, we can develop this further and promote them as if they are some kind of products – but this would not make them brands, but merely trademarks. Marketing can initiate a design of a logo, a slogan, new livery and an advertising campaign to launch and promote these 'new' brands (Anholt, 2010: 9), but this in itself cannot make a city or a nation a successful brand (Muratovski, 2012: 197). In order to further clarify this, I will use Kavatzaris' definition of 'successful branding':

> The key to successful [city and nation] branding is to establish a link between the brand [the city or the country] and the consumer [citizen/inhabitant/visitor/investor], such that there is a close fit between the consumer's own physical and psychological needs and the brand's functional attributes and symbolic values.
> (Kavatzaris, 2004: 65)

If we take into account some of the most successful 'city brands' such as New York, Paris, London, Rome, Barcelona or Athens, we can argue that these cities are highly recognisable not because their image is created by marketing communications, but because their image is a reflection of the sociocultural and physical character of the cities themselves. Even the imagery that is evoked by the mere mention of these cities' names adds intangible value to their brand equity and to that of the countries where these cities are built (Greenberg, 2000: 230; Parkerson and Saunders, 2005: 243–244). The success of these cities is not a product of conscious modern-day marketing, and what is more, these cities do not need any branding exercises in terms of corporate identity construct or corporate communications in order to become 'visible' and remain 'competitive'. Their very success challenges certain schools of thought that cities need marketing in a traditional sense in order to remain competitive as tourist and business destinations (Muratovski, 2012: 197).

Along these lines, Brenda Parkerson and John Saunders (2005: 247) argue that the most important differentiating elements for a city are likely to be of sociocultural and 'manmade' [*sic.*] character. According to them, the uniqueness of these elements is the key to providing competitive advantage over other cities and in creating brand equity. Furthermore, Robyn Mayes (2008) also argues that city branding should involve changes to the 'physical fabric of places' – informing how places can be experienced and used (Mayes, 2008: 129).

Branding and Architecture

According to Klingmann (2007: 3), branding and architecture have developed an 'intimate relationship'. For example, leading commercial brands such as Louis Vuitton, Prada, BMW and Audi progressively employ city architecture in terms of commissioning iconic or highly recognisable buildings as a key element of their new marketing strategies. By the same token, cities and nations take cues from the world of commercial branding in an attempt to enhance their images and to elevate their positions on the world stage.

In a consumer society, 'needs' are surpassed by 'desires' and the acquisition of basic goods is replaced by a search for emotional satisfaction, a search for an identity or distinctiveness, and an aspiration to belong. From a communication design perspective, this becomes an issue of trademarked generic products that people buy to fulfil their daily needs, versus emotionally charged brands that people buy to fulfil their innermost desires (Muratovski, 2012: 197). If we make a parallel to this, it can be argued that buildings fulfil needs, while architecture, on the other hand, fulfils desires (Gobé, 2001: p.xxviii, cited in Klingmann, 2007: 312).[7] Architecture, according to Klingmann (2007: 312), can also be seen as a catalyst that brands its user. It supports and boosts identity and aspirations of clients and fulfils their economic and social ambitions through new structures, interfaces and networks that facilitate growth and transformation. Architecture is in a sense a promotional medium and an identity definer. It is a medium that promotes social relationships as well as individual enterprises, and can be used as a symbol of territorial identity (Klingmann, 2007: 312–313). In this sense, it can be argued that architecture has the capacity to deliver the totemic values that a city or a nation needs in order to become a brand (see Muratovski, Chapter 1 for reference on branding and totemism).

Donald McNeill and Mark Tewdwr-Jones (2003) argue that architecture has the power to affect the cultural meanings of places. According to them, architecture can even be seen as one of the principal vehicles for national(istic) expressions of identity. From a commercial perspective, or in terms of corporate branding, architecture can also be used in conjunction with corporate identity. For example, in terms of corporate identity, the architecture of the corporate headquarters, offices or stores needs to be aligned with the idea of the brand – especially when it comes to design and visual appearance (Kirby and Kent, 2010).

From both an architectural and a branding perspective, buildings are already understood as symbols of 'good taste', 'power' and 'status' (Berg and Kreiner, 1990). This is evident in financial and corporate headquarters within public institutions (Brauer, 2002), the commercial sector (Kelly, 2003) and the retail industry (Kirby and Kent, 2010). In return, this creates a perception that the building is a 'marketing object' (Glendinning, 2004), or that the building has become a branding device (Chung et al., 2001). This 'architectural commodification' (Kirby and Kent, 2010: 433) has sparked the appearance of a new type of architecture: 'the expressive landmark' (Jencks, 2005), or 'iconic architecture' (Sklair, 2010).

A. E. Kirby and A. M. Kent (2010: 437) argue that the 'sense of permanence' contributes to a great extent to the communicative power of architecture. For example, certain architecturally designed or engineered buildings – with the Eiffel Tower or the Sydney Opera House being such examples – have a power to generate enormous public interest. Such buildings have become brands in their own right, while at the same time being landmarks that can communicate the vision of their cities and promote their countries of origin. To draw attention to their landmarks (and consequently their cities), city and state administrators have worked with advertising agencies, publishing houses, broadcasters and other emerging media industries to create an extensive 'critical infrastructure' of a range of media, including urban guidebooks, reviews, websites and various TV programmes and documentaries. As shifts in global, national and local economic bases have forced cities and countries to market themselves internationally in search of new sources of revenue, the concept of city and nation branding has not only helped to 'sell' these urban identities, but it has also inspired the creation of new ones (see Greenberg, 2000: 229; see also Muratovski, 2013b, 2013c).

Built environments, and iconic architecture especially, has become so central to the image of the city brand that, according to Kim Dovey, cities without icons are like corporations without logos (Dovey, 1999: 158–159). However, the modern-day phenomenon of city branding is not always an ideal solution. While branding can be seen as a powerful strategy when it comes to crafting a unique corporate identity, in many cases it has done exactly the opposite. More often than not, city- and nation-branding strategies have failed to establish emotional connections between the place and the stakeholders by imposing standardised solutions on the urban and suburban landscapes. While today's 'brandscapes' – as Klingmann calls them – have managed to raise their profiles and generate attention, they have also resulted in a culture of the copy, imitating one another in their offerings and aesthetics (Klingmann, 2007: 3).

In an attempt to make their cities economically viable and to promote an image of distinctiveness through building attractions and symbolic icons, political leaders have turned their cities into 'ageographic spaces of consumer activities' (Klingmann, 2007: 280). By repeating standard devices, ranging from marketing communication to building types, these contemporary 're-imagining' strategies tend to create overwhelmingly similar places, which in a way defeats the whole purpose of the branding exercise. While this has already been recognised as a problem in the place-branding literature when it comes to the use of overly similar logos, visuals and slogans (Szondi, 2007), now we can see the same happening with architecture. From city to city, local governments increasingly hire the same 'brand-name' architects who produce the same signature buildings. This in return results in a uniform, indistinctive city image. While this approach is less risky for investors as it minimises financial risk and boosts international recognition, the downfalls are that this brand-name architecture creates a less evocative sense of place. These *déjà vu* urban landscapes are rapidly becoming 'franchises' that vary little from each other (Klingmann, 2007: 280). The renowned Dutch architect and theorist Rem Koolhaas has also expressed his fears that the growing use of high-end architecture as a tool for self-promotion can reduce cities to homogeneous architectural 'theme parks' (cited in Ouroussoff, 2008). Yet, despite all this, it can still be argued that architecture can make constructive use of the methods of branding in order to promote cultural values that respect the heterogeneity of places, but it must align city-marketing activities with broader and more inclusive objectives of urban development (Muratovski, 2012: 201).

City Branding

Empirical evidence shows that cities with distinct cultures and recognisable architectural features are more popular than those without them. Consequently, some cities that lacked those unique features have gone as far as to reconstruct their architecture in an attempt to invent new identities and rebrand themselves so they can improve their positioning on the world stage, or to achieve certain political objectives. China, for example, engaged in extravagant redevelopment of Beijing in lead to the 2008 Olympic Games. In an attempt to position itself as a modern and progressive country, China commissioned some of the most ambitious architectural projects of the time in a bid to present its new image while the world was watching. While there has been very little that is traditionally Chinese in this iconic architecture, the scale and the ambition of the new built environments are unmistakably a statement of national pride (Goldberger, 2008).

Every world-renowned city has benefited from the construction of landmark monuments; Big Ben (London), the Eiffel Tower (Paris), the Statue of Liberty (New York) and Christ the Redeemer (Rio de Janeiro) are great examples of that. These monuments are not only mnemonic signifiers of the cities where they are built, but also iconic symbols of their respective nations as well (Walsh, 2006: 27). If we take into account the fact that early cities often emerged around purposely designed sacral monuments or temples of worship (Mumford, 1961), then we can argue that it is in the nature of the city to rely on architectural propaganda in order to attract inhabitants, visitors and investors. Canberra (the capital of Australia) and Brasilia (the capital of Brazil), both totally planned twentieth-century cities, are clear examples of this. Both cities are artificially created around governing bodies and national institutions (Muratovski, 2013a: 48).

Even though it appears that there is a historical divide between urban branding and architectural propaganda, it can be argued that architectural propaganda (the development of symbolic buildings and monuments with strong mnemonic characters) through the course of time evolved into the contemporary practice of urban branding (the branding of cities through architecture). Robert Venturi, in *Learning from Las Vegas* (1972), expresses a similar view and acknowledges that the use of architecture as propaganda is still present. According to him, architecture, as a vehicle of propaganda, acts as a 'billboard' that conveys certain messages through the choice of style, material, technology or historical reference (Venturi, 1972: 1). Guy Julier (2000) sees architecture in a similar way and, according to him, the exteriors of buildings act as displays of the historical, cultural and commercial achievements of the city and the nation-state (Julier, 2000: 120–121).

In the past, built environments of all kinds have often been used as a demonstration of power and authority, but in a contemporary sense they can play a key role in the marketing of places as they can be used as 'special features' that can attract residents, investors and visitors. For example, the iconic works by Charles Rennie Mackintosh in Glasgow (Scotland) and Antoni Gaudi in Barcelona (Spain) are already part of the marketing of these cities (Sklair, 2010). Cities that are defined by their rich architectural and cultural heritage are seen as unique, attractive and lively because of their distinctive urban planning, inimitable architecture and cultural mix (Klingmann, 2007: 273). Furthermore, cities need good built environments and architecture in order to project desired aesthetic and experiential values, and to meet the needs of the public and the local businesses. This is measured by how well they can contribute to the people's overall well-being and can function as a source of civic pride, enhance the sense of community or embody vision, direction and development (see Klingmann, 2007: 274). Cities that possess these qualities will remain appealing for residents and visitors alike, despite the variance in the economic cycles. That is why many businesses often associate their own names with them, as is often the case with cities such as New York, Paris and London (Parkerson and Saunders, 2005: 243–244).

A number of emerging cities have recognised the value of iconic architecture as a way of promoting themselves as urban brands, with Bilbao (Spain) being often used as a landmark example in the literature (Sklair, 2010). Frank Gehry's Guggenheim Museum in Bilbao, which opened in 1997, was hailed as 'the most important building of its time' (Guggenheim, 2013). While Gehry's Guggenheim does not function particularly well as an exhibition space, it provides an exceptionally effective marketing tool for Bilbao. At the very beginning, the building was not conceived merely as an art museum, but as a strategy of Bilbao's city leaders to create an iconic, identity-enhancing structure that would act as a premier tourist destination in order to revive the city's economy (Klingmann, 2007: 67). The so-called 'Bilbao effect' inspired cities from around the world to follow suit.

Part 3: Case Studies

In this section, three emerging nations will be presented: United Arab Emirates, with particular focus on Dubai – an autocratic monarchy and former British colony; Turkmenistan – a totalitarian state and former Soviet republic; and Macedonia – an EU candidate member and a former Yugoslav republic.[8] Even though these three nations are fundamentally different to one another – politically, geographically and culturally – they do share one thing in common. All three of them have invested heavily in the development of new and ostentatious built environments in an attempt to define their identities and manifest their visions for the future.

Dubai, United Arab Emirates

Since the discovery of oil in 1966 and its independence from Britain in 1971, Dubai has evolved into a global city and an international business hub. Even though Dubai started its development in the 1980s, in the 2000s, the city's construction pace became highly aggressive (Suddath, 2009). As Dubai's oil reserves decreased, the city-state turned to massive urban developments to reinvent itself as tourist destination and to attract real estate investors (Fattah, 2007; Ouroussoff, 2007; Walker, 2010; Kaika, 2010: 458).

Even though Dubai commanded the fewest financial resources in the Emirates, it commissioned the grandest projects of them all (Jana, 2006). As a result, Dubai got the world's attention it sought. However, not all of this attention was positive. *The Guardian*, for example, described Dubai as a 'surreal, hallucinogenic fairy tale' (Rose, 2009), and *The Independent* referred to it as an 'adult Disneyland' (Hari, 2009). Nevertheless, with its aggressive pursuit of 'bigger' and 'better', Dubai now rivals Las Vegas as the most extravagant desert city and attracts millions of visitors (Lewis, 2009).

The driving force behind Dubai's urban transformation is Dubai's Crown Prince, Sheikh Mohammed Bin Rashid Al Maktoum. The Sheikh has vested the country's resources, and his authority, into making this project a reality. His smiling face is widely displayed around the city, reminding residents and visitors that it is him who is building this city (Hari, 2009). Unfortunately for the Sheikh, projects such as the world's tallest skyscraper, the artificial ski resort in the desert, world's first luxury underwater hotel and an artificial archipelago of private, residential islands – the biggest development of its kind in the world – have significantly drained the nation's budget and have brought his state to the brink of an economic collapse.[9] This, in turn, forced Dubai to seek financial assistance from its wealthier neighbours such as Abu Dhabi to complete at least some of the projects (McIntyre, 2009).

While there are now signs of economic recovery and Dubai's world rankings have improved (see Knight Frank, 2012), the city is expected to face another problem in the near future: the Sheikh has built his showcase metropolis in a place with no useable water. Without any surface water, very little aquifer and with some of the lowest rainfall in the world, Dubai is forced to consume its seawater as the only option. The vast desalination plants around the Gulf make this the most expensive water on earth; it costs more than petrol to produce. The costs of producing desalinated water are not only financial but also environmental. The amount of carbon dioxide that goes into the atmosphere during production is the main reason why a resident of Dubai has the biggest average carbon footprint on the planet – double than that of an American (Hari, 2009). Regardless of this, Dubai has neither invested in better clean water production technologies, nor in water storage facilities. With only enough water stored to last the city for a week, Dubai has spent all its resources on building castles in the sand, literally – considering that in a case of rising sea levels all their artificial islands will be gone. Other issues such as reports of human rights abuse cast another dark shadow on Dubai's urban developments. A number of the reports claim that the government ignores, and even protects and encourages exploitation and slavery of foreign workers who have come to build the city in a hope for a better life (Hari, 2009). In spite of this, Dubai succeeded in becoming one of 'The Most Important Global Cities' and was ranked tenth in 'Quality of Life' category in *Knight Frank's Wealth Report* (2012), preceding cities such as Vienna and Toronto.

Dubai's actions have inspired its wealthy neighbours to follow suit. The economically stronger Abu Dhabi, not wanting to stay too far behind, was quick to establish its own vision for the future. Over the next decade, Abu Dhabi aims to become one of the great cultural centres of the Middle East. Even though this is a less ambitious project than Dubai's, Abu Dhabi will still make a significant impact on the world stage. The 'latter-day Xanadu', as Hassan Fattah (2007) described it in *The New York Times*, would boast four museums, a performing arts centre and nineteen art pavilions designed by celebrated architects like Frank Gehry, Zaha Hadid, Tadao Ando and Jean Nouvel. The development plans to include franchises of the popular Guggenheim and Louvre museums, as well as an arts institute created by Yale University. With this, Abu Dhabi hopes to transform itself into an international arts capital and tourist destination (Ouroussoff, 2007; McIntyre, 2009).

Both Dubai and Abu Dhabi are closely followed by Qatar. With its bid for the 2022 World Cup, Qatar unleashed its equally wild urban ambitions. With the help of the architectural studios of Foster + Partners (led by the British architect Lord Norman Foster) and Albert Speer and Partners (the son of Hitler's chief architect), Qatar has vowed to build twelve new carbon-neutral, futuristic stadiums that can be disassembled and shipped to various locations in the Middle East to make a total of 22 stadiums. They also plan to build seven satellite cities adjacent to the twelve stadiums, which will be surrounded by solar panels that will generate enough power to supply the neighbouring buildings (Walker, 2010).

The unveiling of major architectural works in these 'emerging' cities has generated enormous publicity. These high-profile buildings have had a positive social and economic impact on the cities themselves, and have also put them on the 'fast track' to join the rankings of well-recognised city brands such as New York, Paris and London (Sari, 2004: 23).

Ashgabat, Turkmenistan

A particularly interesting and not widely documented case of similar nature can be found in post-Soviet Turkmenistan and its capital, Ashgabat. During Soviet times, Ashgabat was an ordinary socialist city – nothing more than a minor province in the vast Soviet Union. Located on the outskirts of the Karakum desert, the city was characterised primarily by low buildings, except for few experimental twelve-storey apartment buildings. There were no trade centres, commercial buildings, office blocks, well-furnished hotels or even sufficient housing of an acceptable standard (Muradov, 2009: 46).

After Turkmenistan's independence from the Soviet Union in 1991, things changed significantly, both in political and urban terms. Turkmenistan's constitution today declares the country to be a secular democracy and presidential republic, even though in reality this is an authoritarian state dominated by a president. The country's first president Saparmurat Niyazov, who was a 'President for Life' until his death in 2006, had absolute power in the country. His successor Gurbanguly Berdimuhamedov, who proclaimed himself as 'Hero of Turkmenistan', continues to rule the country in a similar fashion (U.S. Department of State, 2012).

Soon after becoming the president of the Turkmen Soviet Socialist Republic, Niyazov granted himself supreme powers. Without the central control of the Soviet Union, he was able to exercise an unparalleled influence. The country's wealth, which was now at his sole disposal, was used for the commission of a string of grandiose memorials and buildings in the capital Ashgabat – all of them erected in the glory of the state and its ruler – himself. In doing so, Niyazov made his personality cult inseparable from the identity of the nation.[10] The Arch of Neutrality and Central Asia's largest temple, the Mosque of Turkmenbashi's Soul, are excellent examples of this. While the Arch of Neutrality is formally a memorial that celebrates the country's position of neutrality, on its top, Niyazov erected a giant golden statue of himself that rotates 360 degrees every 24 hours following the sun. The Mosque of Turkmenbashi's Soul is a place of worship, yet at the same time it serves as a tribute to Niyazov who also preferred to be called 'Turkmenbashi', the 'father' of the Turkmen people (Rowat, 2008). These memorials are accompanied by many other similar mega-buildings and environments created in a new revivalist style that brings together neo-Islamist architecture with LeCorbusier-inspired urban planning (Muradov, 2009: 46).

This new and unusual style has crowned the roofs of the new residential buildings with pyramids, cones, pointed domes and other geometrical forms. State and spiritual buildings such as the Presidential Palace and Ruhiet Palace, theatres, mosques, museums, the Cultural Centre (named after Niyazov), the National Library, the Museum of the First President of Turkmenistan, banks, ministries and healthcare facilities have also become a subject of highly enhanced expressiveness of form through marble decorations and vertical bands of glass with gold-plated gratings. Even many of the old buildings, formerly plastered or made up of grey reinforced concrete panels, have been encased with new marble tiles. According to the state-governed analytics journal, *Turkmenistan International Magazine*, the excessive use of marble in Ashgabat's architecture is not a tribute to fashion, but a 'natural reaction to the boring aesthetics of modernism' – a return to a classical architecture merged with the triumph of symmetry that is characteristic to the Islamic world and the centuries-old architectural heritage of Turkmenistan (Muradov, 2009: 46).

One of the most widely used elements in Turkmenistan's built environments today is the octagonal polygon – the 'Oghuz-khan's Star'. This geometrical element, which can be found in the traditional architecture in Turkmenistan and throughout the region, underlies the composition of layouts and the facades of many newly built edifices. The 'Star' is used in the designs of the Monument to the Constitution of Turkmenistan where it serves as a symbol of the firmness of the foundations of the state; it is incorporated in the spatial composition of the Palace of Marriage where it symbolises the earth; it can be found on the TV tower in the form of a glass screen that acts as a solar energy collector capable of providing electricity for the decorative lights of the tower (Muradov, 2009: 47); and it can be seen even in the structure of the enormous indoor Ferris Wheel at the Alem Entertainment Centre (Vershinin, 2012).

In addition to geometric symbolism, numeric symbolism is evident in Turkmenistan's built environments. For example, the total height of the Constitution monument, including the spire, is 185 metres, symbolising the date of adoption of the Constitution – 18 May (the fifth month). Also, this figure has another meaning; 185 UN member states have recognised the neutral status of Turkmenistan. The tetrahedral tower is 91 metres tall, indicating the year of independence of the country. The tower rises from a 27-metre base (which is shaped as the Oghuz-khan's Star), and is accompanied by a 10-metre platform. These parameters (27 and 10) represent the date and the month of establishment of the Turkmen state (Muradov, 2011: 74).

After Niyazov's death in 2006, some aspects of his personality cult were dismantled and replaced by new ones venerating his successor Gurbanguly Berdimuhamedov (BBC, 2012). For example, the Arch of Neutrality with Niyazov's golden statue has been moved to the outskirts of the city and is now being replaced by a new monument (Fitzpatrick, 2011). The importance of controlling the built environments in Turkmenistan can be seen in the fact that Berdimuhamedov quickly positioned himself as a visionary patron who sees Ashgabat as 'a symbol city of the new revival era' (cited in Muradov, 2009: 47). In the government's media section called *Turkmenistan: The Golden Age*, a recent press release named 'New look of Ashgabat as a symbol of magnificent changes in the motherland' completely ignores Niyazov's legacy of built environments and attributes everything exclusively to Berdimuhamedov. Here, Berdimuhamedov is portrayed as 'the initiator of the grandiose reforms and changes launched throughout the country in the epoch of the new Revival' (TDH, State News Agency of Turkmenistan, 2011). Unlike Dubai, Turkmenistan's built environments are inner-directed. Their purpose is not to attract tourists or foreign investors or to position Ashgabat on the world stage but to strengthen the idea of the nation and to glorify the president as a nation-builder.

Skopje, Macedonia

Since the fall of the Ottoman Empire, Macedonia has been seen as a 'bone of contention' in the Balkans, and as a result, its territory was divided among Yugoslavia, Bulgaria, Greece and Albania (Cox, 2006: 554). Since Yugoslavian Macedonia proclaimed its independence in the 1990s, the revival of the Macedonian identity and the sovereignty of the Macedonian state have been seen as a threat by the neighbouring countries. The situation has been critical for Macedonia ever since (Perry, 2001).

The political actions by Macedonia's neighbouring countries since its independence – Greece, Bulgaria, Serbia, Albania and Kosovo (now a newly founded republic) – demonstrate that each of the key Macedonian identity elements has been under coordinated and systematic attack. For example, Greece is disputing the name of the country (*The Economist*, 2011), the existence of the Macedonian minority in Northern Greece (Loring, 1994), the ancient history of Macedonia and its national symbols (Loring, 2010), and has forced Macedonia to change its flag and constitution under the pressure of a severe economic embargo (Perry, 2001: 6). Greece also vetoes Macedonia's EU and NATO membership until these issues are resolved in its favour (Pop, 2011). Bulgaria, even though less aggressive than Greece in its attempts to undermine the Macedonian identity, claims that Macedonian language is a Bulgarian dialect, fails to recognise the Macedonian minority in Bulgaria as a separate ethnic group, and disputes Macedonia's official history from the medieval period to the early twentieth century (Mahon, 1998). Serbia does not dispute these issues, but the Serbian Orthodox Church undermines the legitimacy and the autocephaly of the Macedonian Orthodox Church and vetoes its recognition by the other Orthodox churches. This action is demoralising for the majority of the Macedonian population who are Orthodox Christians (Ivanov, 2011). Kosovo raised a number of disputes over its border demarcation with Macedonia, and this represents a direct threat to Macedonian territorial sovereignty (Illmer, 2009). While there are rarely any open issues with Albania directly, the Albanian minority in Macedonia is perceived as an internal risk factor. The ethnic Albanians often act against the Macedonian constitution by not adhering to it: they have instigated an armed conflict and terrorist attacks on an ethnic basis; they have changed the names of the toponyms where they are the dominant ethnic community; they frequently undermine or ignore the use of the official Macedonian language; and they raise the flag of a foreign country (Albania) on national institutions and territories where they are dominant minority. These actions are often interpreted as subversive activities whose purpose is to weaken and undermine the Macedonian national identity and to annex Macedonian territories for the cause of 'Greater Albania' (Perry, 2001; Neofotistos, 2004; Ringdal, Simkus and Listhaug, 2005; Tanevski, 2005; Buzur, 2006). As a result, the current state of the Macedonian national identity has reached a critical point.

This 'special warfare' against Macedonia can also be seen as a form of neocolonialism – an extension of the colonising process by which the country has been exposed for centuries by the same neighbours. Ludija Georgieva (2006), professor at the Department of Security, Defence and Peace Studies at the Macedonian state university, argues that if the national identity remains under attack and the country fails to defend its identity successfully, its existence as an independent nation-state can be brought into question. According to her, threats aimed at the national identity are also threats aimed at the national security because problems associated with the national identity can cause conflicts between various ethno-cultural groups that live in that country, can lead to secession, can lay down the foundations for potential annexation or can produce operational difficulties for the government (Georgieva, 2006: 36).

According to the president of Macedonia, Gjorgje Ivanov, the country is not prepared to back down on the issue of the national identity.[11] Ivanov (2005) posits that once a nation accepts an identity as its own, the identity remains a legacy for future generations as part of their being. According to him, no force, no threats and no decrees can change that feeling. There are many examples to support this argument in the face of the nations that have been under colonial rule for centuries and have been treated as 'forgotten nations'. Once able to freely express themselves, their ethnic revival and search for roots inevitably brings back their forgotten, assimilated or forcibly changed identities – Ivanov argues (2005: 97). But the identity issue is not the only problem that Macedonia is currently facing.

As an aspiring EU candidate member, Macedonia has also been faced with cultural issues related to EU integration. As the European Union becomes stronger and its internal borders are opening, its external borders are closing – especially for countries that do not resonate well with the 'European' identity, such as Macedonia or Turkey, for that matter (see Pieterse, 1991; Kemming and Sandikci, 2007). The European Union already has problems imposing its 'umbrella' identity over the plethora of independent states that it represents, each with its own distinctive cultural identity, and they do not want to invite countries that do not share common core values and a 'European' culture. This Europeanisation has triggered a 'voluntary' change even within the European Union itself. Cities such as Leeds (UK) underwent a massive transformation as the United Kingdom integrated with the European Union in 1992. Leeds transformed itself from a typical industrial Victorian city into a modern European city no different from Düsseldorf (Germany), or Rotterdam (Netherlands) – to its detriment as some architectural critics have argued (Julier, 2000: 117–119). Even large and well-established cities such as Athens (Greece) and Barcelona (Spain) underwent similar urban 'facelifts'. In the same spirit, the Commission of the European Union has even established the European Capital of Culture Award in 1985 to do precisely that – promote an idea of a European culture (European Commission, 2011). Nevertheless, according to Jan Nederveen Pieterse (1991), what is being recycled as European culture is actually a nineteenth-century 'imperial myth formation' that is essentially elitist in nature (Pieterse, 1991: 5).

Faced with political and cultural challenges, Macedonia has decided to inscribe its identity in stone, concrete and steel, and to create a new image for itself at the same time. In doing so, Macedonia's capital city Skopje is currently being re-built to look like a nineteenth-century city. What makes this even more interesting example is that in 1963, a devastating earthquake destroyed between 75 and 80 per cent of Skopje, and instead of rebuilding the city as it was prior to the earthquake (typically European and neoclassical in style), a decision was made that Skopje should be rebuild as a utopian, futuristic metropolis by using the principles of urban planning of Tokyo (Muratovski, 2013b, 2014).

In an international competition, the Japanese architect Kenzo Tange, famous for his award-winning urban plan for Tokyo, was selected to lead the reconstruction of the city centre. In a true utopian spirit, different nations from all around the world joined forces and reconstructed the surrounding suburbs of the city in contemporary variations of their own national styles. Furthermore, selected architects constructed some of the most iconic examples of futuristic architecture in the central district (Tange and Kultermann, 1970). Even world-renowned artists such as Pablo Picasso and Alexander Calder showed their support by donating their artworks to the newly built Museum of Contemporary Art in Skopje. This was also the first time during the Cold War that opposing nations joined forces under the banner of the United Nations General Assembly to work on a joint project – the building of Skopje. Yugoslavia used Skopje to show the world the true meaning of 'united nations', and Skopje became known as the 'City of Solidarity' (BBC, 2008).

Until Macedonia's independence in the early 1990s, Skopje was a unique, cosmopolitan city where one could marvel extraordinary examples of visionary international architecture and urban planning. And now, 30 years later, the new political elites have decided to reverse this trend and introduce a pro-European vision for the city, and subsequently for the identity of the nation. As a result, the Macedonian government under the leadership of Prime Minister Nikola Gruevski has decided to reconstruct the entire central district of Skopje in a quasi-baroque style. On 1 February 2010, when the government introduced 'Skopje 2014', as they have called the project, their opening words were: 'Remember the look of the capital's centre today. It will never be the same again' (Nova Makedonija, 2010, translated from Macedonian by the author).

This ambitious revivalist project includes the commission of an excessive number of new sculptures of art, monuments of national heroes and important figures, baroque-inspired state buildings, new bridges, wax museum dedicated to the Macedonian struggle for independence, an Arch of Triumph, decorative fountains and a colossal statue of Alexander the Great (one of the largest statues in Europe). Not only has each of the new buildings been given an instant 'heritage' look, which is neoclassical or baroque in appearance, but the surrounding buildings that were built in a typical socialist style of the 1970s have also been given a similar-looking 'facelift'. This also includes the Parliament, which is being upgraded with nineteenth-century style Crystal Palace-looking domes so that it can appear more 'stately' (Nova Makedonija, 2010). In addition to this, in order for the 'look' to be complete, the government replaced the ordinary single-platform public buses with a new fleet of custom-made, vintage-looking double-decker buses. Interestingly, in the 1950s, Skopje really did have original British red double-decker buses servicing the city; the current ones are replicas made in China (Taleski, 2011).

The speed of this project, conducted without proper consultation with architectural and cultural historians and urban designers, has led to some peculiar initiatives such as the commissioning of a baroque-inspired multi-level car parks (Smilevska, 2010), and a baroque-inspired Ferris Wheel (Denkovska, 2010). Given that there are no historical references in terms of style that the architects and the constructors can use to replicate such types of structures (since there were neither cars nor Ferris Wheels at the time of baroque), the end result can best be described as kitsch.

With Skopje 2014, the Macedonian government aspires to develop a 'preferred' Macedonian identity alongside a 'desired' European image. In turning to the past, Macedonia aims to define its national identity, while at the same time it tries to present itself as a quintessential European country that belongs in the European Union. From a political point of view, Skopje 2014 makes sense since its purpose is to strengthen its national identity and to help the country build its European image. The problem is that this point of view does not take into consideration neither cultural nor economic factors (Muratovski, 2013b, 2013c).

As Skopje becomes progressively more 'packaged', the result becomes an imitation that exceeds the original to the point that the original no longer matters because it has lost its authenticity (see Julier, 2000: 149), which is probably why CNN has described Skopje 2014 as a 'theme park' (Davies, 2011). In addition to this, spending a fortune on buildings and monuments that have no return on investment factor, during a global economic crisis, is highly questionable – regardless of how noble the idea is. That is why Dan Doncev, an economic analyst and former member of the Macedonian parliament, believes that Macedonia is running the risk of facing the faith of the Rapanui people of the Easter Island – a small Polynesian island civilisation that spent all its resources on erecting monumental statues (Doncev, 2010). If we take into consideration that Macedonia has around 30 per cent unemployment rate and very limited natural resources, then this is not a far-fetched scenario. Most critics of Skopje 2014, mainly from the opposition, question whether the funds spent on this project would have been better invested in production facilities, technology, infrastructure, hospitals, schools and libraries instead. Yet, this comes in stark contrast with the overwhelming support by the ordinary people who find pride in rediscovering their history inscribed in the new built environments that began to emerge around them (see Davies, 2011; De Launey, 2014). At the time of completing this chapter (April, 2015), Skopje is still under construction with new buildings and monuments being consistently added to the building schedule. Debates over the appropriateness of this project and the logic behind continue to rage, but the government remains seemingly unfazed by the criticism. The indications are that as long as the current government remains in power, this project will continue to expand further.[12]

Discussion

Emerging nations are politically 'peripheral' and they rely on the moral, financial and political support of more developed regions or nations – or the so-called 'centre nations' (see Szondi, 2007). In their transition, emerging nations aspire to become centre nations themselves, and in the process they often employ various public diplomacy efforts in order to achieve that status. In the first instance, these efforts are inner-directed and they often facilitate the question of identity: Who are we? Once this question is answered, the efforts become outer-directed, and the next question raised is the question of image: How do we want to be seen by others? If emerging nations fail to answer these questions themselves in a strong and consistent manner, then others will try to define their images and identities for them; and this is never an outcome that one nation can desire. That is why many emerging nations often resort to symbolic manifestations of their new identities through the use of built environments – as a way of marking their existence in space and time.

While there is no doubt that building monuments and landmark buildings can help emerging nations to define their identities, establish themselves as nation-brands and attract visitors and investors in return, this is never a straightforward process. In this process, the national identity and the nation's image can often be at odds with each other and strong national identity at home does not necessarily mean a positive national image abroad. A number of political, historical, financial, environmental and cultural issues need to be taken into consideration before any major decisions are made.

Dubai's world ranking, for example, has come at great financial and environmental cost, and abuse of human rights. The rapid globalisation of Dubai cityscape often ignores traditional culture, and this might irritate some conservative stakeholders who may feel disconnected from their own culture that is becoming increasingly westernised.

Turkmenistan, on the other hand, pays attention to its culture and traditions, but perhaps too much, which is why Ashgabat may never reach the global status of Dubai. But then again, Turkmenistan, unlike Dubai, is an inner-directed state. The extravagance of the built environments serves only to impress the local population, and not the world. With its own urban style, inspired by local culture and tradition, Ashgabat ignores global trends and subjects itself to the dreams of grandeur.

Macedonia is a special case. While the country neither has financial stability nor natural resources like Dubai and Turkmenistan, it follows the same path as them at great risk to its own economy, which is already in bad shape. While it would have made more sense for Macedonia to upgrade and revitalise the existing built environments that were constructed after the 1963 earthquake and reclaim its international status as a cosmopolitan place, the government has made a very controversial choice instead; Skopje, with its fake heritage buildings, has lost its authenticity and now resembles a real-life Disneyland – even though it is significantly less entertaining.

What we can learn from the United Arab Emirates, Turkmenistan and Macedonia is that built environments can be an effective form of nationalistic propaganda. Even with all their flaws and associated controversy, the built environments in these countries are now powerful mnemonic elements representing national identities, and they will remain as such for the future generations.

Conclusion

Despite some similarities with product branding and corporate branding, nation branding is a distinctive form of branding that brings together various social, cultural, political and commercial perspectives. At the core of the nation-brand stands the national identity, which is neither permanent nor clearly defined entity. Regardless of this, national identities have a significant impact on how a country is perceived at home and abroad – and this is particularly important when it comes to public and international relations, tourism, foreign investments, and international reputation and prestige. The power of communication that built environments and iconic architecture have should not be underestimated. Cities are much more than places for living. Nation-states use the design and urban planning of their cities to manifest their identities, their visions for the future and their connections to the past, and even inscribe these concepts in space and time. In line with this, cities should be seen as 'mirrors' that reflect the social, cultural, commercial and political aspirations of the governing elites – and the idea of the nation brand.

References

Andreyeva, S., 2007. Sochi presents another Olympic project – "Federation Island". *The Voice of Russia*, [online] 25 November. Available at: http://english.ruvr.ru/2007/11/25/164080.html. Accessed 22 October 2012.

Anholt, S., 2010. Editorial: definitions of place branding – working towards a resolution. *Place Branding and Public Diplomacy*, 6:1, pp.1–10.

Ashworth, G. and Kavaratzis, M., 2009. Beyond the logo: brand management for cities. *Brand Management*, 16:8, pp.520–531.

BBC, 2006. Obituary: Saparmurat Niyazov. *BBC News*, [online] 21 December. Available at: http://news.bbc.co.uk/2/hi/asia-pacific/6199021.stm. Accessed 10 December 2010.

BBC, 2008. 1963: thousands killed in Yugoslav earthquake. *BBC on This Day*, [online] 26 July. Available at: http://news.bbc.co.uk/onthisday/hi/dates/stories/july/26/newsid_2721000/2721635.stm. Accessed 10 December 2010.

BBC, 2012. Has Turkmenistan changed at all? *BBC News*, [online] 12 February. Available at: http://www.bbc.co.uk/news/world-asia-16958817. Accessed 7 October 2012.

Berg, p.O. and Kreiner, K., 1990. Corporate architecture: turning physical settings into symbolic resources. In: p.Gagliardi, ed. 1990. *Symbols and artefacts: views of the corporate landscape*. New York: Aldine de Gruyter. pp.41–67.

Brauer, G. ed., 2002. *Architecture as brand communication*. Basel: Birkhauser.

Buzur, S., 2006. Geographies of ethnopolitics: unravelling the spatial and political economies of "Ethnic Conflict". *Occasional Paper no. 7/06*. South East European Studies at Oxford, European Studies Centre, St. Anthony's College Oxford. pp.1–29.

Cannadine, D., 1983. The context, performance and meaning of ritual: the British monarchy, c. 1820–1977. In: E. Hobsbawm and T. Ranger, eds. 1983. *The invention of tradition*. Cambridge: Cambridge University Press. pp.101–164.

Castells, M., 1997. *The power of identity*. Oxford: Blackwell.

Castoriadis, C., 1987. *The imaginary institutions of society*. Cambridge: Polity.

Chung, C. J., Inaba, J., Koolhaas, R. and Leong, S. T., 2001. *Harvard Design School Guide to Shopping*. London: Taschen.

Cox, J. K., 2006. A Balkan trilogy. *East European Politics and Societies*, 20:3, pp.550–561.

Davies, C., 2011. Is Macedonia's capital being turned into a theme park? *CNN*, [online] 10 October. Available at: http://edition.cnn.com/2011/10/04/world/europe/macedonia-skopje-2014/index.html. Accessed 9 November 2011.

de Bourrienne, L. A. F., 1832. *The life of Napoleon Bonaparte*. Philadelphia, PA: Carey & Lea.

De Launey, L., 2014. The makeover that's divided a nation. *BBC News*, [online] 30 August. Available at: http://www.bbc.com/news/magazine-28951171. Accessed 29 March 2015.

Denkovska, A., 2010. Барокни кошнички за панорамско тркало (Baroque cabins for the Ferris wheel; summary in English). *Nova Makedonija*, [online] 9 November. Available at: http://www.novamakedonija.com.mk/NewsDetal.asp?vest=11910954201&id=14&prilog=0&setIzdanie=22128. Accessed 9 November 2011.

Diamond, J., 2003. Archaeology: propaganda of the pyramids. *Nature*, 424, pp.891–893.

Doncev, D., 2010. "Скопје 2014" и Велигденски Остров ("Skopje 2014" and the Easter Island; summary in English). *Utrinski Vesnik*, [online] 9 February. Available at: http://www.utrinski.com.mk/default.asp?ItemID=2F74CAAFED8F0542928122E5F13997EF. Accessed 24 October 2012.

Dovey, K., 1999. *Framing places: mediating power in built form*. London: Routledge.

Edensor, T., 2002. *National identity, popular culture and everyday life*. Oxford: Berg.

European Commission, 2011. European Capital of Culture. *European Commission*, [online] Available at: http://ec.europa.eu/culture/our-programmes-and-actions/doc413_en.htm. Accessed 17 January 2011.

Fattah, H., 2007. Celebrity architects reveal a daring cultural Xanadu for the Arab world. *The New York Times*, [online] 1 February. Available at: http://www.nytimes.com/2007/02/01/arts/design/01isla.html. Accessed 9 December 2010.

Fitzpatrick, C. A., 2011. Turkmenistan: golden Turkmenbashi statue is back. *EurasiaNet*, [online] 7 November. Available at: http://www.eurasianet.org/node/64458. Accessed 21 October 2012.

Gary, p.B. and Talcott, R., 2006. Stargazing in ancient Egypt. *Astronomy*, 34, pp.62–67.

Georgieva, L., 2006. Менаџирање на ризици (*Risk management*; summary in English). Skopje: Faculty of Philosophy, Ss. Cyril and Methodius University of Skopje.

Glendinning, M., 2004. *The last icons: architecture beyond modernism*. Glasgow: Graven Images.

Gobé, M., 2001. *Emotional branding*. New York: Allworth Press.

Goldberger, P., 2008. Out of the blocks. *The New Yorker*, [online] 2 June. Available at: http://www.newyorker.com/arts/critics/skyline/2008/06/02/080602crsk_skyline_goldberger. Accessed 23 October 2012.

Greenberg, M., 2000. Branding cities: a social history of the urban lifestyle magazine. *Urban Affairs Review*, 36:2, pp.228–263.

Guggenheim, 2013. About. *The Solomon R. Guggenheim Foundation*, [online] Available at: http://www.guggenheim.org/bilbao/about. Accessed 13 September 2013.

Hankinson, G., 2010. Place branding research: a cross-disciplinary agenda and the views of practitioners. *Place Branding and Public Diplomacy*, 6:4, pp.300–315.

Hari, J., 2009. The dark side of Dubai. *The Independent*, [online] 7 April. Available at: http://www.independent.co.uk/voices/commentators/johann-hari/the-dark-side-of-dubai-1664368.html. Accessed 7 October 2012.

Hobsbawm, E., 1983. Introduction: inventing traditions. In: E. Hobsbawm and T. Ranger, eds. 1983. *The invention of tradition*. Cambridge: Cambridge University Press. pp.1–11.

Hobsbawm, E. and Ranger, T. eds., 1983. *The invention of tradition*. Cambridge: Cambridge University Press.

Illmer, A., 2009. Macedonia and Kosovo break the ice in border dispute. *Deutsche Welle*, [online] 18 October. Available at: http://www.dw-world.de/dw/article/0,,4802159,00.html. Accessed 30 December 2011.

Ivanov, G., 2005. The name Macedonia. *Politicka Misla*, 26:10, pp.91–96.

Ivanov, G., 2011. Macedonia and Serbia's prospects are in the EU – meeting with the Serbian President Boris Tadic. *Media Centre of the President of the Republic of Macedonia Dr. Gjorge Ivanov*, [online] 16 December. Available at: http://www.president.gov.mk/en/media-centre/news/965-2011-12-16-14-19-40.html. Accessed 30 December 2011.

Jaffe, D. E. and Nebenzahl, I. D., 2006. *National image and competitive advantage: the theory and practice of place branding*. Copenhagen: Copenhagen Business School Press.

Jana, R., 2006. Dubai's architectural wonders. *Business Week*, [online] 2 March. Available at: http://www.businessweek.com/innovate/content/mar2006/id20060302_615308.htm. Accessed 9 December 2010.

Jencks, C., 2005. *The iconic building*. London: Francis Lincoln.

Jensen, O. B., 2007. Culture stories: understanding cultural urban branding. *Planning Theory*, 6:3, pp.211–236.

Julier, G., 2000. *The culture of design*. London: Sage.

Kaika, M., 2010. Architecture and crisis: re-inventing the icon, re-imag(in)ing London and re-branding the city. *Transactions of the Institute of British Geographers*, 35:4, pp.453–474.

Kavaratzis, M., 2004. From city marketing to city branding: towards a theoretical framework for developing city brands. *Place Branding*, 1:1, pp.58–73.

Kavaratzis, M., 2009. Cities and their brands: lessons from corporate branding. *Place Branding and Public Diplomacy*, 5:1, pp.26–37.

Kavaratzis, M. and Ashworth, G., 2005. City branding: an effective assertion of identity or a transitory marketing trick? *Tijdschrift voor Economische en Sociale Geografie*, 96:5, pp.506–514.

Kelly, K. E., 2003. Architecture for sale(s). *Harvard Design Magazine*, 17, pp.1–6.

Kemming, J. D. and Sandikci, O., 2007. Turkey's EU accession as a question of nation brand image. *Place Branding and Public Diplomacy*, 3:1, pp.31–41.

Kirby, A. E. and Kent, A. M., 2010. Architecture as brand: store design and brand identity. *Journal of Product and Brand Management*, 19:6, pp.432–439.

Klingmann, A., 2007. *Brandscapes*. Cambridge, MA: MIT Press.

Knight Frank, 2012. The Wealth Report. *Knight Frank*, [online] Available at: www.google.com/url?sa=t&rct=j&q=&esrc=s&source=web&cd=1&ved=0CCEQFjAA&url=http%3A%2F%2Fwww.thewealthreport.net%2FThe-Wealth-Report-2012.pdf. Accessed 7 October 2012.

Koolhaas, R., 1994. *Delirious New York: a retroactive manifesto for Manhattan*. New York: Monacelli Press.

Lewis, P., 2009. Dubai's six year building boom grinds to a halt as financial crisis takes hold. *The Guardian*, [online] 13 February. Available at: http://www.guardian.co.uk/world/2009/feb/13/dubai-boom-halt. Accessed 9 December 2010.

Library of Congress, 2010. Original plan of Washington, DC. *American Treasures of the Library of Congress*, [online] Available at: http://www.loc.gov/exhibits/treasures/tri001.html. Accessed 10 December 2010.

Loring, D. M., 1994. A new tack needed to resolve old conflicts. *The Age*, 5 March, p.28.

Loring, D. M., 2010. The Macedonian minority of Northern Greece. *Cultural Survival*, [online] 19 March. Available at: http://www.culturalsurvival.org/publications/cultural-survival-quarterly/greece/macedonian-minority-northern-greece. Accessed 5 December 2011.

Mahon, M., 1998. The Macedonian question in Bulgaria. *Nations and Nationalism*, 4:3, pp.389–407.

Mayes, R., 2008. A place in the sun: the politics of place, identity and branding. *Place Branding and Public Diplomacy*, 4:2, pp.124–135.

Mayo, J. M., 1996. The manifestation of politics in architectural practice. *Journal of Architectural Education*, 50:2, pp.76–88.

McIntyre, D., 2009. Dubai bailout may come from rich neighbor Abu Dhabi. *Daily Finance*, [online] 28 November. Available at: http://www.dailyfinance.com/story/dubai-bailout-may-come-from-rich-neighbor-abu-dhabi/19256609/. Accessed 16 December 2010.

McNeill, D. and Tewdwr-Jones, M., 2003. Architecture, banal nationalism and re-territorialization. *International Journal of Urban and Regional Research*, 27:3, pp.738–743.

Mumford, L., 1961. *The city in history: its origins, its transformations, and its prospects*. New York: Harvest.

Muradov, R., 2009. Different Ashgabat. *Turkmenistan International Magazine*, 1:2, pp.46–47.

Muradov, R., 2011. Symbols of renewal. *Turkmenistan International Magazine*, 5:6, pp.74–75.

Muratovski, G., 2008. Corporationalism: subjective creation of national identities and nation-brands. *2008 ACUADS conference: sites of activity: on the edge.* Adelaide, Australia, 1–3 October 2008. Adelaide: University of South Australia.

Muratovski, G., 2010. *Design research: corporate communication strategies – from religious propaganda to strategic brand management.* Ph.D. University of South Australia.

Muratovski, G., 2012. The role of architecture and integrated design in city branding. *Place Branding and Public Diplomacy*, 8:3, pp.195–207.

Muratovski, G., 2013a. Urban branding: the politics of architecture. *Design Principles and Practices: An International Journal – An Annual Review*, 6:1, pp.45–58.

Muratovski, G., 2013b. The use of built environments in the formation and change of national identities: the case of Macedonia and 'Skopje 2014'. *Postcolonial Europe*, [online] Available at: http://www.postcolonial-europe.eu/en/attitudes/154-the-use-of-built-environments-in-the-formation-and-change-of-national-identities-the-case-of-macedonia-and-skopje-2014. Accessed 1 September 2013.

Muratovski, G., 2013c. Theme park in a Fortress: architecture and politics in Macedonia. *The Conversation*, [online] Available at: http://theconversation.edu.au/a-theme-park-in-a-fortress-politics-and-architecture-in-macedonia-9354. Accessed 1 September 2013.

Muratovski, G., 2014. Keynote address: the utopian city. *'Think Outside' G20 Cultural Celebrations Program – part of the G20 Leaders Summit 2014.* Brisbane, Australia, 5 November 2014. Brisbane: Asia Pacific Design Library and Queensland Government Department of the Premier and Cabinet.

National Register of Historic Places, 2001. Washington, DC: the L'Enfant and McMillan plans. *National Park Service, US Department of the Interior*, [online]. Available at: http://www.nps.gov/nr/travel/wash/learnmore.htm. Accessed 10 December 2010.

Neofotistos, V. P., 2004. Beyond stereotypes: violence and the porousness of ethnic boundaries in the Republic of Macedonia. *History and Anthropology*, 15:1, pp.47–67.

Nova Makedonija, 2010. Скопје 2014: нов град (Skopje 2014: the new city; summary in English). *Nova Makedonija*, [online] 2 February. Available at: http://www.novamakedonija.com.mk/NewsDetal.asp?vest=25101030253&id=14&setIzdanie=21902. Accessed 10 December 2010.

Olins, W., 1990. *Corporate identity: making business strategy visible through design.* London: Thames & Hudson.

Oommen T. K., 1997. *Citizenship and national identity: from colonialism to globalism.* London: Sage.

Ouroussoff, N., 2007. A vision in the desert. *The New York Times*, [online] 1 February. Available at: http://www.nytimes.com/2007/02/01/arts/design/04ouro.html. Accessed 9 December 2010.

Ouroussoff, N., 2008. City on the Gulf: Koolhaas lays out a grand urban experiment in Dubai. *The New York Times*, [online] 3 March. Available at: http://www.nytimes.com/2008/03/03/arts/design/03kool.html. Accessed 9 December 2010.

Parkerson, B. and Saunders, J., 2005. City branding: can goods and services branding models be used to brand cities? *Place Branding*, 1:3, pp.242–264.

Perry, D., 2001. Macedonia: small potatoes or a big deal? *The International Spectator*, 36:2, pp.5–12.

Pieterse, J. N., 1991. Fictions of Europe. *Race and Class*, 32:3, pp.1–10.

Pinkney, D. H., 1955. Napoleon III's transformation of Paris: the origins and development of the idea. *Journal of Modern History*, 27:2, pp.125–134.

Pop, V., 2011. UN court: Greece broke the law in Macedonia name dispute. *EU Observer*, [online] 5 December. Available at: http://euobserver.com/15/114506. Accessed 30 December 2011.

Ricoeur, P., 1991. Narrative identity. *Philosophy Today*, 35:1, pp.73–81.

Ringdal, K., Simkus, A., and Listhaug, O., 2005. Disaggregating public opinion on the ethnic conflict in Macedonia. *Disaggregating the study of Civil War and transnational violence*. San Diego, CA, 7–8 March 2005. San Diego: Institute of Global Conflict and Cooperation at the University of California.

Rose, S., 2009. Towering follies: the Dubai architecture you couldn't make up. *The Guardian*, [online] 3 December. Available at: http://www.guardian.co.uk/artanddesign/2009/dec/03/dubai-architecture. Accessed 21 October 2012.

Rowat, A., 2008. Travel: Ashgabat, Turkmenistan. *Wallpaper**, [online] 28 October. Available at: http://www.wallpaper.com/gallery/travel/ashgabat-turkmenistan/17050587/. Accessed 10 December 2010.

Sari, E., 2004. Architecture and branding. *Dialogue: Architecture+Design+Culture*, 83, pp.22–99.

Sklair, L., 2010. Iconic architecture and the culture-ideology of consumerism. *Theory, Culture and Society*, 27:5, pp.135–159.

Smilevska, M., 2010. Хорор катна гаража среде Скопје (Horror-like multi-storey parking in the middle of Skopje; summary in English). *Alfa TV*, [online] 28 June. Available at: http://alfa.mk/default.aspx?mid=36&eventid=24304&egId=6. Accessed 9 November 2011.

Smith, A. D., 1986. *The ethnic revival in the modern world*. Oxford: Basil Blackwell.

Suddath, C., 2009. Brief history: Dubai. *TIME Magazine*, [online] 14 December. Available at: http://www.time.com/time/magazine/article/0,9171,1945354,00.html. Accessed 25 October 2012.

Sudjic, D., 2006. *The Edifice Complex: how the rich and powerful shape the world*. London: Penguin Press.

Szondi, G., 2007. The role and challenges of country branding in transition countries: the Central and Eastern European experience. *Place Branding and Public Diplomacy*, 3:1, pp.8–20.

Taleski, M., 2011. Double Decker buses help revive Skopje's flair. *Southeast Europe Times*, [online] 28 March. Available at: http://www.setimes.com/cocoon/setimes/xhtml/en_GB/features/setimes/features/2011/03/28/feature-03. Accessed 9 November 2011.

Tanevski, B., 2005. The problem between the Macedonian and Albanian ethnic groups in the Republic of Macedonia and its future. *New Balkan Politics: Journal of Politics*, [online] Available at: http://www.newbalkanpolitics.org.mk/napis.asp?id=36&lang=English. Accessed 9 February 2012.

Tange, K. and Kultermann, U., 1970. *Kenzo Tange*. Zurich: Verlag fur Architectur Artemis.

TDH, State News Agency of Turkmenistan, 2011. New look of Ashgabat as a symbol of magnificent changes in the motherland. *Turkmenistan: The Golden Age*, [online] 20 November. Available at: http://www.turkmenistan.gov.tm/_eng/?id=43. Accessed 21 October 2012.

The Economist, 2011. Macedonia's name dispute: call it what you want. *The Economist*, [online] 10 December. Available at: http://www.economist.com/node/21541400. Accessed 30 December 2011.

U.S. Department of State, 2012. Background note: Turkmenistan. *Bureau of South and Central Asian Affairs*, [online] 23 January. Available at: http://www.state.gov/r/pa/ei/bgn/35884.htm. Accessed 7 October 2012.

Venn, C., 2002. Narrative identity, subject formation, and the transfiguration of subjects. In: W. Patterson, ed. 2002. *Strategic narrative: new perspectives on the power of personal and cultural stories*. New York: Lexington Books. pp.29–50.

Venturi, R., 1972. *Learning from Las Vegas*. Cambridge, MA: MIT Press.

Vershinin, A., 2012. Turkmenistan claims largest Ferris wheel record. *The Guardian*, [online] 19 May. Available at: http://www.guardian.co.uk/world/feedarticle/10249812. Accessed 21 October 2012.

Walker, A., 2010. Qatar's World Cup: engineering marvel; PR nightmare? *Fast Company*, [online] 12 June. Available at: http://www.fastcodesign.com/1662812/qatars-world-cup-engineering-marvel-pr-nightmare. Accessed 9 December 2010.

Walsh, K., 2006. Branding the cities of god. *Brand Strategy*, September, p.27.

Zizek, S., 1989. *The sublime object of ideology*. London: Verso.

Notes

1. For the purpose of this study, built environments are defined as human-built structures and surroundings ranging from urban design and buildings, to parks, monuments and public art.
2. For the purpose of this study, architecture is defined as the style in which a particular built environment is designed or constructed.
3. According to Eric Hobsbawm (1983: 1–2), invented traditions are a 'set of practices, normally governed by overly or tacitly accepted rules and of a ritual or symbolic

nature, which seek to inculcate certain values and norms of behaviour by repetition, which automatically implies continuity with the past'.
4. Please note that there is a distinction between a monument and a sculpture – not all monuments are necessarily sculptures.
5. The Pyramid of the Sun, built by the Teotihuacan civilisation in the Valley of Mexico, was never matched by the later, more powerful, Aztec Empire. Instead, much like Cheops's successors in Egypt, the Aztecs invested in long-distance trade, outlying colonies, military conquest, garrisons, intensive agriculture and crafts production. The story is similar with Peru's earliest state – the Moche and with Japan's first state – Yamato. The Moche built Peru's largest pyramid, the House of the Sun (*Huaca del Sol*), yet their more powerful successors, the Chimu and the Incas, who enjoyed unquestioned actual control, never saw a need for such ostentation. Instead, the Incas constructed a vast road system, storehouses, and irrigation canals, and invested in their military capacity (Diamond, 2003: 891). Like Cheops and the Moche, Emperor Nintoku of Yamato constructed the largest *kofun* in Imperial Japan – a megalithic tomb in the form of a large, keyhole-shaped earthwork mound. As this structure was built in the early years of the Yamato state, the *kofun* had no other purpose than to impress Yamato's neighbours (Diamond, 2003: 891).
6. The Lincoln Memorial is a particularly interesting example where a colossal statue of the sixteenth president of the United States, Abraham Lincoln, more suitable for a Greek or a Roman god than a president, is placed in a temple on a top of a hill overseeing the city. The Washington Monument, on the other hand, is an ancient Egyptian symbol – obelisk – associated with the cult of the sun and symbolises the Egyptian sun god Ra – their greatest deity (see Gary and Talcott, 2006: 62–67).
7. While all buildings possess some architectural elements, not all buildings are architecturally significant. By the same token, while all trademarks possess certain brand elements, not all trademarks are brands, in a sense that generic trademarks fail to engage the consumers in the same way as branded trademarks (e.g. Coca-Cola vs. the supermarket Cola).
8. I would liked to acknowledge the ongoing name conflict between Republic of Macedonia (the constitutional name of the country) and the Hellenic Republic (Greece). In this chapter, I will use the name Macedonia – a name that has been recognised by 133 countries (61 per cent of all UN member states) to date (2015).
9. Inspired by the newly 'designed' coastline of Dubai, Russia aspired to undertake a similar project nearby the luxury resort city of Sochi. Like 'The World' island in Dubai that represents a map of the world, Russia is developing its own offshore resort in the Black Sea called 'The Federation', which resembles the map of the Russian Federation. The Russians have commissioned the same architect that Dubai used for their own island, Erick van Egeraat, and they stated that their island would be the 'most beautiful' artificial island in the world. The project was planned for completion in time for the 2014 Winter Olympics in Sochi (see Andreyeva, 2007). However, one

10. Niyazov's ambitions and demonstrations of power have not been affixed solely within the domain of the built environments. He named cities, airports and even a meteorite after himself. His book, the *Ruhnama* – a collection of his thoughts on Turkmen identity, history and destiny – was required reading in the curriculum of schools and universities, and it even serves as a 'spiritual guide' in mosques. In addition to this, Niyazov named some of the months and days of the week after himself and his family and introduced increasingly personal laws, such as a ban on young men wearing beards and long hair and a ban on make-up for female news reporters and anchors (BBC, 2006).
11. Prior to his election as the president of the Republic of Macedonia, Prof. Gjorgje Ivanov, Ph.D., served as the Head of the Political Science Department at the Macedonian state university – Saints Cyril and Methodius University of Skopje, as an academic, he has published extensively on the 'Macedonian issue' prior to his election in 2009 and his re-election in 2014.
12. The government under the leadership of Prime Minister Nikola Gruevski was first elected in 2006; it has remained in power by continuously winning the parliamentary elections, the presidential elections and the local elections that have been held since then.

Chapter 3

Race, Advertisements and YouTube: Identity and Nationality

Kathleen Connellan

Abstract

This chapter exposes the racial content in three fast-food advertisements for analysis. The advertisements' presence and uptake on YouTube provides the specifically global popular culture environment that is the focus of the contextual analysis. Two Nando's and one KFC advertisement set in South Africa and Australia are presented as case studies. The analysis and discussion use a combined critical race theory and Foucauldian approach so that racial signifiers are rendered more visible. A transcription of the dramatic dialogue and a close description of the visuals provide the raw material for discursive revelations of national identities, belongings and exclusions. The backdrop of migration, prejudice and corruption is brought to life in stories that have immediate resonance in countries that love sport, cars and jokes. And it is the use of humour that is paramount in the application of a critical race lens; humour in the advertisements is used to avoid a direct confrontation with the paramount issue of race and racism. This humour is shown to be a significant device in the advertising of a type of food that is consumed by crowds; that is groups of people who are thrown together but portrayed in the advertisements as being intrinsic to a society of belonging – belonging to a culture of continuous enjoyable consumption. Everyone in these advertisements is therefore given passports to enjoy a ubiquitous state of satisfaction. However, an analysis of the advertisements' transcripts reveals a consistent presence of race and class distinction. Through the style of analysis employed here, the chapter highlights the social implications of divisiveness that advertising to target markets based upon race and national affiliation can perpetuate.

Keywords

race, YouTube, fast food, advertising

Introduction

Popular culture is often communicated through stories. Narrative traditions in advertising have always been a powerful mechanism for drawing people into the consumption of particular products. When advertising was at an interesting zenith in the mid-twentieth century in the United States, followed by the United Kingdom and its colonies, the stories were situated within specific and recognisable cultures of conservatism. Now that the capitalist world has become global and is no longer so neatly segmented into nation-states – as large-scale immigration and refugee populations change the social landscape of countries – the question of how these stories are told is an interesting one. Importantly, in this chapter I acknowledge that one of the most obvious outcomes of these changes is that populations of many countries that might have seen themselves as racially discrete in the twentieth century are now much more diverse. Nonetheless, products are still advertised to racially distinct market segments because people relate to the familiar, and the familiar is often embedded in a common narrative.

The writings of Michel Foucault on historical and discursive formations underpin my approach in this chapter. The Internet is arguably the epitome of discursiveness. I use Foucault's thoughts on race and the subject as an infinite network of power relations to read and analyse the visual, verbal and performed narratives of YouTube advertisements together with textual and performed responses to them. My methodological framework is also informed by critical race theory as it sheds additional light on the interplay of subjectivities in contested spaces. I apply these theories to case studies of advertisements so as to identify the prominent features and devices used for narrative, characterisation and commercial communication.

Popular culture and business, the theme of this book series, engage with everyday consumption in an atmosphere of free enterprise and profit. The term 'popular' comes from the Latin *populous* meaning people, which then through the French and Italian translations implies the common people, that is ordinary human beings. Combine common people with culture, which signifies a level of cohesion, and add 'business' in the twenty-first century and you arrive at a massive demographic, a potentially huge market. It is in this market that YouTube advertising is finding its niche. But what is YouTube? Can it really 'work' across business and cultures in an ostensibly global economy?

I have chosen examples from two countries, but the discussion is a global one that addresses the ways in which advertising is constructed in a world of shifting identities. The ideological environment and national imaginaries of South Africa, Australia and America form the backdrop to my discussion of racial separation, reversal and integration in the narrative plots of the YouTube case studies. Both South Africa and Australia are testimonies to varying degrees of racial power dynamics, including the use of humour to undermine racial tension. I wish to engage with this touchy theme of race and racism in the case studies and discussions. Before presenting the case studies of selected YouTube advertisements, I now provide a brief explanation of advertising and YouTube as a combined force in popular culture.

Advertising is one of the many voices of popular culture; it is a system of signification that invites ordinary people into a story and therefore an experience that could satisfy a need or compunction they might have. Bignell notes that:

advertisements encourage us to participate by decoding their linguistic and visual signs and to enjoy this decoding activity. Ads make use of signs, codes, and social myths which are already in circulation and ask us to recognise and often to enjoy them.
(Bignell, 1997: 33, emphasis added)

Bignell's words remain true almost two decades later; however, the media landscape has expanded exponentially with the growth of online communication. This has made it imperative for advertisers to have a strong presence on the Internet. Increasingly, people have smart phones and mobile devices that allow them to be online most of the time, and YouTube is the perfect platform for advertisers to reach an impetuous and impatient market.

Officially launched in June 2005 in California's Silicon Valley, YouTube is an online success story that now also offers a space for people to broadcast themselves, extending its function to include 'a platform for public self-expression' (Jarrett, 2008: 134). Millions of people visit YouTube to upload or download music and videos, and it is the cheapest and quickest way to hear and see the latest hot topic in popular culture. Many advertisers have purchased rights to overplay their advertisement in the first few seconds of videos, and viewers are only given the option to skip the advertisement some seconds in. The catchiness and liveliness of short YouTube videos is an irresistible template for advertisers, where they can also immediately get feedback on the advertisement from the comments beneath.

Advertisers mimic the impromptu drama of amateur videos taken on mobile devices. These videos capture a moment in someone's life, but advertisers also recreate scenarios that are prominent topics in the general media. These topics include crime and its associated dramas; the competitive excitement of international sport; and mass migration as a result of political upheaval. Advertisers also try to trigger responses through emotional connection to some of our biological, physiological and psychological needs (Maslow, 1943: 370–371). Food, safety and belonging are crucial in Maslow's hierarchy of human needs and each one of these can be identified in the two Nando's South Africa advertisements and the one KFC Australia YouTube advertisement discussed below.

Methodology

I combine Foucauldian and critical race theory as an overall methodology for discussion and analysis. Three case studies present detailed descriptions and dialogue of three separate advertisements. These advertisements were originally designed for television and were subsequently posted onto YouTube. The existence of YouTube means that an advertisement meant for a particular audience (such as Australia and South Africa) is also viewed elsewhere. For example, the Australian KFC advertisement discussed in this chapter was widely viewed in the United States, something that would not have happened a decade ago. Therefore, it is the YouTube environment that is the focus of the analysis. The online comments are also a feature of YouTube and form a crucial part of the case studies in this chapter. The comments selected are the most typical and the most responded to. I chose case studies as a method because it allowed me to present a contemporary phenomenon in a real-life context. I selected fast-food advertisements for their non-elite position in culture and because their brand, venues, services and satisfaction have become a part of popular culture through repeated advertising that targets ordinary people. After a desktop survey of fast-food advertisements produced in 2012, I selected those that featured race, ethnicity and national identity to provide the content for a critical race reading. This does not mean that the advertisements made for these globally recognised brands are also globally representative of racial attitudes, but they are an indication of how race is used by advertisers and they provide an opportunity to analyse and reflect on a topic that is so often avoided.

Case Study 1: Nando's Traffic Cop, South African TV Advertisement

The advertisement (Black River FC Advertising Agency, 2012) starts with white text on a black screen and a voice-over saying, 'Nando's always takes flack for telling it how it is. This time we're telling it how it isn't.'[1] The scene moves to a well-built traffic officer running to a car he has waved down. A robust and lively greeting takes place between the officer and an urbane black man at the wheel of an expensive foreign car, dropping to momentary seriousness when the officer says the words 'licence please'. Silence ensues as the licence is scrutinised, then more laughter with the officer acclaiming, 'it is you here [...] looking beautiful and handsome at the same time'. The visibly relieved driver laughs equally loudly and continues the banter to extract an 'ah [...] [beautiful and handsome] a-ll the time' from the officer. Encouraged, the driver then says 'but you are a nice guy, let me buy you lunch'. There is more silence and momentary unease as the officer looks shocked and displeased, saying, 'you buy me lunch?! Why do you want to buy me lunch? I can buy *you* lunch'. Unease again, followed by more relieved laughter with some repetition of the repartee. Then the scene moves swiftly to a busy Nando's interior with an obviously multiracial clientele. The officer and the urbane driver in his smart suit are sitting down to 'a quarter chicken and chips and a roll for just R21.95. It shouldn't be but it is'. The back-and-forth power play continues as one puts a chip into the other's mouth.

Selected Online Comments[2]

The comments listed below the YouTube video from November 2012 to July 2013 frequently focused upon the readers' mirthful satisfaction about the police officer–smart guy exchange in parody. One wrote: 'Hahaha [...] License please hmmm [...] serious business lol' and another wrote: 'What makes this halirous is this police officer is a JMPD [Johannesburg Metropolitan Police Department] loooooooooool'. The abbreviated text for laughter and laughing out loud accompanied by other references to how funny the audiences found this advertisement constitutes the key response. Another aspect that caught the attention of viewers is the background industrial landscape (water tower and chimneys), which some mistook for a nuclear plant until other commenters corrected them. One commenter particularly appreciated the acting, saying: 'pause at 0.14 and look at his eyes'. A large majority of comments actually quoted the dialogue directly and chose excerpts such as 'Licence please hahah'; 'I can buy you lunch. lol'; 'You look beautiful and handsome at the same time'; several commented on Nando's ads: 'D Nandoz is boss'; 'I love Nandos commercials'; and one comment zoned in on the price, saying 'R21 is less than £2 sterling […] bargain'.

Case Study 2: KFC's Cricket Survival Guide

The advertisement begins with a small still icon of a red cricket ball inscribed with 'KFC's' in thick white lettering and below the ball against a black background 'cricket survival guide'.[3] A yellow cricket hat sits on the ball with two crossed cricket bats behind the ball. There is a jingly dance rhythm in the background and the still then jumps to a scene with a single white man sitting down in a crowded stadium wearing an Australian green and gold top. He is surrounded by several black (West Indian) fans, some dancing to music. His expression is one of confused frustration; he covers his face with both hands in seeming despair and then shouts at the camera: 'Need a chip when you're stuck in an awkward situation?' A large container of chips and chicken then appears, which he holds up to the dancing West Indian supporters around him. They take a chip each and the music is momentarily quieter. He smiles at the camera, saying 'too easy'. Another, deeper voice comes over (the voice of KFC?) saying 'KFC's crowd pleaser' in a tone that rises and then drops gently in cadence, suggesting everything will be alright now.

Online and Offline Commentary

This advertisement attracted considerable attention especially in the United States and stirred up controversy regarding its racist overtones. According to *The Guardian*, a UK newspaper, 'the clip has quickly found its way around the world on the internet, prompting stinging criticism in the US where fried chicken remains closely associated with age-old racist stereotypes about black people in the once segregated south' (Clark, 2010). Andrew Clark of *The Guardian* notes that 'KFC Australia has come out fighting, saying that the commercial was a "light-hearted reference to the West Indian cricket team" which has been "misinterpreted by a segment of the people in the US"' (2010).

The Young Turks, an online news show that addressed the controversy of the KFC advertisement, was posted onto YouTube in January 2010. The two young US hosts Cenk Uygur and Ana Kasparian (2010) asked incredulously 'This is Australia?' They then proceeded to debate the definitions of 'racist' against the backdrop of the KFC advertisement, agreeing that if something is racist then 'the target' is 'made to look bad', saying that in this advertisement it is clearly the case where 'stereotypes are pushed'. They continued to describe the advertisement as movie commentators would for films, noting in facetious and sarcastic tones that the white guy is 'so civilised' sitting down in his own seat. He just wants to watch the game while these 'black folk' who 'probably didn't even buy their tickets' are so 'unruly, uncivilised and rowdy', jumping up and down. They just will not calm down unless you give them 'some damn fried chicken [...] too easy'. The hosts repeated these last two words (too easy) several times. They appeared to consider (by their amazed and amused tones) that these two words, accompanied by the placatory action of the chip offering, are the pinnacle of this racist video. After the repartee on racism, the male host said that at the outset he wanted to give the advertisement the benefit of the doubt but, now that they had unpacked it bit by bit, he had to agree that it is racist. 'But what do you do about it?' he asked the audience, which is invited to provide feedback. The hosts reflected upon how ridiculous the video is but also admitted that people actually think this way (despite the female host saying 'yes but this is Australia' – indicating that the take on race in Australia is different to that of the United States). She did not elaborate on the distinction but went on to blame 'the media' for 'pushing' the idea of race as portrayed on the video.

An Australian Broadcasting Corporation panel talk show, *The Gruen Transfer*, reviews TV advertisements, and comprises critical representatives from selected advertising design studios in addition to the hosts. One of their shows included a discussion of the KFC advertisement presented in this case study (2010). They began the discussion by referring to the American view that the advertisement is racist, and panellist Todd Sampson – an advertising expert – said that, apart from the advertisement being bad in terms of quality, it was pulled off the air not because it was racist but because 'people were outraged that it was racist'. He said that Australians do not require an 'American filter' for everything they do, noting that the racial stereotype of dancing black people eating fried chicken is an American one. Sampson said that the advertisement needed to be pulled because KFC is an American company and the advertisement ended up being offensive to Americans despite it being made in Australia. The global nature of the Internet was blamed for the reactions and outcomes: 'It's a great example of negative PR, so negative PR travels a lot faster than positive PR so normally when you get angry at an ad you tell ten friends and you say "I really didn't like it", now you tell 10 million people in 3 seconds'. The woman on the panel said that she would like to talk for the West Indians, saying she was married to a (white) West Indian (this racial clarification was extracted laughingly by the rest of the panel). She said that she rang some of her husband's 'people' to find out a bit more before coming onto the panel that night and she stated it is 'not racist; it is fact':

black West Indians do eat fried chicken. 'There is a KFC on every street corner'. This then led to a discussion of whether it 'would be racist for a black man to feed a bunch of Aussie guys meat pies to keep them quiet'. Responses included feigned indignation by one of the 'Aussie' men on the panel who said, 'yes, I would find that racist!' This and most of the panel discussion was filled with intermittent laughter from panel members.

Selected Online Comments

The public comments on the KFC video are full of anger with several vitriolic exchanges between commenters. American commenters point out the faults of Australians in online text format but most comments are unrepeatable due to the frequency and level of foul language. However, one of the recent comments addresses the touchiness of race relations in the workplace, implying that racist readings of the KFC video are a reflection of this: 'The United States is so obsessed with political correctness and over sensitiveness towards minorities. Now when you have minorities and non-minorities together such as in the workplace it's uncomfortable as hell! Everyone is afraid of offending each other!' Another comment that is partially repeatable appears to respond to an attack on Australians as racists: 'So Americans made stereotypes about black people in America and decided they apply to all black people and it's racist to use any of the black stereotypes that America invented?' One comment makes light of the angry commentary, saying: 'I find this video offensive because I'm not haveing some of that delicious chicken!'

Case Study 3: Nando's South Africa Diversity Advertisement

The opening scene shows long Highveld grass blowing in the wind with a typical South African thorn tree in the middle ground; the sun is low on the horizon of distant hills.[4] All that can be heard are faint bird sounds. To the right there is a makeshift wooden sign upon which the word 'Arrivals' is hand painted. There is evidence of a high razor wire fence with a large hole in it. A male voice-over breaks the stillness with 'You know what is wrong with South Africa? All you foreigners' and on the word foreigners, the torso of a black African man rises out of the long grass in the foreground. His face is alert; he momentarily disappears only to rise up again carrying a suitcase in each hand. He and several others like him run with luggage through the grass. As he steps through the hole in the fence with his suitcase, the voice-over, which has continued slowly, says ominously, 'you must all go back to where you came from'. And with those words the man vanishes in an audible puff of smoke. The voice-over continues as the scene cuts to a long line of Africans queuing along a sidewalk beside a nondescript building but in front of a tent marked 'Immigration' where processing takes place. The people vary slightly in their stance and dress. Two men are running on the spot in running gear; one woman is dressed in ankle-length floral fabric with a matching headdress. There is a man standing very upright in a suit and other men and women all dressed in casual, clean and neat attire, including two men in white Muslim robes. The voice-over continues with 'you Cameroonians, Congolese, Pakistanis, Somalis, Ghanaians and Kenyans' and as each nationality is named, one or two of the people in the queue disappear in an audible puff of white smoke. The scene cuts to three black men, one in a white vest sitting on the front steps of a building and two others standing close by; two young white people are in the interior of a white Mercedes in the foreground. As the voice continues with 'and of course you Nigerians', all three of the black men vanish into puffs of smoke to the surprise of the white couple in the Mercedes who also turn into smoke clouds as the voice says 'and you Europeans'. The scene moves to a high vantage view of Johannesburg with a large 'plaza' down in the foreground. The voice continues without a pause, saying 'let's not forget all you Indians and Chinese'. On the word Indians, smoke comes out of all the plaza windows and along the roads inside the area of the plaza; then as the camera shifts to vans being unloaded in the grounds, on the word 'Chinese' the people around the packing containers go up in smoke. The voice and scene move to a well-built middle-aged white man in a hat with his dog in the front of a ute, or *bakkie* as they are called in South Africa. He goes up in smoke when the voice says 'even you Afrikaners' (the dog remains). The voice picks up pace with 'Bantus, Swazis, Xhosas, Sothos, Tswanas, Vendas, Zulus, everybody'. All these black South Africans go up in smoke and then on the word 'everybody', the scene moves from an urban setting to the open country and an indigenous San man with a leather pouch/*karros*, bow and arrows standing alone in the countryside. A cream *bakkie* drives past leaving dust and smoke on a gravel road but the San is still there. He turns to look at the passing *bakkie*, frowns at the camera and a new voice-over in the Khoisan language says (with subtitles) 'I'm not going anywhere, *$!@# [you] found us here'. And with this he turns and runs off across the vast earth-toned landscape towards the setting sun. The scene cuts to a plate of Nando's food: 'real South Africans love diversity, that's why we have introduced two more items, new peri crusted wings and delicious Trinchado and chips'.

Selected Online Comments

Text that is attributed to Nando's runs as follows:

> Nando's #Diversity campaign, where the flame-grilled chicken brand forces South Africans to question Xenophobia and intolerance - the fact is, if we go back far enough in time, we were all once foreigners in SA. This Winter, Nando's has teamed up with Cheesekids to create pop up soup kitchens in parts of SA that have been affected by Xenophobia, to walk the talk in galvanising our message of creating 'dialogue between the diverse'. You too can volunteer to join our soup kitchens by visiting www.souperstars.co.za.

A comment (from a commenter with an African name) offers a puzzled response to the allegations that the advertisement is racist:

> Im not sure I understand. Granted I am not of European descent [...] but I dont see what is racist about this commercial. And I dont understand when you say the truth is always racist when told by white people. Thats just not true. The truth is the truth no matter who tells it. And a racist statement is racist no matter who says it.

Other responses from people with African names include: '7 months later and no body killed anyone because of this ad yet'; 'You white people have been barbarians. But my history tells me that no empire has lasted forever and you will one day go down'; 'It's easy to talk especially when you know south African history aht your grandad made up so that they can say we are all foreigners. You stupid white people are just angry because your stupid lil plan to have our land and resources all to yourselves forever is a FAIL'; 'South Africa is for South Africans period!' And a commenter with an Afrikaner name and a photo image of a dog similar to the one in the advertisement replies:

> It all depends on your customized version of what is South African right? The Europeans colonized the USA barely 50 years before they came to South Africa. Are you saying that the Americans of today are not American? The fact they totally killed off the REAL natives so nobody is left to tell them to go home? Are you not ecstatic that we didn't kill YOU off? I can assure you we totally could if we wanted to. Maybe the San should tell you to go home.

This Afrikaner comment is followed by two African (in name) comments that include 'LOL' among shorthand for expletives such as 'WTF'. And at the end of the above selection, there is a single comment on a favourable currency comparison for the price of the Nando's dish advertised: 'its ridiculous cheaper' in South Africa.

General Analysis

Popular culture is essentially about the familiar, and in the current commercial world of overwhelming choice, even the most familiar fast-food chains need to maintain their relationships with their customers. This is especially true when the customer base includes diverse ethnicities and cultures. Advertising agencies are not only employed to retain old customers but also to reach out to new ones. The positioning of the subject is therefore at the heart of advertising. In Foucauldian terms, the subject is the full but fluid complexity of the individual person in society. In business this would be the customer, the client and the consumer; however, these market-based terms divest human beings of their intrinsic subjectivity. Foucault notes that there are two types of subjectivity:

'subject to someone else by control and dependence, and tied to his own identity by a conscience or self-knowledge. Both meanings suggest a form of power which subjugates and makes subject to' (1982: 212). In other words, the individual subject (you, me) is open to persuasion from outside ourselves and from inside ourselves, depending on our allegiances and classifications.

The case studies of Nando's and KFC presented above offer us the opportunity to identify ways in which subjectivities of race are dramatised to engage the consumer market (and all of its subjects). As Butler notes, 'when we are speaking about the "subject" we are not always speaking about an individual: we are speaking about a model for agency and intelligibility, one that is very often based on notions of sovereign power' (2006: 45). And here the sovereign power is that of a late capitalist business model that stands (albeit precariously) as the arbiter of desire in a competitive market of competing identities. In the following, an analytical discussion of the prominent features emerging from the videos and their accompanying commentary in the context of YouTube and the Internet is presented.

The use of humour comes across as the strongest device common to all three videos. Humour is imbricated across all the other key themes that emerged: paradox, stereotyping, nationality/identity, truth/history and price/quality. I will discuss these themes one by one alongside the signification of race in all three advertisements.

Paradox and Irony

Sound, action and expression are used in the powerful paradox of serious versus funny in the play of tensions with the traffic officer and the driver he has stopped on the highway (case study 1). The paradox of power in the form of the law (police) and wealth (expensive car and clothing) swings wildly from one moment of repartee to the next, maintaining a kind of hysteria for the audience who is kept in suspense as to which way the jokes will swing. Being stopped by a police officer on the highway is a common and unwelcome occurrence in South Africa and therefore the conversation is a variation of one that South African viewers of the advertisement have quite possibly had themselves. The Nando's voice-over, 'Nando's always takes the flack for telling it how it is. This time we're telling it how it isn't', prepares the audience to expect the opposite to what usually happens, and in this case the policeman is the one who takes the driver to lunch, not the other way around. The traffic officer repeats the driver's words with shock at being insulted, which is evident in his tone and facial expression: 'let me buy you lunch? I can buy *you* lunch'. The unease that follows is relieved with laughter, which acts as a linking agent between each side of the paradoxical back-and-forth power play. The precarious nature of the paradox and the tipping point of power are excruciatingly prolonged in the service of theatre. The high irony enacted has nothing to do with fact and everything to do with farce. It is the ultimate sophist stage play: 'which appear to refute; […] which appear to subject him to a paradox; […] which appear to make him fall into verbiage' (Foucault, 2013: 43). Additionally, the fact that Nando's has selected a black traffic officer and a black driver is symbolic of the new democratic post-Apartheid South Africa where the balance of power has shifted from white to black. However, Nando's clearly admits that they are not presenting the real situation, and therefore conceding that, if they did, it would be the black police officer taking the bribe of a Nando's lunch from the wealthy black man. The interweaving of black race as power but still open to corruption, which is presented as a kind of bargaining in the video, positions the rule of law and democracy of post-Apartheid South Africa as a paradox in itself. This paradox is akin to Foucault's explanation of the contingency between the police, the state and economy. 'The governmentality of the *politiques* gives us police, and the governmentality of the économistes introduces us, I think, to some of the fundamental lines of modern and contemporary governmentality' (Foucault, 2007: 348). Foucault then points to the 'artificiality of governmentality of police' (2007: 349), which is a kind of mentality that is contorted to govern according to the pressures and weaknesses of the state, the people and their compounded desires.

In the short Australian KFC advertisement (case study 2), paradox is illustrated in race and power dynamics. This is achieved by positioning the white Australian male as an object of pathos, whereas in normative terms he is a symbol of white race privilege. He is strategically there as a clean white young man who means no harm, and is innocently and commendably trying to support his nation's team.

> For those in power in the West, as long as whiteness is felt to be the human condition, then it alone both defines normality and fully inhabits it [...] the equation of being white with being human secures a position of power. White people have power and believe that they think, feel and act like and for all people; white people, unable to see their particularity, cannot take account of other people's; white people create the dominant images of the world and don't quite see that they thus construct the world in their own image; white people set standards of humanity by which they are bound to succeed and others bound to fail. Most of this is not done deliberately or maliciously.
> (Dyer, 1997: 9)

The above description presents whiteness as benign, as something that is simply there with no need to declare itself. However, in the advertisement the white male is outnumbered. This position is often rendered laughable in gendered representations when, for example, a single man is outnumbered by many women. In this advertisement, the single white guy is humiliated because of the focus on how this white man 'who represent[s] the normative dominant position on two of the main axes of power [race and gender], can best confront [his] internalised privilege and [...] embodied dominance' (Pease, 2004: 119). KFC comes to the 'rescue' and uses racial irony adeptly to magnify itself (or its food) and its role as a saviour in this 'awkward situation'. The advertisement is one in a series entitled 'cricket survival guide', but the irony is that the survival guide is not for the West Indians, who are presented as quite happy, but rather for the pathetic figure of the white Australian male. Irony is a device that hits with immediacy and can be augmented more effectively with music, movement and colour than spoken words, which take too long in an advertisement designed to be short and sharp. Irony is also most commonly supplemented with humour, but KFC's defence that it was 'light hearted humour' was not entirely successful. Members of the Australian advertising panel discussion mentioned above attempted to resurrect the humour by emphasising that it was not a good advertisement anyway, and by pretending outrage at the racism if they as white 'Aussie' blokes were placated with meat pies by a black man at a sports match. The paradox of this advertisement is present in the dichotomy of frustration/despair versus relief of the white Australian male, but the paradox is made more clear when the American and Australian responses are compared: outrage at the racist approach from American viewers and talk show TV panel, but humour (feigned or otherwise) from the Australian panel who, in a disavowal of racism, said that the advertisement was pulled off the air not because it was racist but because 'people were outraged that it was racist'.

The title of the 'Diversity Ad' (case study 3) is a paradox in itself. '7 months later and nobody killed anyone because of this ad yet' (online comment) is a chilling indictment of the power of advertisements that are laced with racial, ethnic and religious prejudice. This advertisement ironically tries to avoid prejudice by including every current national and linguistic South African group possible and then systematically to make each one disappear in a puff of white smoke. The protagonist voice-over has a black South African accent rather than a (white) English or Afrikaans accent. It proclaims with thick irony that all these South Africans are foreigners, thereby rendering everyone as alien except for a lone indigenous San who proclaims that he is not going anywhere. This is the paradox presented: if everyone leaves, then no one except a few San will be left. The story of migration and the dramatic reality of refugees fleeing for their lives across African bushlands are synonymous with refugees arriving dangerously in many foreign countries from across treacherous seas and deserts. Ahluwalia emphasises the constant movement of the displaced and, drawing from Edward Said, he stresses that this state is an experience of restless exile, one of never fully arriving (2010: 9). The fragility of this continual state of unbelonging is reinforced by the voice-over words, 'go back to where you came from'. Ironically, these words also constitute the name of a television programme made for SBS (Special Broadcasting Service) Australia, where a mixed group of Australians (often including high-profile personalities) literally retraces the journeys of real refugees who landed on Australian shores so that they and the viewing public get a sense of the dire situations endured by refugees.

Stereotyping

Conjuring up a recognisable image of the self posits a continual challenge for advertisers, and when the medium cannot be fixed into a relatively discrete space (like television) or controlled by a specific rendition of the spectacle, it is even more difficult. The advertiser's strongest device, rhetoric (Darley, 2000: 53; Dyer, 1982: 127), may no longer have the conceptual power it used to, given the shifting platforms of communication. Nonetheless, despite the fluidity and volatility of the Internet as a platform for communicating narratives for commerce, the mirrored self remains a benchmark. For the purposes of representation, this self is the 'sum of our symbolic interactions' (Kavoori, 2011: 138). In the process of stereotyping, these symbolic signifiers are magnified so that they are immediately recognisable and for comedy this is taken to the point of the ridiculous, thereby ostensibly condoning outright ridicule. The signifiers are markers or catchy signs of identity made obvious in appearance and mannerisms.

The South African traffic officer is stereotyped to the point of high parody along with the smooth, slick black businessman. Appearances are most important in a developing country such as post-Apartheid South Africa; therefore, affluence is signified here by personal grooming and a smart car. However, the precarious nature of affluence, and consequently the fragility of the stereotype, is caught by the policeman's teasing words to the driver, 'beautiful and handsome at the same time' followed with a reassurance for the sensitive ego of the driver: 'ah [...] beautiful and handsome *a-ll* the time'. Constant laughter heightens the hilarity and hyperbole of the stereotyped narrative in addition to the characters. The laughter at the statements and expressions is echoed by online comments with repeated and extended 'lols' (laugh out loud) and 'hahaha's'. Stereotyping that picks out specific details for caricature, as is the case in political cartoons, is a process of decentring the subject of representation for the purposes of play (Foucault, 1998: 346). While the art of the political cartoon is slightly removed from the YouTube content discussed here, their theories of mockery do apply as the use of stereotype is a sophisticated tool. Nonetheless, Navasky (2013) draws our attention to the problem that some people equate the use of stereotype to the reinforcement of stereotype.

Stereotyping is more racial in the Australian KFC advertisement where the white male, who is typified as blond, blue-eyed, young, sporty and slightly confused by his situation, is not in control and comfortable. From a whiteness studies angle, it is unusual for white racial attributes to be highlighted because one of the most significant features of whiteness is its ability to render itself unremarkable and thereby normal, as already mentioned. The reversal of white race to the minority and consequently 'other' in the KFC advertisement's scenario is obviously a device that is fully comprehended by the advertisers and used to attract attention. The stereotyping of the West Indian supporters as a homogenous group all behaving in the same way robs them of individuality and, unlike the portrayal of the single white Australian, this is a common albeit problematic racial representation. According to Clark in *The Guardian* newspaper, 'age-old [white American] racist stereotypes about black people in the once segregated south' of dancing and singing are enacted in the advertisement (Clark, 2010). One of the American TV talk show panellists engaged in a debate on definitions of racism, announcing that stereotyping is a case where 'the target' is 'made to look bad', and saying that in this advertisement it is clearly the case where 'stereotypes are pushed'. An Australian commenter noted, 'So Americans made stereotypes about black people in America and decided they apply to all black people and it's racist to use any of the black stereotypes that America invented?' Racial stereotyping makes everyone nervous because of extreme sensitivity to the issue of racism; however, the panels and some of the comments highlight the basic defensive strategy of blaming others in order to assume one's own innocence. As Appiah noted, 'almost everybody agrees that racism is morally bad [but] it is far from clear that most of us share a view about why it is wrong' (2002: 11). Faucher and Machery add:

> It is a mistake to view racism as a simple phenomenon, motivated by a single type of emotion [...] psychology suggests that people's attitudes toward a particular racial group typically result from a combination of emotions that depend upon on the problems that this group is seen as posing and on the stereotypical characteristics associated with this group. (Faucher and Machery, 2009: 59–60)

Short advertisements such as this one usually 'have the ability to mask the real structure of society, which is based on differences' (Bignell, 1997: 39). But now in a late post-structural and global consumer society, mythical meanings have become a feature. This masking complicates any semblance of firm societal structures. The well-worn adage by Karl Marx and taken up by Marshall Berman (1983), 'all that is solid melts into air, all that is holy is profaned, and man is at last compelled to face with sober senses his real conditions of life and his relations with his kind' (Marx and Engels, 1848: 7), is so much more true when even stereotypes shift rapidly. With YouTube, any attempt at masking and pretence gets caught up in the fluid interchange of commentary and also the movement of the clips and vlogs[5] across cultures that might not fully comprehend mythical overlays, thereby possibly exposing stereotypes in unexpected ways.

The 'Diversity ad' is based upon stereotype and cliché; it uses environment, dress and activity combined with the voice-over to assign nationalities to endorse the types. The long golden grass of the South African Highveld and the wide branches of the ubiquitous thorn tree (*doring boom*) are familiar images that typify the often romanticised African savannah and are therefore easily recognisable. So too is the association of Chinese tradespeople importing goods and offloading them in yards for distribution, the Indian entrepreneurial retailers doing business, the white robes of Muslim faithful, the abundant brightly coloured cloth for West African women and the neat suit signifying clichéd respectability. I also address these national and ethnic identity signifiers below.

Nationality/Identity

The South African traffic cop bears the mark of nationality obliquely through stereotyping, cultural identification and shared experience as discussed above, but in the 'Diversity ad' South African nationalism and nationality is turned into a burlesque when one by one each migrant is identified by country or language, rendering them all 'foreigners' because 'South African' applies to no-one except perhaps the original hunter-gatherers. This narrative touched a raw nerve and resulted in an array of online comments that are racially self-identified, for example: 'You stupid white people are just angry because your stupid lil plan to have our land and resources all to yourselves forever is a FAIL' and 'South Africa is for South Africans period!' This racial vitriol continued in a reply from a white Afrikaner who says 'you' (meaning black South Africans) should be thankful that the white settlers did not kill you all off as was the case with the Americans. Identifying as South African appears to be most important to the commenters and yet the seemingly misplaced humour calls upon them all to consider who they really are, thereby unsettling a deeply seated need to belong. But nationalism itself can be regarded as a misplaced phenomenon because the nation-state is a construct so frequently based upon conflict. Ahluwalia asserts that nationalisms are fictions premised upon 'an invented identity' (2006: 110); however, he also notes that identity often 'remains tied to the nation' (2001: 70). It is clear that nationalism and identity remain paradoxical and can be, as Amartya Sen says, a 'boon or curse' (2008: 44). Racial identity is blatantly marked out in the video and, as stated above, each individual is characterised by dress, activity and national or linguistic label. The runners are no doubt parodied as Ethiopians because of Ethiopia's Olympic successes in athletics. Some are not so simple to identify visually because the local black South Africans who migrated south of the Sahara prior to European settlement are not identified by tribal dress, neither do they need to be in the migrant queue. The narrator rapidly rattles off the names of these tribes so that it is difficult to hear if he is indeed including all the Southern African tribal groups.

The Australian KFC advertisement also exaggerates national and racial identity by dressing the Australian cricket fan in national colours, positioning him as a solitary mascot for his country while ensuring that the West Indian supporters also wear their county's colours somewhere on their already colourful apparel. Wagg (2007: 11) cites *The Spectator*: 'In football, by and large, it's the fans that are racist but in cricket it's the establishment. It's institutionalized racism. The smell of imperialism is in your nostrils all the time'. This indictment stretches beyond the advertisers, the brand and the product to a national identity that has its roots in empire, particularly because Australia is still a part of the British Commonwealth of Nations. The particular Australian identity is further amplified by the Australian accent and the vernacular/slang words 'too easy' so often used by Australians to smooth over situations or accede that everything is in order. The utterance of these two words, which was taken up repeatedly by panellists, is what Foucault would call the 'enunciative statement'. It exists within a discursive field and contains a *'repeatable materiality'* (emphasis in the original) but it can only be attributed with authentic meaning in its 'original form' (Foucault, 2010: 102). 'Original form' (in Foucault's lectures) belongs to a more stable platform than Internet and YouTube advertising, but in a Baudrillardian (1984) sense the repeated form becomes a simulacrum that attains a renewed materiality in every new context. The Australian–American national differences and loyalties are also acutely apparent in the online comments and the panel discussions referred to earlier. There are three primary nationalities involved in this YouTube phenomenon. If it had been left as a simple advertisement, then it would only be Australia and the West Indies but, despite the advertisement being taken off the air for TV, the clip became viral on the Internet and was taken up by Americans who identify with KFC and who took umbrage at the racialisation of the West Indian supporters, and the national reach became broader. This type of dispersal has been made possible by the Internet and more specifically the 'deep' and 'parallel texts' (Kavoori, 2011: 8) that characterise YouTube through processes of 'referentiality' (Kavoori, 2011: 6). Identities are then dropped into this deep and parallel network of capillaried power relations (Foucault, 2004: 27) through text, image and utterance, one bouncing off the other and linking to the next. Kavoori notes that we could theoretically spend a lifetime following the links on the Internet, but in this amorphous space identities emerge as distorted, exaggerated, mutilated and removed from any living reality (2011: 8).

Truth/History

Foucault (2013) regards reality and truth as twin but contested concepts in philosophy and history. In Foucault's lectures on the 'will to know', he points out that the entire Platonic platform of philosophy never really presented options for the contest between the real and the true. It is only with Aristotle, who exposed the game of sophistry as false reasoning, that we begin to see how advertising can utilise the classical methods of the Sophists. Therefore, to extend what I have already mentioned above under 'Paradox and Irony', sophistry is the art of disguise, 'the semblance of reasoning' (Foucault, 2013: 51). The symbolic subject, be it in the symbol of law enforcement, authority, affluence, supplanted identity or nation, is the material substance for this game of truth as evidenced in design (Connellan, 2012). In the South African traffic cop advertisement, Nando's is quite clear at the outset that they are twisting truths, but, despite this acknowledgement, it is evident that there are several parallel truths enacted in the course of the video. The clever use of inversion and humour ensures that the audience is never entirely sure of who is in the right. The traffic officer might not be legitimate, the licence may be a fake, the car might be stolen, the driver might not be what he appears to be and so on – these are some of the everyday dramas that feed popular culture and urban mythologies. In case study 2, history and truth linger in the background; the uncomfortable histories of slavery and its songs of resistance in America are the dark side of the racist outrage about this video where whiteness is 'innocently' inverted. In case study 3, the varying and contested histories of migration, and African as well as European settlement, are presented as pointless but taken up with ire by commenters. One commenter questioned why 'the truth [...] is always racist when white people tell it' and emphasised that, despite being of 'non-European descent [...] the truth is the truth no matter who tells it'. References to the 'made up' histories are rendered laughable with the typical 'LOL' inserted to make the point. Commentaries such as these on YouTube are sometimes called 'phatic communication' (Hartley, 2009: 136) because they check 'the connection between speakers' but do not create 'new knowledge' (Hartley, 2009: 135). In this way, comments spin threads that can be taken up without the need for factual verification and the conversations (as in this case of truth/history) become highly personalised.

Price/Quality

It is not possible to say whether online comments about value for money, which interrupt the at-times angry commentary regarding racism, are planted by the companies or not. For example: 'I find this video offensive because I'm not haveing some of that delicious chicken!' comes in the heat of furious comments about the Australian KFC advertisement and might also be there to provide light relief. There are also comments about price and currency comparisons for the Nando's South Africa meals, which point out that the South African price is very cheap. Price and more specifically money in this instance are introduced into the commentary as one aspect of exchange, because people in their various predicaments or diversities are also presented by the advertisers as contributing to the whole exchange experience. In this way, the commercial transaction becomes a social one and price is not given centre stage in the drama but is deflected, with money becoming part of the 'material memory [and] deferred exchange' (Foucault, 1994: 181). The advertisements themselves ensure that the narrative culminates in an answer to all the problems, that is the inevitable Nando's or KFC plate of food presented with all the appropriate highlights and colour to evoke the texture, aroma and taste of the food. So here, in a Barthesian sense, the myth materialises and delivers: 'The meaning is always there to *present* the form; [but] the form is always there to *outdistance* the meaning' (Barthes, 1973: 133). In other words, it is the narrative and message (getting out of a traffic fine, having fun at a sports game, accepting diversity) that carry the form and figures in the advertisements, but it is the form and figures (characters and food) that are intended to last for the target audience. This is the intention of advertisers but the case studies presented in this chapter show (through the comments and feedback) that in a post-Barthesian world (YouTube and the Internet) the meaning and the message may in fact outdistance everything. For example, the Australian panel emphasised that whether advertisements were good or bad 'negative PR travels a lot faster than positive PR so normally when you get angry at an ad you tell ten friends and you say "I really didn't like it", now you tell 10 million people in 3 seconds'. This is a factor that must affect the brands: negative reactions keep them in the public eye even if it is for the 'wrong' reasons.

In case study 1, the meal is integrated as a crucial part of the narrative: it is the object/form of the bargain. When the story unwinds, it is not just to a plate of food but to the convivial interior of a Nando's restaurant, a place of conversation and gaiety. In case study 2, the KFC carton of chips and chicken is also the instrument of bargaining, the harbinger of peace. However, case study 3 uses the narrative build-up to disguise suspense and present new dishes that accommodate diverse tastes for the different migrants that make up South Africa. Nando's South Africa also make it clear in their online statement that theirs is a concerted campaign to combat xenophobia not only by extending their menu but specifically through their collaborative pop-up soup kitchens at grassroots sites. 'Pop-ups' are a growing feature of both informal and formal economies, providing avenues for individuals to set up stalls and sell merchandise or services. The 'dystopian realities' of an uneven world are brought into focus not only by Nando's grass-roots initiative but also and especially by the contrast with 'the utopian possibilities' shown on YouTube (Jenkins, 2009: 124). The images of satisfied customers happily eating their Nando's or KFC are far removed from the hunger and struggle of the really poor.

Conclusions

In this chapter, I have brought a Foucauldian and critical race reading to a sample of fast-food advertisements on YouTube. The three advertisements earned their period of fame on the Internet through emotional responses to race and identity. The dramas of everyday life and one of the most basic human needs (food) are served up as platters of vibrant but contesting identities. This contest of identities among all of the characters, be they stereotyped in the ads, magnified on television or articulated via the commentary, is one of the power to be who 'we' think we are and what we think is our sovereign right. Additionally, in a changeable world of unrest, the boundaries of identity become a highly sensitive zone of conflict. As Butler notes, 'what was once thought of as a border, that which delimits and bounds, is a highly populated site, if not the very definition of the nation, confounding identity in what may well become a very auspicious direction' (2006: 49). Advertisers are keenly aware of sensitised boundaries and in order to reach their audiences, they have to touch a nerve, which in these advertisements is subjectivity and race.

Foucault (2010) writes that in the processes of analysis, we (researchers/students) might naturally credit the discourse we analyse with coherence and that in doing so we are constantly on the lookout for contradictions, disruptions and disturbances. We then look for patterns in the contradictions but, he cautions, we should 'not give too much weight to small differences' (Foucault, 2010: 149) but see them against a larger expanse of events. In the advertisements discussed in this chapter, the paradoxes of type, nationality, truth and history operate at macro- and micro-levels, from outside of ourselves (or the characters we might recognise) and from within. The paradoxes need to be spoken of 'rather to overcome the contradictions, and to find the point from which they will be able to be mastered' (Foucault, 2010: 149) but this is not to say that all distinctions of race, agency and subjectivity should be smoothed over. For Foucault, there is both the rational path of discovering a 'systematicity' and the path that is more 'affective' and 'imaginary' (Foucault, 2010: 150).

We have seen how the many layers of the Internet provide a medium for discovery at both the rational and affective levels of sensitivity. National imaginaries of belonging are vowed and disavowed in a continuum of exchanges that have no determined end. The infinity of the Internet, which is the fluid space that YouTube operates in, determines its own peaks and troughs in its own time. There is no one mastermind behind it and as such it presents the perfect example of what Foucault describes as the discursive field. This is cleverly described by Kavoori, in his guide to reading YouTube critically, as a field that is infinitely referential through a process of participatory 'chaining', an 'interchangeable quality and structural mutability', which is YouTube's distinguishing feature (Kavoori, 2011: 7). In this way, YouTube moves beyond early postmodernist preoccupations with surface play to incorporate levels of depth that are also partially achieved through narrative.

The common narratives of being pulled over on a highway by a police officer, being frustrated at a sports match or witnessing refugees and migrants entering a country all utilise the devices of stereotype and spectacle to create a hyper-reality. Added to this is the pervasive technique of humour that, with the assistance of irony, highlights and attempts to dilute difference. In this theatre of layered surfaces that is the Internet, we can remind ourselves of Foucault's thoughts on theatres of truth where he says, 'Irony rises and subverts' while 'humour falls and perverts' (1998: 346). The sum of these dramatic techniques makes the advertisements double as entertainment. Darley (2000) notes that the early (twentieth-century) cinematic spectacle is returning in the digital contemporary context. And in YouTube, the spectacle combines with a narrative rendition of 'the short', which Kavoori (2011) claims is one of the YouTube 'genres'. 'The Short as a genre on YouTube is a complex mix of narrative intentions and contradictions' (2011: 119), which is evidenced in the case studies included for analysis in this chapter. Therefore for business and commerce globally, YouTube provides a creative platform for engaging with markets but one that ultimately keeps the balance of power between 'consumer' and 'producer' constantly in motion.

References

Ahluwalia, P., 2001. When does a settler become a native? Citizenship and identity in a settler society. *Pretexts: Literary and Cultural Studies*, 10:1, pp.63–73.

Ahluwalia, P., 2006. Inventing home: (re)membering the nation. *Sikh Formations*, 2:2, pp.103–114.

Ahluwalia, P., 2010. *Out of Africa: post-structuralism's colonial roots*. London and New York: Routledge.

Appiah, K. A., 2002. Racism: history of hatred. *New York Times*, [online] 4 August. Available at: http://www.nytimes.com/2002/08/04/books/review/04APPIAT.html. Accessed 27 March 2015.

Barthes, R., 1973. *Mythologies*. Translated from French by J. Cape, 1972. London: Paladin.

Baudrillard, J., 1984. The precession of simulacra. In: B. Wallis, ed. 1984. *Art after modernism: rethinking representation*. New York: New Museum of Contemporary Art. pp.253–281.

Berman, M., 1983. *All that is solid melts into air: the experience of modernity*. London: Verso.

Bignell, J., 1997. *Media semiotics: an introduction*. Manchester and New York: Manchester University Press.

Black River FC Advertising Agency, 2008. *Nando's – traffic cop – South African TV ad*, 1.06 minutes. [video online] Available at: http://www.bestadsontv.com/ad/11266/Nandos-Only-R2195-Meal-Traffic-Cop. Accessed 9 September 2013.

Black River FC Advertising Agency, 2012. *Nando's – South Africa – Diversity Ad*, 53 seconds. [video online] Available at: http://www.youtube.com/watch?v=cBIDkW2_FnQ. Accessed 9 September 2013.

Butler, J., 2006. *Precarious life: the powers of mourning and violence*. London and New York: Verso.

Casimir, J., and Denton, A., 2010. *The Gruen Transfer*, Series 3 ABC TV. [video online] Available at: http://www.abc.net.au/tv/gruentransfer/ and https://www.youtube.com/watch?v=96Btq4pBouo. Accessed 27 September 2013.

Clark, A., 2010. KFC accused of racism over Australian advertisement. *The Guardian*, [online] 7 January. Available at: theguardian.com. Accessed 9 September 2013.

Connellan, K., 2012. Parrēsia: between principles and practices in design. *Design Principles and Practices Annual: An International Journal: Annual Review*, 6:1, pp.11–22.

Darley, A., 2000. *Visual digital culture: surface play and spectacle in new media genres*. London: Routledge.

Dyer, G., 1982. *Advertising as communication*. London: Methuen.

Dyer, R., 1997. *White*. London and New York: Routledge.

Faucher, L. and Machery, E., 2009. Racism: against Jorge Garcia's moral and psychological monism. *Philosophy of the Social Sciences*, 39:1, pp.41–62.

Foucault, M., 1982. Afterword: subject and power. In: H. Dreyfus and P. Rabinow, eds. 1982 *Michel Foucault: beyond structuralism and hermeneutics*. New York: Harvester Wheatsheaf. pp.208–226.

Foucault, M., 1994. *The order of things: an archaeology of the human sciences*. Translated from French by A. Sheridan, 1970. New York: Vintage.

Foucault, M., 1998. *Aesthetics, method and epistemology: essential works of Michel Foucault 1954 – 1984*. Translated from French by R. Hurley. London and New York: Penguin.

Foucault, M., 2004. *Society must be defended: lectures at the Collège de France 1975–1976*. Translated from French by D. Macey, 2003. London: Penguin.

Foucault, M., 2007. *Security, territory, population: lectures at the Collège de France 1977–1978*. Translated from French by G. Burchell, 2002. New York: Palgrave Macmillan.

Foucault, M., 2010. *The archaeology of knowledge: and the discourse of language*. Translated from French by A. M. Sheridan Smith, 1972. New York: Vintage.

Foucault, M., 2013. *Lectures on the will to know: lectures at the Collège de France 1970–1971 and oedipal knowledge*. Translated from French by G. Burchell, 2013. New York: Palgrave Macmillan.

Hartley, J., 2009. Uses of YouTube: digital literacy and the growth of knowledge. In: J. Burgess and J. Green, eds. *YouTube: online video and participatory culture*. Cambridge: Polity. pp.126–143.

Jarrett, K., 2008. Beyond broadcast yourself: the future of youtube. *Media International Australia, Incorporating Culture & Policy*, 126: February, pp.132–144.

Jenkins, H., 2009. What happened before YouTube. In: J. Burgess and J. Green, eds. *YouTube: online video and participatory culture*, Cambridge: Polity. pp.109–125.

Kavoori, A., 2011. *Reading YouTube: the critical viewers guide*. New York: Peter Lang.

KFC, 2010. *KFC's cricket survival guide*. [TV ad.] subsequently titled: *The racist KFC ad in Australia*. [video online]. Available at: http://www.youtube.com/watch?v=FftZt-Dw_hQ. Accessed 9 September 2013.

Marx, K. and Engels, F., 1848. *The Communist Manifesto*. Translated from German by S. Moore, 1888. Reprint 2013. London: Swenson & Kemp.

Maslow, A. H., 1943. A theory of human motivation. *Psychological Review*, 50:4, pp.370–396.

Navasky, V. S., 2013. *The art of controversy: political cartoons and their enduring power*. Toronto: Knopf.

Pease, B., 2004. Decentring white men: critical reflections on masculinity and white studies. In: A. Moreton-Robinson, ed. 2004. *Whitening race: essays in social and cultural criticism*. Canberra: Aboriginal Studies Press. pp.119–130.

Sen, A., 2008. Is nationalism a boon or a curse? *Economic and Political Weekly*, 43:7, p.44.

Uygur, C. and Kasparian, A., 2010. *The Young Turks*, [YouTube] 4 January. Available at: http://www.youtube.com/watch?v=ZaIhf41ctkM. Accessed 27 September 2013.

Wagg, S., 2007. "To be an Englishman": nation, ethnicity and English cricket in the global age. *Sport in Society*, 10:1, pp.11–32.

Notes

1. Copyright permission to insert stills was requested but received no response. The advertisement has since been archived and can be accessed through registration at http://www.bestadsontv.com/ad/11266/Nandos-Only-R2195-Meal-Traffic-Cop.
2. I have not noted spelling or typographical errors with the customary 'sic' in parenthesis so as to preserve the integrity of the original and specifically because it is commonplace for online commentary to use all sorts of shorthand and abbreviations and not to pay attention to grammar and spelling. As is the case with text messaging, 'errors' have become a distinct stylistic feature of some informal Internet communication.
3. Copyright was requested and denied by KFC Australia.

4. Copyright to reproduce stills was requested but no response was received.
5. A vlog is a video blog.

Chapter 4

The Use of Gold Rush Nostalgia on Wine Labels: Brief History of New Zealand's Central Otago Wine Region

Lloyd Carpenter

Abstract

Central Otago's landscape was transformed by miners in the 1860s, seeking riches from the streams, hills and riverbeds, while some early pioneers experimented with planting vineyards. When the gold ran out, wine was forgotten and farming, stonefruit and tourism took over, but in the early 1980s a new transformation began as vintners realised that classic 'terroir' conditions of Burgundy, Champagne and Bavaria were emulated in the dusty Otago countryside. Rabbit-blighted, barren sheep farms were planted in verdant vineyards, and Central Otago wines became famed for their quality, but by the mid-2000s, some winemakers began to look backwards to set themselves apart in their marketing endeavours, rediscovering their golden past. Beginning with a summary of how and why the region developed its wine story, this chapter examines the process whereby Central Otago vineyards are exploiting nostalgia for the province's golden heritage to market their wine and discusses their efforts and motivations for employing elements of popular culture to create a romantic, myth-laden past on which to create brand identity and market segmentation.

Keywords

nostalgia, heritage, gold, landscape, marketing, wine, Otago, wine labels

Introduction – The Central Otago Gold Rush

New Zealand's history changed in 1862 when Horatio Hartley and Christopher Reilly thumped 87 pounds of gold onto the Dunedin gold-buyer's counter-top, creating banner headlines around the world and sparking the Central Otago gold rush. Before long, the new gold finds celebrated at Hartley's Beach, Nokomai Valley, Shotover Gorge, Arrow River, Conroy's Gully, Skipper's Canyon and Frenchman's Point were the subject of earnest discussion at dining tables, shop counters and public bars throughout Australasia.

Miners flooded into Otago from Australia and around the world, each dreaming of emulating the achievements of the first prospectors. Central Otago proved very rich in places, and while the 87-pound haul made the area famous, subsequent reports revealed that this was not the only such find, nor was it the biggest: 'the finds obtained by many of the [Dunstan] miners would even astonish those who have seen that "jewellers shops" of Ballarat, or the results of a days washing from claims in the far famed Eaglehawk, Bendigo' (Otago Daily Times, 1862: 5). One prospector testing the gravels of the Kawarau River observed that 'the farther they got on to the bed of the river the gold became heavier and more plentiful' and exclaimed 'that he'd be blow'd if there wasn't tons of gold in the bed of the river' (Otago Witness, 1862: 8).

New towns appeared, with wood-framed, canvas-sided hotels, and stores hastily opened for business, but as a reporter commented, 'it is not to be expected that the viands are of the most recherché description' (Otago Daily Times, 1863: 9). Some miners, defeated by the capricious nature of gold deposition or horrified at bad goldfields meals, grew vegetables, planted fruit trees and opened restaurants in the nascent gold towns. A couple of miners with experience in Victoria had even bolder plans.

French Vignerons at the Dunstan

Loire Valley-born James (born Jacques) Bladier arrived in Victoria in the mid-1850s and planted a vineyard at Campaspe (South Australian Register, 1859: 2). Bladier, a pioneer of the Bendigo wine industry (De Castella, 1886: 102), was bankrupted when a sludge channel embankment collapsed and inundated his garden. After sequestration of his estate in 1863, he emigrated to the Dunstan to begin afresh (Bladier, 1860; Argus, 1861, 1863). He bought a section near the mouth of the Waikerikeri Valley, which he declared to Dunstan Goldfields Warden Vincent Pyke, was 'less liable to frost than either the South of France or the district of Bendigo in Australia, and highly favourable to the culture of some species of the vine' (Pyke, 1864), and obtained a small subsidy from the Otago Provincial Government to import 600 grapevine cuttings from Victoria to plant the first vineyard at the Dunstan (Otago Daily Times, 1864a). With his brother Theodore, he planted fruit trees, vegetables and tobacco, which, with his grapes, flourished in the local climate (Otago Daily Times, 1865).

Another Frenchman, Jean Desiré Feraud, bought the plot beside Bladier and named it 'Monte Christo'. After an apprenticeship in the Grasse perfume industry, Feraud who came from a vigneron family in Vence and (Advertiser, 1893) shifted to Ballarat in the early 1850s where he opened the Lafayette Bakery on Main Street (Trumpeter, 1855). Like many in Ballarat, Feraud jumped at the fresh opportunities offered in Central Otago, where he developed a large sluicing claim at Manuherikia. This claim at Frenchman's Point 'turn[ed] out almost fabulous quantities of gold', yielding 20–24 ounces per day throughout 1864 (Otago Daily Times, 1864b: 5, 1864c).

Bladier did not see his vines produce a crop, because in June 1865 he sold his property to Feraud and shifted to Lake Mahinapua, near Hokitika (Daily Southern Cross, 1867). He continued gardening, selling produce from his store in Revell Street, which unsurprisingly included the first grapes grown in Westland (West Coast Times, 1867). In

1869, he purchased and ran Hokitika's famous Café de Paris (West Coast Times, 1869) until the early 1880s, when he returned to Bendigo to purchase a partnership in a vineyard and was elected chairman of the Winegrowers Association of Victoria (Argus, 1886).

Feraud was elected the first mayor of Clyde in 1866 (Otago Daily Times, 1866) and submitted his red wines to the Paris exhibition of 1867 where he was awarded a first award (Otago Daily Times, 1890). He sold his claim in 1871 to turn his attention to his farm, declaring that he was 'erecting a large building [...] and intends therein to commence the manufacture of colonial wine, French liqueurs, and cordials' (Tuapeka Times, 1871: 4). A year later, the *Tuapeka Times* editor declared Feraud's 'ducal grape wine, cherry brandy, orange bitters, and orange wine' to be 'excellent in every respect' (Tuapeka Times, 1872: 6), while the *Dunedin Evening Star* said his light Madeira is a 'very excellent wine, [that seemed] likely to become a favourite beverage with everyone who enjoys a pure light wine' (Dunedin Evening Star, 1872: 2).

A visitor from Dunedin wrote 'the Monte Christo Garden presents a charming and agreeable feature with its bright green patches of high cultivation, amidst almost a desert of sand, rocks, and gravel, which compose the Dunstan Flat' (Otago Daily Times, 1874: 5). Despite a brief brush with insolvency in 1873, by 1876 Feraud was bottling 2000 gallons of wine and 400 gallons of cider, tinning a large quantity of jams and jellies and selling three tons of peaches each season (Tuapeka Times, 1876). In the early 1880s, he was rewarded with prizes for his liqueurs, fruit syrups and wines at International Exhibitions in Australia (Sydney Morning Herald, 1880; Argus, 1881).

Even as he was receiving these awards, Feraud's work was undone by gold in the Waikerikeri Valley. The leased part of his farm was needed for a sludge channel, and in 1879 petitions to appropriate his land under the aegis of the Gold Fields Act were filed in Wellington (Baylea et al., 1879). In 1881, Feraud bowed to the inevitable, auctioned his stock and received £300 from the Government Gold Fields Committee for the extinguishing of the lease (Feraud, 1882). He shifted to Dunedin, where he manufactured fruit liqueurs, cordials and aerated waters, supplying the hotel and restaurant industry there. In 1891, he sold his business and shifted to Adelaide, where, as 'John D. Feraud', he worked as a 'wine manufacturer and distiller liquoriste' and advised local vintners (Advertiser, 1892: 10). In 1893, he worked with local gardeners to distil oils and perfumes from their crops in the hope of developing an export industry (Advertiser, 1893).

In 1894, New Zealand Government Pomologist J. C. Blackmore reported on the horticultural potential of Central Otago, recommending what Bladier and Feraud had already found: the cultivation of grapes should proceed (Otago Witness, 1894). This was confirmed by Romeo Bragato, head of the viticultural section of the Victorian Department of Agriculture. Bragato asserted Conroy's Gully to be 'the spot where the grape could be produced to greater perfection than anywhere else in the colony' (Otago Witness, 1895a: 4) and told the Otago Chamber of Commerce that 'there was no country on the face of the earth which produced better Burgundy grapes than were produced in Central Otago' (Otago Witness, 1895b: 4).

Unfortunately for Bragato's dream, the potential for a viticulture industry in Central Otago was subsumed by a combination of an outbreak of phylloxera in vines, high returns for wool, hydraulic elevation mining on river terraces and the swallowing of the prime riverside land by dredges. When the gold ran out, fruit-growing, sheep farming and horticulture replaced mining and the idea of developing a wine region to rival California and Victoria was forgotten. Throughout the twentieth century, Central Otago became synonymous with stonefruit production, to the point that when Cromwell's business area was relocated when the Clyde dam was built in 1990, the choice for a defining icon near the new town entrance was a giant fruit sculpture. The once-lauded suitability for vine cultivation lay buried in the pages of Bragato's notebooks and in old newspaper reports of his, which were about Feraud and Bladier's efforts, until dusted off by the now-iconic 'Pinot Pioneers' of Central Otago (Oram, 2004).

Hesitant steps, both with and without government support, led to the first rebirth of Central Otago winemaking in the late 1960s and into the 1970s, but it was not until the 1980s that the modern era began as new vine-growing pioneers appeared. Stories of how the Mills family developed the Rippon vineyard at Wanaka, Ann Pinckney planted the first Pinot Noir vines at Queenstown, Alan Brady and the Hay brothers developed rabbit-ravaged properties at Gibbston Valley and Bill and Gill Grant's William Hill and Verdun Burgess' Black Ridge transformed the landscape near Alexandra have passed into New Zealand winemaking legend (Oram, 2004: 6–7, 77–82, 89–101; Cull, 2001: 39, 81; Saker, 2010: 63–64, 229, 242, 279; Brady, 2010: 58, 73–81). Their battle with climate, pests, naysayers and governmental bureaucracy is still celebrated, and defines the modern Central Otago vintners as 'winemakers on the edge' (Cull, 2001: 12).

The late 1990s saw another surge, as the success of the pioneers attracted corporate finance and expertise, bringing a level of professionalism to what had been a learn-as-you-go, bottom-up industry development (Caple, 2011: 89–96, 139–144, 167–178, 187–197; Oram, 2004: 26–42; Saker, 2010: 229). This allowed for vineyard developments at Bendigo, Lowburn, Bannockburn and across the Alexandra region, launching large enterprises such as Mt. Difficulty, Quartz Reef and Peregrine (Saker, 2010: 229, 268–271; Brady, 2010: 197, Oram, 2004: 128–143) along with a proliferation of new boutique vineyard operations such as Jeff Price's 3 Miners and Grant Taylor's Valli. Acres of Riesling, Pinot Noir and other varietals were planted, transforming a parched, marginally profitable, merino-farming landscape into swathes of verdant green. Gates that used to merely state a run number for rural mail deliveries or the names of the sheep farmers resident there now bore newly painted signs advertising a winery and tasting room. Some vintners earned a reputation among the cognoscenti of the wine world as makers of an exceptional product, and Central Otago itself emerged as a byword for excellence in wine (Harmon, 2005: 3).

Wine writers began echoing the words of Feraud's customers and confirming the most enthusiastic of Bragato's opinions; Oxford Companion to Wine editor Jancis Robinson said, 'After several years of being curmudgeonly about New Zealand Pinot Noir I am now thrilled by the number of exciting Pinots that are emerging from these two islands, particularly from this, the most southerly wine region in the world in the south of the South Island' (Robinson, 2003), while London-based *Times* wine writer Jane Macquitty wrote 'at last Burgundy has a serious New World rival' (Macquitty, 2003). In 2007, Bald Hills Wines won the ultimate International Wine Challenge '2007 Champion Red' for its 2005 Pinot Noir, effectively naming it the best red wine in the world (Manins, 2007), and when Wild Earth Wines of Bannockburn repeated the feat in 2008, the rest of the world, if it had not already done so, took notice (Otago Daily Times, 2008).

As Caple (2011) found in her Central Otago wine-marketing doctorate, their achievement is as improbable as it is remarkable:

> [*the*] Central Otago Wine Region, [is] a New World wine region that has seen much global success and has established a regional brand. [...] The success of the region is an enigma because there is a deficiency in the region of experienced wine industry managers, vintners, and viticulturalists. Somehow the boutique producers have collectively devised a strategy for regional branding and wine quality management without an abundance of experience in the wine industry.
>
> (2011: 97)

Central Otago Wine

The bottles from more than 50 vineyards, wineries and contract producers bear the label 'Central Otago Wine', which has become code for premium quality. As Caple (2011) found,

> [...] the wineries in the Central Otago wine region have succeeded in competing and yet collaborating to achieve a sense of a unique regional place, one which all the wineries seemingly share. The image of place and its connection to quality wine production has given the region global recognition.
>
> (2011: 78)

'Central Otago Wine' has been developed as a regional brand with what Pritchard and Morgan identified as the separate aims of the place as a brand in and of itself, and as a destination brand, developed with tourism in mind (1998: 215–229).

The Internet websites of Central Otago wine companies reveal a passion for their environment, heritage and wines. Each pours, according to their website prose, their heart and soul into making wines fit for today's discerning palate. The swathe of national and international awards won over the past 25 years would suggest that their enthusiasm is not mere bragging.

However, after the nurturing of vines is complete, the battle with the harsh, fickle climate is won, the crop is harvested and the transformative magic of the oenologist is wrought on the result, the wine is bottled and shipped to retailers, where the winery has one chance to communicate all they have done to the potential consumer: the wine label (Kotler and Armstrong, 1996: 293; Cutler, 2006: 2).

The Wine Label

The wine world has come a long way in a short period of time, and it is within recent memory that all a label offered was the provenance, vintage, producer, grape variety and a few other technical details (Brostrom and Brostrom, 2009: 145; Barber, Ismail and Taylor, 2007: 76). The winemaker's label persuades the consumer to make the first purchase; the winemaker's product persuades them to make a second (Barber, Almanza and Donovan, 2006: 219), as Larson says in her *Generation Wine* study,

> Even if a winery has developed an exquisite and flavorful wine, the success of the brand still lies in the hands of the consumer. If a wine label does not spark curiosity, the quality of the wine will not matter because it will not get picked up off the shelf.
> (2012: 14)

With a label affixed to the front and the back of the bottle, a Central Otago winery must impart information that communicates all their passion, information, point of difference and why the consumer should buy what is a highly discretionary purchase.

But the gold medal achievements from vineyards across Australasia have turned past expectations on their head, and Central Otago wines have emerged with a reputation for a premium product commanding price points above their competition (Baker, 2011). The proliferation of local brands means that the battle for the consumer dollar has forced innovation and creativity in marketing, especially on the label (Sherman and Tuten, 2011: 221, 231; Brostrom and Brostrom, 2009: 145), and the complexity of this market means that the label must, according to Bertrand,

> [...] not only capture the unique personality of the winery, the wine and the brand but also catch the attention of shoppers in environments ranging from wine boutiques to club stores. The label must present well on the dinner table, as well, whether at home or in a restaurant.
> (2006: n.p.)

Labels have evolved from a means of merely communicating basic information, to where '[...] wine is fashion, and beverage aisles are our runway [...] [to] reach a point where marketing and merchandising play as important a role as making the product itself' (Sugarman, 2009: n.p.).

Enter any specialist wine retailer or the wine aisle of a supermarket and '[...] your eyes [are] assaulted by' the visual cacophony of labels and packages, each seemingly more colourful than its neighbour (Franson, 2006: n.p.) as wineries seek to differentiate their products to stand out in the marketplace (Lockshin, 1997: 386–387). To the dismay of Central Otago's avowedly artisan winemakers, producing an excellent product is insufficient; marketing and product design are critical elements of the market, all the more critical because most wine purchasing decisions are made in-store (Thomas, 2000: 12; Banks et al., 2007: 1, 22).

Thomas (2000: 54) noted a range of motivations impelling wine buying, from indulging oneself to celebrations and social gatherings, to dining out or buying a gift and even curiosity. Bruwer, Li and Reid highlight a stratified market for wine according to consumer experience and motivations (2002: 234–237), making communication via the label critical (Charters, Lockshin and Unwin, 1999: 193–194). Given that quality-related attributes can only be evaluated by consumption, the consumer is forced to rely upon extrinsic cues such as price, packaging and brand (Barber, Dodd and Ghiselli, 2008: 124–127, 136; Barber, Almanza and Donovan, 2006: 219). Kidd implies that the packaging of the wine as well as the wine itself has a life beyond the purchase (1993: 201), adding a social importance to purchase choices and contributing to a feeling of unease for inexpert wine shoppers (Olson et al., 2003: 40–52; Johnson and Bruwer, 2007: 278). No one wants to hear that their choice of wine purchase committed a social faux pas, and this intimidates some consumers into doubting their ability to choose. Perusing the wine label then becomes part of a risk reduction strategy (Johnson and Bruwer, 2003; Sutanonpaiboon and Atkin, 2012: 2; Barber, Ismail and Taylor, 2007: 74, 76–77, 83), or leads some to the conservative fall-back choice of repeating the purchase of a familiar wine (Bruwer and Wood, 2005: 193–211). Olsen, Thompson and Clarke (2003: 40–52) found that consumers read labels, rather than seeking guidance from other information sources, while Barber and Almanza (2006: 83–98) note that a direct relationship exists between the perception of the wine label design and the decision to purchase. This means the winemaker can intervene in the consumer choice process by designing extrinsic product attributes in the packaging (Orth, 2002: 80–82; Sutanonpaiboon and Atkin, 2012: 5) and can respond to consumers' product perception by making label changes without changing the wine (Lockshin and Rhodus, 1993: 13–25). This then makes the information conveyed by the Central Otago wine producer's label critical. For some, a point of difference had to be found that took this further.

A Point of Difference

After declaring their wine to be a 'Central Otago Wine', winemakers, especially those in newly emergent wineries, sought an additional semiotic to make them stand out from the crowd on their label. For a significant number, this difference lay in Otago's golden past. When Caple (2011) interviewed winery owners, winemakers and people involved in the marketing of Central Otago wine, she found that there was a prevalent identification with

[...] the risk-taking attitude of the pioneers in the gold-digging era with their pioneering experiences in the wine industry [...]. They empathise with the risks the gold-miners took in their efforts, as they had their own struggle with growing grapes and refer to themselves as wine pioneers.

(2011: 210)

Some went further, taking names, images, colours, symbols and identities iconic to the Central Otago gold rush and putting them on their labels. For these wineries, the 'backstory' of their wine is intrinsically – and explicitly – linked to the activities, personalities and dreams of the gold miners of the gold rush. Sarah Eliott of Terra Sancta Wines at Bannockburn uses their property's lineage in the gold rush to contextualise their product and 'do more than just say "Here's some wine, please try it"; offering the culture of our place – and its proximity to the gold workings – to add to the experience in the tasting room' (Eliott, 2012), while Jeff Price of 3 Miners is unequivocal: '[...] the gold rush was always our starting point; our company is called "Miners' Lane" after the bridle path which crossed our property, and our name came from the three mining claims that were worked on the boundaries of our property' (Price, 2012). Bannock Brae offers a 'Goldfields Dry Riesling' and a 'Goldfields Pinot Noir', although they do not provide a narrative to go with the name.

The websites of several other wineries directly reference the gold rush, like Lowburn Ferry highlighting that their property was owned by 'George Partridge in 1867 – a goldminer who had come from Australia to work in the goldfields at Quartz Reef Point – having travelled inland by the Dunstan Trail over the mountains from Dunedin on foot, carrying his swag' (Lowburn Ferry, 2012: n.p.) and Packspur Vineyard (2012), who '[...] takes its name from the track that was used to pack supplies over the Pisa range, from the Lowburn Valley to the goldfields of the dry Cardrona' (n.p). Quartz Reef notes their link with the historic gold town of Bendigo while emphasising their unique terroir to produce wines that 'exhibit a symphony of flavours [...] [that] capture attention and entertain so that you forget everything else' (Quartz Reef Wines, 2011: n.p.); Aurora declares that their land was '[...] originally named South Chinaman's Creek in recognition of the Chinese migrant workers who camped here when they worked on the Bendigo gold fields' and observe that 'the unusual shape of our wine labels was inspired by the old gold certificates from this era' (Aurora Vineyard Limited, 2012: n.p.), while Desert Heart's name '[...] was chosen to pay tribute to the land, because Pinot Noir, more than any other grape reflects where it is grown, and to the historical reference to the name of Bannockburn, 'Heart of the Desert', from the gold rush era' (Desert Heart, 2012: n.p.).

Some wineries provide a comprehensive mining history at their property, such as Kawarau Estate near Cromwell and Davishon Wines from Alexandra. Davishon operate as Alexandra Wines and, given that their vineyard borders the original Monte Christo Estate on the Dunstan Flat, claim the inheritance of Jean Desiré Feraud, providing a comprehensive biography of his work there. They are not the only ones to highlight Feraud's legacy; many use a potted history of his work and that of Bragato to identify with the 'winemaker on the edge' ideal, but Davishon are the only winemakers to use Feraud's name on one of their wines (Davishon Vineyard Limited, 2012). The most explicit use of the goldfields history is Kawarau Estate Wines, whose vineyard is on the slopes of the Pisa Range on the western side of Lake Dunstan. Kawarau discovered the name of the miner who owned and farmed their land, a remarkable character called Bonadventure de Bettancour. As well as providing a survey of the historic ownership and use of their land, their narrative offers a lineage that confers a sense of rootedness and belonging. It is Kawarau who explicitly uses images of gold miners at work on their labels, and provide an intriguing, though understated, link of their own to the gold rush as their reason for doing so:

> Wendy Hinton and Charles Finny, owners of Kawarau Estate, have long links to this region. Wendy's mother [...] Hazel's aunt Gabrielle Parker was the first wife of William McMillan, father of Murray, the present owners of Mt Pisa station. Charles' pioneering ancestors – the Blacks and the Maces – established two towns in the area – Blacks (Ophir) and Macetown. Wendy and Charles are determined to keep the region's rich heritage alive – that is why they celebrate the region's pioneers on every bottle of Kawarau Estate wine.
>
> (Kawarau Estate, 2012: n.p.)

A more subtle link is offered by some companies, utilising the semiotics of a goldfields name to make their links to the past. Perseverance Estate at Muttontown (near Clyde, and the site of the first settlement when the Dunstan gold rush began) takes its name from the Perseverance Dredge, a current wheel-powered craft that was one of the first to operate on the Clutha, which worked a claim just metres from the modern vineyard. They use a picture of the dredge on their label in an unconscious homage to McLoughlin's Cromwell Brewery, who in the midst of the local dredging boom of the late 1890s added a silhouette of a river dredge to their stout labels (Perseverance Estate, 2012).

Schist Cottages

One of the most enduring legacies of the gold rush is the ruins of old miners' stacked schist cottages dotted around the district. Four wineries use these iconic images on their labels: Bannockburn's Domain Road, Hawkshead at Gibbston and Dry Gully Wines (who also employ a gold rush semiotic with a 'Pick and Shovel' label for their Pinot Noir) at Earnscleugh, while Gibbston Valley Wines, who have a vineyard on the Schoolhouse Terrace at Bendigo, use the iconic cottage from Bendigo's Welshtown on their Schoolhouse Pinot Noir.

Several wineries utilise these historic stone structures for tasting rooms, such as Three Miners (who also constructed a trailer-mounted miner's cottage as a mobile tasting room), Gibbston, Kawarau and Terra Sancta. Misha's Vineyard took a different path, taking a two-pronged approach to their engagement with the region's golden past: offering, in addition to a narrative outlining their path to vineyard ownership and development, a summary of the history of wine-growing in the area and a carefully constructed mythological Chinese character, *Ah Foo*:

> Not much detail is recorded of the history of this character who came to Bendigo in Central Otago to find fortune in the goldfields. With just the remains of his house now reconstructed on Misha's Vineyard, on the Lakefront Terraces overlooking Lake Dunstan to work from, the legend of Ah Foo is a blend of facts and fiction, bringing to life a story that would apply to many of the Chinese who came to New Zealand in the 1860's.
>
> (Wilkinson, 2012: n.p.)

This narrative constructs a past that includes family details and photographs, passage from Canton to Ballarat, the vicissitudes of mining life there and the eventual move to Bendigo in Otago, via Dunedin and Gabriel's Gully (Wilkinson, 2012). To support the legend, an extensive schist 'ruin' of a typical miner's hut was constructed in the middle of the vineyard from stone located on the property. This is used for tastings and to anchor the vineyard's metanarrative that is framed around marketing and winemaking explicitly (but not exclusively) aimed at Asian tastes: 'Having spent 16 years living in Asia, the idea of producing a range of superb wines suited to Asian as well as Western foods, and to be able to do so in the stunningly beautiful country of New Zealand, became our ultimate challenge' (Wilkinson, 2009). Given the success they have had in the Chinese market, it seems their approach is bearing fruit (O'Hara, 2012).

This use of goldfields imagery on Central Otago wine labels has more than the semiotic of history and place implicit in their use; they are, at least in part, tapping into the immense marketing power of nostalgia in their portrayal of an idealised past.

Nostalgia

Muehling and Sprott define nostalgia as 'an individual's yearning for an idealized past' (Muehling and Sprott, 2004: 25), and while, strictly speaking, the use of stylised goldfields imagery involves the employment of a constructed memory, the emotion that the marketing targets is the same as that targeted by traditional 'remember when'-style nostalgia campaigns. Rather than Holbrook's 'yearning for yesterday' (Holbrook, 1993: 253), this use of nostalgia portrays an ideal whose veracity cannot be challenged, since the events and people portrayed are 150 years earlier and allow a safely distant, vicarious experience of the historic events (Muehling and Sprott, 2004). Holak and Havlena describe how nostalgia in marketing aims, through the 'association with the past' to 'create a network of connections to the individual that do not exist for other objects' and note that the intent is to focus 'specifically on preferences toward objects rather than on the memories evoked by those objects' (1998: 218).

Present-day wine consumers do not and cannot access memories of a distant past when they were miners or when they were new colonists in the dusty, gold-built towns of Central Otago, but the association with the romantic, exciting past via the imagery allows them to mentally visit the era, but without the dirt, danger or effort that marked that life. As one American columnist commented, 'We want to relive those thrilling days of yesteryear, but only because we are absolutely assured that those days are out of reach' (Rosenblatt, 1973). But the real power in the use of nostalgic imagery is how nostalgia grafts resonant associations onto new commodities (Chrostowska, 2010: 56), aiming to create a positive consumption experience by adding, what Stern calls, 'the "sizzle" of pastness' to the otherwise commonplace (Stern, 1992: 14). This allows the consumer to identify with the gold rush past that is perceived (or presented) as a repository of authenticity, or more desirably, enables them to transcend time and connect to that past (Belk et al., 1989: 10–11). This then turns their nostalgia into a vehicle for commodification that, Hewison argued, 'reinforces the longing for authenticity in order to exploit it' (Hewison, 1987: 29).

When it came to new products, Zimmer noted the prevalence of invention to construct a background that evokes nostalgia as a means to establish legitimacy (Zimmer, Little Griffiths, 1999: 259–267), while Naughton and Vlasic emphasised the effectiveness and power of this as a marketing decision to build brand meaning and loyalty (Naughton and Vlasic, 1998: 58–64; Muehling and Sprott, 2004: 26). This is, Chrostowska (2010: 53) argues, working 'on the premise that they are reproducible and transferable, and, in ideological term, that emotions, no matter how they are manipulated, retain their naturalness and remain a counterweight to materialism'. For an emergent wine business, perhaps established by new residents in the area and looking at five-year-old vines and shiny stainless-steel processing vats, the use of various goldfields images and narratives allows them to re-invent themselves as intrinsically belonging, appropriating roots that are widely perceived as legitimate, in an example of Laura Oswald's 'culture swapping' to establish their new identity (1999: 303).

Images of the Gold Rush

The choice of gold rush imagery employed to muster nostalgia is a combination of a remembered, imagined and reinterpreted past, which in memory is often more benevolent, loving and problem-free than the actual past was (Creighton, 2001: 10744–47). Depictions of the gold rush highlight the desirable, nice aspects of the era.

Miners celebrate gold finds, they do not mourn a mate crushed under a sluice face slump or drowned in the Clutha; they are not digging a water race on starvation wages to open up new ground, or carting loads of spoil on a shoulder yoke from claim to rocker beside an Otago river. Photographs show miners working their own claim, not working for wages for a syndicate of wealthy Dunedin investors. No one illustrates a quartz miner working ten hours with a mate 400 feet underground, using a hand-operated rock drill to the inconsistent light of two cheaply made candles, then ascending a ladder at the end of his shift, climbing the equivalent of a 38-story building to emerge into the sunshine he has lived without for a day (Lawson, 1882).

Women gaze demurely out of photographs, dressed in the magnificence of Victorian fashion – which may or may not have been hired from the photographer for the purpose – hiding that they face childbirth with amateur midwifery care, spending their days cooking over a choking coal fire or washing loads of washing in a freezing water race, hands rendered cracked and bleeding by the hard work they are put to, praying that today it is their husband who returns, not his mates coming to inform about an accident. Given that nostalgia is by definition predicated on a sense of loss, the goal of the employers of nostalgic imagery is to recapture the past in an idealised abstraction without evoking painful memories (Holak and Havlena, 1998: 223; Holak, Havlena and Matveev, 2006: 198–199) or reinforcing any perceptions of failure in the present (Brown, 2003: 66).

As Caen (1975) once commented, this nostalgia is 'memory with the pain removed', with the intention, says Davis (1979), of '[…] bestowing an endearing luster on past selves that may not have seemed all that lustrous at the time' (1975: 41), and after the marketers have worked their magic on images and words, offer what Chrostowska (2010: 54) says is a '[…] departure from the definite past for the indefinite', and at its extreme, '[…] is a revolt against the past as *fait accompli*, against the past's facticity'. But as Lowenthal (1996: 13) suggests, in 'celebrating some bits and forgetting others, heritage reshapes a past made easy to embrace. And just as heritage practitioners take pride in creating artifice, the public enjoys consuming it. Departures from history distress only a handful of highbrows. Most neither seek historical veracity nor mind its absence'.

Modern representations are carefully shaped to perpetuate the evocation of positive imagery of the gold rush, such as the Otago Goldfields Heritage Trust's annual 'Cavalcade' re-enactment of the earliest migration of miners to Central Otago, but with carefully documented health and safety procedures, mapped (and GPS-aided) routes and not a bushranger or starving, failed miner to be seen. The region's gold rush narrative similarly follows an assiduously clean-scrubbed cheerful positivity, embracing the pick of popular myths in its museums, historic reserve interpretation and heritage tour offerings, unconsciously confirming the choice of the wine label designers in selecting a romanticised mining imagery to sell their product.

Conclusion

With the sesquicentennial of the Central Otago gold rush in 2012, a fresh wave of commemorations, re-enactments, conferences and community celebrations reminded locals and the rest of New Zealand of the region's golden era. It is therefore hardly surprising that a number of Central Otago's 'Pinot Pioneers' embracing their 'Vineyards on the Edge' identity have turned to and identify with imagery from their local gold rush for their wine labels. Their use of the immense power of nostalgia to carve out a marketing niche for their wines is therefore as understandable as it is deftly used.

References

Advertiser, 1892. Winegrowing in South Australia, *Advertiser*, 25 Jun. p.10.

Advertiser, 1893a. Adelaide news, *Advertiser*, 7 Jan. p.5.

Advertiser, 1893b. Distillation of perfumes, *Advertiser*, 14 Feb. p.6.

Argus, 1861. New insolvents, *Argus*, 2 Nov. p.7.

Argus, 1863. Estate of Theodore and James Bladier, *Argus*, 21 May, p.8.

Argus, 1881. List of awards and medals, *Argus*, 20 May, Supplement, p.3.

Argus, 1886. Winegrowers' Association of Victoria (from our correspondent.) Stawell, *The Argus*, 23 Aug. p.6.

Aurora Vineyard Limited, 2012. Aurora Wines: the vineyard, [online] Available at: http://www.auroravineyard.com/TheVineyard/tabid/72/language/en-US/Default.aspx. Accessed 16 June 2012.

Baker, C., 2011. Otago defies gloomy wine industry outlook. *Southland Times*, 27 Aug., p.17b.

Banks, G., Kelly, S., Lewis, N. and Sharpe, S., 2007. Place 'From One Glance': the use of place in the marketing of New Zealand and Australian wines. *Australian Geographer*, 38:1, pp.15–35.

Barber, N. and Almanza, B., 2006. Influence of wine packaging on consumers' decision to purchase. *Journal of Foodservice Business Research*, 9:4, pp.83–98.

Barber, N., Almanza, B. and Donovan, J., 2006. Motivational factors of gender, income and age on selecting a bottle of wine. *International Journal of Wine Marketing*, 18:3, pp.218–232.

Barber, N., Dodd, T. and Ghiselli, R., 2008. Capturing the younger wine consumer. *Journal of Wine Research*, 19:2, pp.123–141.

Barber, N., Ismail, J. and Taylor, D., 2007. Label fluency and consumer self-confidence. *Journal of Wine Research*, 18:2, pp.73–85.

Baylea, J. C. and others of Waikerikeri Valley, 1879. Petition, Reports of the Gold Fields Committee, – No. 127, Session I. *Appendix to the Journals of the House of Representatives*, Session II, I-03, p.5.

Belk, R., Wallendorf, M. and Sherry, J., 1989. The sacred and the profane in consumer behavior: theodicy on the Odyssey. *Journal of Consumer Research*, 16:1, pp.1–38.

Bertrand, K., 2006. Brand Packaging Association: intoxicatingly lovely wine labels conquer retail noise, [online] Available at: http://www.brandpackaging.com/articles/intoxicatingly-lovely-wine-labels-conquer-retail-noise. Accessed 8 June 2012.

Bladier, J., 1860. Victoria Parliament, Parliamentary paper: petition from Mr. James Bladier to the chief secretary, Victoria Parliament Legislative Assembly, 2 May, Melbourne, Section A. no. 34.

Brady, A., 2010. *Pinot Central*. Auckland: Penguin.

Brostrom, G. and Brostrom, J. eds., 2009. *The business of wine – an encyclopaedia*. Westport, CT: Greenwood.

Brown, S., 2003. No then there: of time, space, and the market. In: S. Brown and J. F. Sherry, eds. 2003. *Time, space, and the market: retroscapes rising*. Oxford: Taylor & Francis.

Brown, S., Doherty, A. M. and Clarke, B., Stoning the romance: on marketing's mind-forg'd manacles. In: S. Brown, A. M. Doherty and B. Clarke, eds. *Romancing the market*. London: Routlege.

Bruwer, J., Li, E. and Reid, M., 2002. Segmentation of the Australian wine market using a wine-related lifestyle approach. *Journal of Wine Research*, 13:3, pp.217–242.

Bruwer, J. and Wood, G., 2005. The Australian online wine-buying consumer: motivational and behavioural perspectives. *Journal of Wine Research*, 16:3, pp.193–211.

Caen, H., 1975. Nostalgia. *San Francisco Chronicle*, 15 Apr. p.26.

Caple, S., 2011. *An investigation into the role of collaboration in the development of a regional brand*. Ph. D. University of Otago.

Charters, S., Lockshin, L. and Unwin, T., 1999. Consumer responses to wine bottle back labels. *Journal of Wine Research*, 10:3, pp.183–195.

Chrostowska, S., 2010. Consumed by nostalgia? *SubStance*, 39:2, p.56.

Creighton, M., 2001. Anthropology of nostalgia. In: N. Smelser and P. Baltes, eds. *International encyclopedia of the social & behavioral sciences*. 16. 2nd ed. Amsterdam: Elsevier. pp.10744–47.

Cull, D., 2001. *Vineyards on the edge*. Auckland: Longacre.

Cutler, L., 2006. Wine label design: What makes a successful label. *Wine Business Monthly*, [online] Available at: http://www.winebusiness.com/wbm/index.cfm?go=getArticle&dataId=44322. Accessed 1 June 2012.

Daily Southern Cross, 1867. Sydney shipping news, *Daily Southern Cross*, 25 Jun. p.4.

Davis, F., 1979. *Yearning for yesterday – a sociology of nostalgia*. New York: Free Press.

Davishon Vineyard Limited, 2012. Alexandra Wine Company: about us, [online] Available at: http://www.alexwine.co.nz/aboutus.html. Accessed 8 June 2012.

De Castella, C., 1886. *John Bull's vineyard: Australian sketches*. Melbourne: Sands & McDougall.

Desert Heart, 2012. Desert Heart – wine caressed by angels: history, [online] Available at: http://www.desertheart.co.nz/history.html. Accessed 28 May 2012.

Dunedin Evening Star, 1872. Wine manufacture, *Dunedin Evening Star*, 24 Aug. p.2, quoted in *Timaru Herald*, 28 Aug. p.3.

Eliott, S., 2012. Terra Sancta Wines Limited, Bannockburn. [telephone interview] (Personal communication, 13 June 2012).

Feraud, J. D., 1882. Petition: reports of the Gold Fields Committee, No. 261, *Appendix to the Journals of the House of Representatives*, Session I, I-03, p.1.

Franson, P., 2006. Labels gone wild. *Wine Enthusiast Magazine*, [online] Available at: http://www.winemag.com/Wine-Enthusiast-Magazine/March-2006/Labels-Gone-Wild/. Accessed 22 October 2011.

Goulding, C., 2003. Corset, silk stockings, and evening suits: retro shops and retro junkies. In: S. Brown and J. F. Sherry, eds. 2003. *Time, space, and the market: retroscapes rising*. Oxford: Taylor & Francis.

Harmon, J., 2005. Presentation to New Zealand Trade and Enterprise for Central Otago Pinot Noir Limited, 3, quoted in Caple, S., 2011, p.92.

Hewison, R., 1987. *The heritage industry: Britain in a climate of decline*. London: Methuen.

Holak, S. L. and Havlena, W., 1998. Feelings, fantasies, and memories: an examination of the emotional components of nostalgia. *Journal of Business Research*, 42, pp.217–226.

Holak, S. L., Havlena, W. and Matveev, A. V., 2006. Exploring nostalgia in Russia: testing the index of nostalgia-proneness. *European Advances in Consumer Research*, 7, pp.195–200.

Holbrook, M., 1993. Nostalgia and consumption preference: some emerging patterns of consumer tastes. *Journal of Consumer Research*, 20:2, pp.245–256.

Johnson, T. and Bruwer, J., 2003. An empirical confirmation of wine-related lifestyle segments in the Australian wine market. *International Journal of Wine Marketing*, 15:1, pp.5–33.

Johnson, R. and Bruwer, J., 2007. Regional brand image and perceived wine quality: the consumer perspective. *International Journal of Wine Business Research*, 19:4, pp.276–297.

Kawarau Estate, 2012. Kawarau Estate wines: our story, [online] Available at: http://www.kawarauestate.co.nz/our-history. Accessed 4 June 2012.

Kidd, I., 1993. The Art of dressing the product. *Australia and New Zealand Wine Industry Journal*, 8:3, pp.201–204.

Kotler, P. and Armstrong, G., 1996. *Principles of marketing*. London: Prentice Hall.

Larson, A., 2012. *Generation Yine: the millennial generation and wine label trends*. Undergraduate dissertation. Faculty of the Graphic Communication Department, California Polytechnic State University, San Luis Obispo.

Lawson, C., 1882. Letter from Bendigo, Otago. [letter] (Personal communication, letter courtesy of Hilary Rowlands, England, grand-daughter of recipient).

Lockshin, L., 1997. Branding and brand management in the wine industry. *Australian and New Zealand Wine Industry Journal*, 12:4, pp.386–407.

Lockshin, L. and Rhodus, W., 1993. The effect of price and oak flavor on perceived wine quality. *International Journal of Wine Marketing*, 5:2/3, pp.13–25.

Lowburn Ferry, 2012. Lowburn Ferry Wines Limited: vineyard information, [online] Available at: http://www.lowburnferry.co.nz/lowburnferry/vineyardinformation.html. Accessed 12 June 2012.

Lowenthal, D., 1996. *Possessed by the past – the heritage crusade and the spoils of history.* New York: Free Press.

Macquitty, J., 2003. Tuck into Central Otago pinot noir. *The Times*, 11 Oct., Wine Section, p.2.

Manins, R., 2007. Pinot noir beats the best in world. *Otago Daily Times*, 25 Sep., p.3a.

Muehling, D. and Sprott, D., 2004. The power of reflection: an empirical examination of nostalgia advertising effects. *Journal of Advertising*, 33:3, pp.25–35.

Naughton, K. and Vlasic, W., 1998. The nostalgia boom. *Business Week*, 23 Mar., pp.58–64.

O'Hara, Y., 2012. Central wineries exhibit at Hong Kong Wine Expo. *The News*, 5 July, p.18c.

Olsen, J., Thompson, K. and Clarke, T., 2003. Consumers self-confidence in wine purchases. *International Journal of Wine Marketing*, 15:3, pp.40–52.

Oram, R., 2004. *Pinot pioneers.* Auckland: New Holland.

Orth, U., 2002. Research Note—targeting the un-experienced and the convenience shopper. *International Journal of Wine Marketing*, 14:3, pp.80–82.

Oswald, L. R., 1999. Culture swapping: consumption and the ethnogenesis of middle-class Haitian immigrants. *Journal of Consumer Research*, 25:4, pp.303–318.

Otago Daily Times, 1862. Dunstan diggings, *Otago Daily Times*, 27 Sep. p.5.

Otago Daily Times, 1863.Taieri diggings, *Otago Daily Times*, 21 Nov. p.9.

Otago Daily Times, 1864a. Local, *Otago Daily Times*, 30 Jul. p.5.

Otago Daily Times, 1864b. Dunstan, *Otago Daily Times*, 11 Jul. p.5.

Otago Daily Times, 1864c. The Dunstan, *Otago Daily Times*, 5 Nov. pp.5–6.

Otago Daily Times, 1865. Clipped from the 'Molyneux Mail' of the 4th inst., *Otago Daily Times*, 8 Apr. p.4.

Otago Daily Times, 1866. Social and domestic, *Otago Daily Times*, 20 Aug. p.6.

Otago Daily Times, 1874. Travelling notes, *Otago Daily Times*, 25 Dec. p.5.

Otago Daily Times, 1890. Advertisements, *Otago Daily Times*, 28 Jan. p.3.

Otago Daily Times, 2008. Central wine named world's best red. *Otago Daily Times*, [online] 5 September. Available at: http://www.odt.co.nz/the-regions/central-otago/21059/central-wine-named-world039s-best-red. Accessed 4 June 2012.

Otago Witness, 1862. Dunstan, *Otago Witness*, 4 Oct. p.8.

Otago Witness, 1894. Fruitgrowing industry in Central Otago, *Otago Witness*, 17 May, p.11.

Otago Witness, 1895a. The Otago Vine Belt, *Otago Witness*, 28 Feb. p.4.

Otago Witness, 1895b. Fruit Growing, *Otago Witness*, 2 May, p.4.

Packspur Vineyard, 2012. Packspur Vineyard Limited: home, [online] Available at: http://www.packspur.co.nz/. Accessed 12 June 2012.

Perseverance Estate, 2012. Perseverance Estate Wines, Alexandra: home, [online] Available at: http://www.perseverance.co.nz/. Accessed 4 June 2012.

Price, J., 2012. Three Miners Wines Limited, Alexandra. [interview] (Personal communication, 8 June 2012).

Pritchard, A. and Morgan, N., 1998. Mood marketing – the new destination branding strategy. *Journal of Vacation Marketing*, 4:3, pp.215–229.

Pyke, V., 1864. Wai-keri-keri. *Otago Daily Times*, 18 Jun. p.9c.

Quartz Reef Wines, 2011. Quartz Reef Wines Limited: home, [online] Available at: http://www.quartzreef.co.nz/home/. Accessed 31 July 2015.

Quartz Reef Wines, 2011. Quartz Reef Wines Limited: our story, [online] Available at: http://www.quartzreef.co.nz/home/history/. Accessed 10 January 2013.

Robinson, J., 2003. Wine of the week: two paddocks Pinot Noir Central Otago. Originally published at [online] http://www.JancisRobinson.com. Republished: Neill, S., 2013. *Two Paddocks blog*, [blog] Available at: http://twopaddocks.com/article-0022.shtml. Accessed 18 April 2015.

Rosenblatt, R., 1973. Look back in sentiment. *New York Times*, 28 Jul. p. 23a.

Saker, J., 2010. *Pinot noir – the New Zealand story*. Auckland: Random House.

Sherman, S. and Tuten, T., 2011. Message on a bottle: the wine label's influence. *International Journal of Wine Business Research*, 23:3, pp.221–234.

South Australian Register, 1859. The Vine on Bendigo, *South Australian Register*, 23 Apr. p.2.

Stern, B., 1992. Historical and personal nostalgia in advertising text: the Fin de siècle effect. *Journal of Advertising*, 21:4, pp.11–22.

Sugarman, P., 2009. Wine labels that work: wine is fashion & beverage aisles are our runway, [online] Available at: http://winelabelsthatwork.com/?m=200909. Accessed 4 May 2012.

Sutanonpaiboon, J. and Atkin, T., 2012. Using region to market wine to international consumers. *Journal of Food Products Marketing*, 18:1, pp.1–18.

Sydney Morning Herald, 1880. Sydney International Exhibition, *Sydney Morning Herald*, 22 Apr. p.8.

Thomas, A., 2000. Elements influencing wine purchasing: a New Zealand view. *International Journal of Wine Business Research*, 12:2, pp.47–62.

Trumpeter, 1855. Advertisements, *Trumpeter*, 30 Aug. p.1.

Tuapeka Times, 1871. Local, *Tuapeka Times*, 7 Dec. p.4.

Tuapeka Times, 1872. Local, *Tuapeka Times*, 11 Apr. p.6.

Tuapeka Times, 1876. Local, *Tuapeka Times*, 19 Apr. p.2.

West Coast Times, 1867. Resident Magistrate's Court, *West Coast Times*, 10 Dec. p.4.

West Coast Times, 1869. Advertisements, *West Coast Times*, 24 Nov. p.3.

Wilkinson, M., 2009. Misha's Vineyard Limited: our journey, [online] Available at: http://www.mishasvineyard.com/reveal/our-journey/. Accessed 5 June 2012.

Wilkinson, M., 2012. Misha's Vineyard Limited: the legend of Ah Foo, [online] Available at: http://www.mishasvineyard.com/reveal/the-legend-of-ah-foo/. Accessed 5 June 2012.

Zimmer, M., Little, S. and Griffiths, J., 1999. The impact of nostalgia proneness and need for uniqueness on consumer perception of historical branding strategies. *American Marketing Association Conference Proceedings*, 10, pp.259–267.

Chapter 5

Mad Men and Women: Construction and Management of Advertising Executives in Popular Culture

Anne Peirson-Smith

Abstract

This chapter examines the mediated constructions of fictional executives working in advertising using a close reading of the television drama series, *Mad Men* portraying a fictional advertising agency, Sterling Cooper Draper Price in 1960s America. Applying organisational theory to representations in popular culture, it will suggest that texts such as *Mad Men* can provide useful insights into management practices at particular periods of historical time by examining three levels of culture operating in the organisation, namely, the observable artefacts, corporate values and workplace assumptions. It will suggest that the themes exploited in each episode across seven seasons, such as marginalisation, sexism, alcoholism, infidelity, work-life balance, lifestyles, consumerism, homophobia, inequity, manipulation, truth, deception, unequal power relations, success and failure, are all relatable for contemporary viewers and have added to the popularity of the series by offering audiences a way of sense-making about their lived experiences and wider societal truths through immersive engagement with cultural artefacts and mediated narratives.

Keywords

Mad Men, popular culture and organisations, popular culture and the workplace, popular culture and professional representation, organisational culture and representation, popular culture and work, gender and organisational culture

Introduction

The critical examination of popular culture representations of the workplace is relatively under-researched. This omission is surprising given that such examinations potentially offer a useful perspective of the professional workplace, activities and behaviours of workers. This chapter examines television series *Mad Men*, produced by US cable station AMC from 2007, situated in a fictional advertising agency, Sterling Cooper (SC) / Sterling Cooper Draper Price (SCDP) in 1960s New York. It suggests that texts such as *Mad Men* provide useful insights into management practices in an agency setting by examining the identities of occupational and social groups in society and how their meanings are negotiated and decoded by audiences (Hall, 1973).

Mad Men is set in the post-World War II economic boom in the United States (Marwick, 1998). This period saw the dawn of the advertising industry and the emergence of the mass media industry against the backdrop of increasing mass production. 1960s advertising orchestrated the consumption patterns for new generations of North Americans who were gravitating to cities for new jobs, homes and lives. As a measure of the advertising industry's key socio-economic role the corporate advertising gross annual budgets increased fourfold between 1945 and 1960, with cars and cigarettes being the top consumables:

> Large families, new suburban homes, televisions and enormous chromed automobiles symbolised the hopes and possibilities of the era, and adverts helped shape popular standards [...] Advertising courted the newly affluent as never before, and Americans pushed mass consumptions to new heights.
>
> (Sivulka, 1998: 240)

The first season of *Mad Men* opens with a late 1950s scenario, when a post-war values system of prudent spending was being replaced by an era of forward looking optimism defined by culture, technology, politics and consumerism. The use of material markers to define identity and success continued to hallmark this decade, as the main consumer base – the white middle class – who tended to judge success by the markers of conspicuous consumption that adorned their homes and appearance.

These themes form the core motifs throughout the series of the drama, characterisation and plot, adding authenticity and an opportunity to critique the inconsistencies and paradoxes of the era (Marwick, 1998). The juxtaposition of consumerism and social consciousness defined the 1960s, providing dramatic context for the series. Against this modernising backdrop, the central creative concepts in advertising campaigns and the 'captains of consciousness' who directed them (Ewen, 1976) had to cater for a new and more critically aware 'individual' consumer, as well as for a broadening demographic of consumer audiences comprising wider ethnicities and different age groups (Schudson, 1984).

These sociocultural issues contrast with the individual pursuits of the consumer that advertising caters for, and the collective appeals to an assumed universal consumption culture based on a mythic dream of success founded on hard work, self-improvement and loyalty to a nation of opportunity. Such themes also define the professional and personal trajectories of the SCDP employees, as the dualist structure of the series is based on the operations and fortunes of the advertising agency and its creative industry. The focus is on employee loyalty, and it positions advertising as a legitimate profession, based on a belief in the legitimacy of the advertisements themselves, both by their advertisers (producers and creators) and consumers. This producer–consumer relationship is located in the power of mythic promises to sell products and services through representational dreams, imaginary futures and the re-creation of new identities. The activities at SCDP exemplify the circuit of production, as promotional advertising texts emerge from within the prevailing culture (Du-Gay, 1997). These advertisements are situated in an endless circuit of promotional messages promising empty dreams, unattainable identities and states of being that are never fulfilled and can only be satiated through increased consumption of advertised objects (Wernick, 1991; Cook, 2001).

Organisational Theoretical Framework

The fictional representation of the workplace in popular culture texts of film and television has more recently been recognised as a valid analytical site because fictional narratives offer 'more dramatic, more intense, more dynamic representation of organisation than management texts' (Hassard and Holliday, 1998: 1). Therefore, *Mad Men* can also be seen from the perspective of organisational theory. The focus on the workplace, and interactions of the characters therein, provides a more emotional, humanised version of an organisation. In contrast, organisational research provides more rational, objective insights, focusing on macro-power relations.

The mimetic value (Taussig, 1993) of workplace representations in popular culture is important here, as audience members may be influenced and impacted by the role models, values and behaviours represented in these media texts, from satisfying the affective needs for entertainment and mediated gratification to mimetic sense-making and professional role modelling. In addition to imparting social and ideological values or telling tales of human success and failure, series such as *Mad Men* offer a blueprint for organisational culture and practice as a way of understanding why these professional practices prevail, and how things are done in contextualised, organisational settings.

Organisational Cultural Framework

Organisational theory using the cultural metaphor as an analytical approach falls into two main approaches. Firstly, the prescriptive approach details what type of culture an organisation has, and to what extent this determines its success or failure (Deal and Kennedy, 1982; Peters and Waterman, 1982). Conversely, conceptual interpretive approaches are concerned with sets of characteristics that define an organisation and attempt to describe and comprehend the inherent complexities in which it evolves and is encountered.

The complexities of organisational culture are evidenced by markers of rituals, stories, metaphors, rules of communication, value and belief systems that are socially constructed and performed by its members. In turn, these are differentiated by internal subcultures that are fragmented and ambiguous, given the dynamic internal and external environments in which organisations operate.

The plot and characters of *Mad Men* support this representation of organisational culture, and it is a useful starting point to analyse the validity of its representation of the workplace, and specifically the historical representation of how an advertising agency on Madison Avenue in 1960s New York operated. The plot of the TV series features an ensemble cast of six to seven core characters (namely Bert Cooper, Roger Sterling, Pete Campbell, Lane Pryce, Harry Crane, Betty Draper, Peggy Olson and Joan Harris) in addition to the main protagonist, creative director Don Draper, whose interactions across all of their professional and domestic domains form the main storylines in each episode. One of the overarching themes throughout the series revolves around the way in which each individual attempts to collaborate professionally and socially by decoding the shared demands of senior management and clients. The drama emerges from consistent anxieties that characters experience in navigating their role in the agency, when managing client accounts and their regular failure to anticipate emerging events on both work and domestic fronts. These operational shortcomings often arise from the flawed leadership of the agency founders and line managers, such as Draper, who sometimes fail to impart the objectives required to implement a successful campaign representing a reflection of the inexact science and ambiguous art form that is advertising. As such, accounts are often lost as clients are disappointed by the work that the creative executives lay before them. In the same way, relationships and marriages form and disintegrate. These crisis situations are counterpoised with high points in the drama when accounts are also won and clients happily sign off on creative campaigns, while advertising awards are acquired when the account and creative team manage to unlock and embrace the shared assumptions and expectations of the internal line managers and the client. Hence, the complexities of organisational culture, and that of the SCDP advertising agency itself, can be usefully examined to determine representations of the workplace and the application of these insights by viewers' into their own lives by examining three levels of culture operating in the organisation, namely the 'observable artifacts, values, and basic underlying assumptions' (Schein, 1985: 15).

Each of these features will now be examined in turn. Firstly, the artefacts and what they say about an organisation; secondly, the espoused collective corporate values in terms of how things should work in the office based on accepted assumptions and their alignment with reality or lack of it; and thirdly the basic ideological assumptions and values that workers hold about the corporation they work in as matched up to their individual, personal agendas.

1. Observable Artefacts

From its first episode the show received positive critical acclaim, especially in its adherence to the painstaking and authentic recreation of the ambiance of this fictitious Madison Avenue advertising agency of the era in terms of the office look and layout, and work clothes which evoked the spirit of the age (Hamilton, 2012), as well as defining the character traits, identity, sexuality and relationships of the main characters. The popularity of the show was also extended beyond the act of viewing to the immersive engagement with fans of the series clamouring to get the *Mad Men* look of Joan's silhouette and Don's sharp suit or acquire retro furniture to recreate Betty Draper's home. However, the series was also equally criticised for being all style and no substance by pedaling mythic nostalgia and trivialising history at the expense of glossing over the past legacy of contemporary social issues in favour of artful scenes of characters behaving badly while always looking good (Mendelsohn, 2011).

Yet, the idea that elements of style and aspects of material culture offer few useful insights into the past as a way of making sense of the present is contested here. Essentially, *Mad Men* uses style and design as narrative tropes to highlight the value of objects in everyday lives and provides insights into expressions of who the characters are, just as any form of human exchange or dialogue does. The vintage aesthetic of the carefully curated items that comprise the *Mad Men* sets enables the viewer to engage with the past through a re-reading of these mediated texts and cultural narratives through a present day, subjective lens operating outside of traditional historical accounts.

Mad Men's advertising agency is located in the image business. Given its symbolic nature, advertising's output and its core work are ambiguous, rendering it necessary for the profession and its executives to demonstrate to each other and their clients that they possess special competences to fulfil this task. In this context, advertising executives are involved in a daily performance as they create their campaigns 'backstage' in agency brainstorming and status meetings and present these creative campaign options 'front stage' in client meetings (Goffman, 1959). The capacity to signal superior competency and distinctiveness within their given field to mark themselves out from clients, competitors and amateurs is located in this habitus (see Bourdieu, 1984). For advertising executives, as with other creative industries workers, this disposition is considered to emanate from demonstrations of good taste and cultural capital that can be visually communicated through tropes such as appearance or office décor (Featherstone, 1991). In this sense, Don Draper is the quintessential advertising man as he appears to intuitively understand the connections between artefacts and desires and the affective significance that they have for consumers. This is evident when he brands Kodak's slide machine device for showing family photographs as 'the Carousel', thereby associating the circularity of family life captured in family photographs with the experiential and transitory fun of the fairground (Season 1, Episode 13, The Wheel).

In *Mad Men* the observable artefacts from Season 1, Episode 1 comprise the props, sets and costumes, including the 'physical layout, the dress code, the manner in which people address each other, the smell and feel of the place, its emotional intensity, and other phenomena, to the more permanent archival manifestations such as company records, products, statements of philosophy, and annual reports' (Schein, 1990: 111).

The Building
The physical environment of the SC advertising agency is a towering symbol of modernism with its rational planning and standardised production echoed in the glass and concrete skyscrapers that define the modern urban landscape. As signifiers of power, they symbolise corporate success by housing large numbers of workers unified in the corporate effort and a private insider world of industry and bureaucracy – the corporate family – accessible by invitation only. Many scenes feature employees arriving or departing the agency in the confined space of the elevator as the boundary between the outside world and the corporate domain. Key scenes also occur in the elevator where characters are forced to communicate with each other or encounter people from outside of their immediate office environment. Characteristically, SCDP is located in iconic Time Life Building, 1271 Avenue of the Americas that would have accorded with reality and adds to the situational authenticity of the plotlines.

The Office Interior
The semi-open office plan with the secretarial pool of 'young ladies' (Wright Mills, 1956: 200) on display in the middle of the floor, flanked by the senior professionals' offices around the parameter wielding occularcentric power (see Foucault, 1977) over their working space is still the model for many ad agencies today. In addition, a hierarchy exists within this executive-secretary configuration. The personal assistant style secretary is positioned as gatekeeper and is seen as guardian of her male boss's office door. This trope exists in almost every episode to signal the importance and power of the male characters who these office ladies are servicing and is used as a way of demarcating 'organisational man' from the other less senior workers in the firm. Uncharacteristically, young secretary Peggy's ascendancy from Season 1 as Don Draper's Personal Assistant to Senior Copywriter from Season 3 is a nod to the increasing feminist movements of the era. But, despite her obvious creative talent and evolving managerial skills, she is still relegated to a small, shared windowless office signifying her lesser organisational status and her gendered role.

Aesthetically, office interiors reflect the mid-century modern period furniture designed with functional, clean lines. Characterisation is also extended through individual employee offices and personal decoration. Significantly, all of Draper's offices in both agency scenarios are sleek, minimal and anonymous as if the physical representation of his office space represses his real personality, which he always appears to keep under control. By way of contrast, the office of eccentric founder of the agency, Bert Cooper (Seasons 1–4), is decorated with seventeenth-century Japanese prints and screens representative of his eclectic taste, cultural capital and deeper worldly wisdom as often evidenced by the approbation of visitors in his sanctum. Equally, Roger Sterling's office in the new Time Building sports an op art black-and-white theme complete with Brigit Riley-esque décor and sleek white Corona chair, Saarinen table and stools. This contrasting décor signifies the character's tendency to shock acquaintances and engage in social and sexual transgression, and also markedly contrasts with Peggy's more natural earth-toned artworks adorning her muted office walls suggestive of her conservative life and aspirations.

Domestic Spaces

Living spaces and interior design styles of the time are presented as evidence of the growing consumerism that the advertising executives are making a living out of nurturing. Most New York apartments in the series, such as Pete Campbell's home in Seasons 1–3, feature furniture and artwork as a way of demonstrating the growing wealth of the ad executive in this era. Throughout the series, the theme of consumption and its aid to homemaking is also highlighted to engage with defining trends of the day. Equally, the homes of the key employees signify the lifestyle choices of the characters, with the younger 'unmarrieds' living in mid-town apartments only gravitating to the domestic safety of the suburbs once their children arrive, which aligns with contemporary practice.

Alcohol, Cigarettes and Drugs

Alcohol and cigarettes are recurring motifs that define the SCP workplace, client servicing and professional debriefings, all appearing to fuel the creative drive in the company as executives are rarely seen without a glass or a cigarette in hand at some point in the working day episode. The conspicuous consumption of whiskey and vodka by senior male executives also comprises an astounding product placement for brands and is evidence of audience manipulation and influence that would enable the Frankfurt school to rest their case. The excessive consumption also signifies post-prohibition prosperity and freedom. For Draper, alcohol is a creative tool, but it is also his emotional and professional crutch enabling him to escape from his past and cope with the pressures of the present whether domestic or work based. As the series progresses we see that the bottle of whiskey is also a permanent fixture on Peggy's desk from Season 3 as a mark of her growing maturity and adoption of masculine traits ensuring survival in a patriarchal environment.

As the series arrives in the mid-1960s, the emerging drug culture features in the plotlines. The creative team experiment with weed to find imaginative solutions for the Bacardi campaign ('My Old Kentucky Home' Season 3, Episode 3) much to the consternation of Peggy's older secretary. This response from an older demographic also represents the generational divide and highlights the incipient bourgeois bohemian culture of the 1960s consumer society in contrast to the puritanical ethos of late nineteenth-century industrial capitalism (Arthurs, 2003).

Serial alcohol abuser Roger Sterling also experiments with LSD ('Far Away Places', Season 5, Episode 6) with life changing effect and a seemingly motivational spur reactivating his commitment to bringing in clients. Essentially, the integration of social drug usage in the storyline serves to highlight the high pressured, high stakes, glamorous world of advertising and a new age of discovery based on a break away from accepted social codes.

Technology
The offices of SCDP's rhythmic heartbeat is metered out by sensory clickety-clicking of painted female fingernails on typewriter keys – the cutting edge communication technology of the time also accompanied by the incessant ringing of Bakelite phones. The senior male players are never seen to be involved in the act of typing or operating the switchboard, as theirs is a world above this for the secretaries are employed to physically encode information or manage machinery. The men think, talk and look, while the office women obey orders, operate and act, which actually affords them some form of agency and power in the workplace through their technical knowledge. In this sense, the patriarchal structure of the workplace is redefined. Only the secretaries use the cutting edge office technology of the era such as the Dictaphone or the copying machine to decode and make sense of the cognitive utterances of their male boss.

Male Appearances
The work-based identities of SCDP staff, at all levels and across genders, reflect the stylish self-consciousness and the signs of conspicuous consumption at work (Nixon, 1997: 12) that advertising industry workers appear to display (see Bourdieu, 1979) in an increasingly hedonistic culture. The binary construction of organisational males versus working females and stay-at-home wives in the series is based on familiar gender stereotyping that provides meaning in framing each in opposition to the other. The traditional patriarchal separation between the dominant, directive professional male boss and the servile female secretary is often central to the characterisation and plot being utilised as a way of attaining workplace authenticity. The senior male executives in the agency are all typical of 'the organisational man' (Whyte, 1956). Essentially, they are reminiscent of the classical corporate executive films from 1930 to 1960, such as *The Executive Suite* (1954) or *The Man in the Grey Flannel Suit* (1956), representing 'the world of executive work in the large, bureaucratic, male dominated corporation where narratives about power, reward and success dominate' (Bell, 2008: 89). The sartorial signifiers, such as the sharply tailored suit, trilby hat, white shirt and silk tie, suggest the expert, dispassionate, successful nature of the characters in charge of the agency. This corporate male uniform also reflects the prevailing trends for post-war consistency and structure in the workplace as a way of resuming some sort of normality after the Depression and the socio-economic disruptions of the Second World War (Hollander, 1993). In terms of professional authenticity, the advertising industry makes a discursive and visual distinction between the clean-shaven account managers who are referred to as 'suits' and the 'creatives' who usually wear anything but a suit, preferring casual dress as their professional wardrobe. Certainly, this is echoed by the staffers as Pete, Roger and Harry are always be-suited with white shirt and tie. Also, top creative Don Draper wears dark Brooks Brothers best tailoring and has spare Arrow shirts in the drawer in case of an all-nighter. When Don becomes partner, his former secretary and second wife Megan comments in Season 5: 'You are so sharp you could cut me with those shoulders',

suggesting the dangerous and inaccessible aspects of his character. Meanwhile, senior copywriters, junior copywriters and art directors consistently wear more casual chinos and sports shirts with longer hairstyles and a more unshaven appearance to signify their creative, independent spirit and the more liberal, bohemian nature of their work.

In another sense, the male suit operates to establish social uniformity in the urban workplace to ensure a type of equality among the post-war middle class – either real or aspiring. The work suit could effectively disguise the 'inconsistencies' of the people beneath it (Creadick, 2006: 278) as it helped '[…] to erase prior identities and allow the wearer to become part of a collective, an indistinguishable member of the social group' (Bell, 2008: 95). Throughout the series Don Draper is constantly evading his true identity. He successfully manages to conceal his dark past from most of his work colleagues and from his first wife for the first three seasons. The act of evasion and identity fraud appears inexorably connected to his office wear, with the donning of the sharp suit being a visual metaphor for a promotional industry that has often been accused of 'paid lying' by inherently pulling the wool over the eyes of consumers to intensify the positive and downplay the negative aspects of the product being promoted as part of advertising's rationale.

Female Appearances
At a basic level, the characterisation of the female office workers at SDP reflects both the standard literary dialectical female typology (Hirschman and Stern, 1994) of the innocent virgin destined for domesticity, as typified by the new, young recruits (Megan as Draper's PA), and the knowing whore whose masculine secular exposure offers an uncertain future based on contested relationships (for example, Joan Harris's ongoing affair with her boss representing his emasculation and her access to insider knowledge).

Hence, clothes contribute significantly to the detailed characterisation of these female characters, with office workers wearing 1960s-style tailored dresses, pencil skirts and blouses depending on rank, which highlights the growing consumer culture that they are buying into when projecting their professional and social identities. Joan Harris, the super-capable office manager, wears bright, bold, tight fitting dresses with a defined decolletage that command the eye as much as her presence. This dress code signifies her ability to be in control of her work team and the capacity to use her sexuality to manipulate her male co-workers or to secure client accounts. On the other hand, Peggy as secretary who makes it good as copywriter wears modest dresses with high necklines in muted natural tones to signify her introverted nature and the ability to secure success based on talent. Equally, we see wives such as Betty Draper and Trudy Campbell in fashionable day 'new look' dresses at home and in hats, furs and tailored coats and pearls when visiting their husbands in the office thereby 'performing' their status and the reflected success of their husbands.

The female secretaries are all turned out in immaculate and highly colourful, tailored dresses with coiffured hairstyles typical of a 1950s to 1960s workplace environment where the female 'with pink fingernails' was expected to serve her male boss along with 'half dozen assorted skirts whisking through the filing cases of his correspondence' (Wright Mills, 1956: 200). Yet, there is also sense in which the feminist themes of the era as portrayed by the series are being introduced (Friedan, 1963). Hence, Peggy, originally as PA to Draper, is portrayed as geeky and dowdy in her style of hair and dress, signifying her hidden depths as a potential copywriter that she eventually becomes following her insightful, gendered feedback in doing office focus group research for the Coty lipstick account. Subsequently, this results in a gradual rebranding of her image as she morphs into a more powerful executive role and adopts the sartorial trappings of organisational success.

The series represents a range of female roles such as PA, secretary, receptionist and telephonist, mistress and corporate wife who all assume their place in the patriarchal workplace, occupying menial servicing roles that men never take up. These female roles of the serving worker (most of the PAs and secretaries), the disciplinarian office manager (Joan Harris) and the androgenous career women (Peggy) are all defined in terms of their relation to their male co-workers and the patriarchal environment in which they work – where dominant and ambitious males are serviced by passive and supportive females. In this demarcated space, women serve to highlight male power in their otherness, in terms of their visible differences, their character traits and ambitions (Wright Mills, 1951). The vagueness surrounding the secretary's job tends to place the focus on what she is, rather than what she does. In this sense, these women were typical of their 1960s 'dolly-bird' role: 'Mini-skirted and made-up they embodied a portable interior phantasmagoria, a new design furnishing that was commonly referred to as "brightening the place up"' (Shonfeld, 2000: 94). However, these office ladies are often characterised as having ambitions to change their social role and climb the ladder often by marrying the boss, which happens with Roger Sterling in addition to Megan and Don Draper, only to end unhappily often due to male infidelities, in a recurring plotline suggesting that men are in control of their work but not of their female relationships. Equally, while the emphasis on characterising female appearance to represent their controlled status and worth invites the viewer to adopt the male gaze, suggesting a neutering of their workplace power in their objectification, in essence their curated appearance can also be read as a source of power and pleasure immune to male control.

Cityscape

The city of 1960s New York is also portrayed with largely patriarchal overtones in terms of its phallic landscape and the gendered spaces that it contains. In this space men meet up in bars to celebrate having made it through the working day and where an occasional female worker, secretary or wife on a dinner invitation may aesthetically lighten up the scene and satisfy the male gaze. Men own the cityscape, while women are relegated to the hearth as we see in the case of Betty Draper in the classic patriarchal mold. Don Draper meanwhile is portrayed as an urban flâneur roaming around New York by night and satisfying his carnal desires across a string of extra-marital affairs, while Betty, defined by domesticity, stays at home and makes dinner, puts the children to bed and sits alone with a drink and a cigarette waiting for her husband to return from his nocturnal urban-based sexual conquests. In this narrative, the city is the preserve of sinners and the hearth is the domain of virtuous vessels.

2. Corporate Value System

The corporate value system is a belief framework underpinning the ways that things are, or how they should be done within the organisation. This factor is less visible than physical artefacts as it is located in the staff behaviours and their alignment with corporate values. It includes such issues as how to fulfil the corporate vision and increase efficiency and effectiveness, how to manage co-workers, how to treat clients and how an organisation differentiates itself from competitors. In many ways, it also drives the plotline of each episode in terms of the differences between these positions and their inconsistencies.

Contextually, the world of *Mad Men* saw the emergence of the post-war manufacturing boom from the 1950s catering for rapidly emergent consumer demand, as workers across wide demographic ranges had disposable income and desired to define their identities and embrace new lifestyles by consumption. As a corollary, a managerial phenomenon of the large modern corporation (Perrow, 1991) and the educated and well-groomed corporate man working in advertising and older service industries (see Boozer, 2002) also emerged to service these new customer needs assisted by new technological developments and corporate systematisation throughout the 1950s and 1960s (Chandler, 1977).

Leadership and Managing Workers
This value system, according to Schein, is usually located in, and defined by the leadership. In the case of *Mad Men*, the original founders have clearly decided that Don Draper is the heir apparent and is made creative director by Bert Cooper, a role that he makes into his own and starts to develop the leadership skills that eventually land him a partnership and the co-founder of SCDP. From these corporate heights, Draper is accorded the role of the value monger of the organisation by increasingly dispensing wisdom about what constitutes good advertising, how to manage clients and what women want from purchasing lipsticks to underwear. As he explains of his professional interactions with his team and his clients, 'People want to be told what to do so badly they listen to anyone' ('Babylon' Season 5, Episode 8).

Despite his obvious personal flaws, Draper is positioned as a leader who gains the trust and respect of his co-workers and creative team firstly because he intuitively knows the business of advertising as a consummate salesman admitting – 'I sell products, not advertising' – and he often articulates this competency in creative brainstorming sessions and client meetings. He is frequently scripted as a latter-day shaman, exposing what consumers want out of life and how advertising provides the solution to these needs –

sentiments that could have come straight out of Ogilvy's *Confessions of an Ad Man* (Ogilvy, 1963). Hence, in 'Smoke Gets in Your Eyes', Season 1, Episode 1 in a meeting Draper explains to major client Lucky Strike and his management team: '[…] advertising is based on one thing: happiness. And you know what happiness is? Happiness is a smell of a new car; it's freedom from fear; it's a billboard on the side of a road that screams with reassurance that whatever you are doing, it's okay. You are okay'.

The focus of Draper's work and its central creative concept is based on the benefits accruing from the product rather than focusing on the physical features, which marked a creative conceptual shift in the ad industry from the mid-1960s among the more progressive agencies headed up by iconic leaders of the time (Ogilvy, 1983). Equally, Draper's visionary creative leadership in the series is illustrated by his ability to deal with Japanese clients or in handling difficult customers, for example. In these narratives he is often portrayed as the protagonist who minimises cultural offence caused by the prejudices of his co-workers or in protecting the agency's corporate vision by closing down the accounts of stubborn clients who refuse to buy into his creative ideas. Draper is also seen to emerge from his detached stoicism and to morph into the motivational guru in order to rally the troops when SCDP business is bad or if major clients are lost and when staff are authorised to work throughout their weekend and holidays on a new pitch. In this sense, Draper's confident stoicism also represents the distillation and personification of the advertising industry itself, that consumers put their faith in, by offering solutions to their problems in the form of aspirational dreams of happiness. He also influences his co-workers to get them to see things his way and fulfil his creative vision in the same way that he is influencing his target prospects to buy consumer products. When client Lucky Strike are facing challenges after the Federal Trade Commission declares cigarettes to be potentially hazardous to health, Draper counsels his team and the client to realise that despite the public perception linking tobacco with cancer that all of their six competitors face the same problem and the only way forward is to differentiate their product by being the first to claim that the tobacco they use is toasted in the production process. Thereby, Draper creates a positive association in the mind of the consumer and gives them permission to smoke Lucky Strike as 'Everyone else's tobacco is poisonous. Lucky Strike's is toasted. It's TOASTED' ('Smoke Gets In Your Eyes' Season 1, Episode 1).

Draper as ad man supremo is also seen to be setting the standards and defining what constitutes team success and failure and is consistently critical of substandard creative output. When his team are working on the Samsonite account and fail to impress him with their over-dependence on a consumer research report to guide their work, he chastises Peggy: 'I'm glad that this is an environment in which you feel free to fail. […] I gave you more responsibility and you didn't do anything. […] You give me something I like' ('The Suitcase' Season 4, Episode 7). As quality controller and creative mentor, his aim is often to take his team from organisational compliance to commitment.

The vision of the organisation is not only protected by Draper, but is also seemingly directed by him, thereby aligning with corporate theory suggesting that strong organisational leaders drive the value system (Morley and Shockley-Zalabak, 1991), which also reflects the origins and evolution of advertising agency management in the mid-twentieth century (Ogilvy, 1983).

Managing Clients
Client relationships are portrayed as a necessary evil and a troublesome necessity required to keep the agency alive. Most clients are portrayed as difficult, naïve, insensitive or depraved. They are often treated as unenlightened and irrational, having wasted the time and spurned the inspired ideas of the creative team. Also, clients become more demanding as the series unfolds, requesting specific music tracks for their TV commercials and even taking to writing their own storylines in meetings. As a relatively new profession in the 1960s wanting to establish and protect its professional space and gain recognition for a community of practice by signalling its difference from plain selling, the senior team are often seen to be at pains to behave in a professional manner and manage clients while taking care to accommodate their wishes. The contested nature of this fragile and frustrating relationship is witnessed on many occasions as when Draper loses his temper with, and dismisses an underwear client who appears resistant to his creative ideas on the basis of being too risqué.

3. Core Assumptions: Individual and Workplace

The third model addresses the assumptions that individual employees hold about the world, how it works and their place in it, which are often taken for granted and normalised on account of cultural conditioning, socialisation and corporate reinforcement of 'how things work around here' (see Schein, 1990: 111). This is also relevant when it comes to establishing professional credibility in a creative industry where abstract outputs do not speak for themselves. In addition, as the role of Draper exemplifies, advertising has historically been built on the backs of the names of the founding fathers of iconic advertising agencies, such as David Ogilvy or Bill Bernbach, who invariably lacked a formal education or a career path in advertising that would normally secure professional legitimacy. Hence, great importance is placed on the personal qualities of the advertising executive in their creative capacity, their innate intuition about what will appeal to customers and their ability to influence the prospects' purchasing decisions. Consequently, the individual advertising guru is a trope that we see legitimised by the industry itself and is a critical part of the characterisation of *Mad Men* as represented by Don Draper - the archetypal ad man across the twentieth century.

Despite the collective nature of the work in advertising agencies, where a community of practice professionals work in teams on client-based accounts to deliver promotional campaigns (see Wenger, 1998), it is the team leader who calls the shots. As Peggy acknowledges of Draper, 'We are all here because of you'. In this corporate culture, meetings constitute a conceptual space where ideas are floated but decisions are made hierarchically. Within management meetings the senior members usually achieve their wishes and junior members are often overruled in the management of accounts and appear to be disconnected from managing the real business of the day. While individuality is the key to generating creativity this is done in carefully controlled forms of hierarchically ordered, quality control scenarios where 'truth' or the creative solution emerges from collective debate and intense moments of conflict among the creative team. In creative meetings individuals and their ideas are aggressively pitted against each other in the process of generating creative copy often with the decision-making buck stopping at Draper's behest. Within the creative team, once the decision is made to go with an idea approved by Draper, the truth is derived from key leaders and the employees are expected to follow orders once a decision is reached (Schein, 1985). This is a hierarchically run family with a benign dictatorship, and is not unlike the way that Draper runs his own family where authority is vertically ordered and wife and children must obey.

Yet, while some of the core characters have their doubts or frustrations with the way that things are being managed in the ad agency and threaten to leave or go for interviews with other competitors, often based on a feeling that they are undervalued, they still return to their jobs after being persuaded to stay in the agency by the senior managers. This highlights the passive aggressive nature of the senior management. Other employees, on the other hand, are dismissed for transgressing corporate values, such as demonstrating a lack of respect for co-workers or indulging in substance abuse.

The advertising agencies of the day and the demographics of the corporate landscape are typically homogenous in terms of gender and culture. Yet, they were being challenged by the emerging sociocultural dynamics within contemporary American culture. The *Mad Men* agency is seen to be adapting, often unsuccessfully, to ethnically different clients or culturally different competitors and potential owners, and this is well exemplified when Sterling Cooper is subject to a merger with a UK advertising firm or has to deal with Japanese client culture.

Conclusion

This chapter has highlighted how a fictional text such as the *Mad Men* television drama series can be used to illustrate the realities of workplace activities and its operations by focusing on the aspects of corporate culture such as artefacts, values and assumptions that are useful in understanding and reading organisational life (Schein, 1990) as the place where so many of us spend most of our waking hours. Specifically, the mercurial nature of the advertising industry and what constitutes corporate success is also represented in terms of the way that the advertising professionals present themselves and behave in the series. The hierarchical organisational leadership in an ad agency such as SCDP is seen to define the rules of the game within this value system. As Don Draper tells his creative team, 'if you don't like what's being said, change the conversation' ('Love Amongst the Ruins' Season 3, Episode 2).

Organisational studies have increasingly recognised the value of stories told within organisations about the organisation itself, or in employees representing markers for investigating the 'realities' of the workplace (Boje, 1991, 1994; Czarniawka, 1997, 1999, 2004; Yiannis, 2008). Such representations also offer a rich narrative resource. Thus, a TV series such as *Mad Men* provides a critical and subversive focus on everyday workplaces and work practices through its plotlines, thereby inviting engagement and critical readings from the audience. This helps to build the dramatic tension and works as a safety valve – by staging both drama and carnival, the series provides both conformity and resistance (see Czarniawka and Rhodes, 2006: 214). Certainly, *Mad Men* is attempting to present ongoing contradictions that prevail in the supposedly glamorous creative industries within the promotional economy that are run by ordinary people selling empty, yet aspirational dreams to other ordinary people to satisfy their hedonistic desires.

Fundamentally, *Mad Men* tends to focus on the emotional aspects of the corporate workplace experience. In the plotlines we recognise and take solace vicariously from the moments and emotions that we often are not privy to in our own lived experiences. Equally, audiences are enticed by an opportunity to view the backstage activities of an industry that has been a major part of our lives as consumers in its attempts to sell us artefacts and commodities that define our identities and lifestyles while shaping our dreams in the endless process of wanting more.

Despite the fact that *Mad Men* is a fictitious take on the advertising industry, its authentic, stylised representation of this community of practice in its historical context appears to align with the realities of professional practice today, which may account for its popularity and success. The universal characterisation offers portraits of relatable co-workers that the viewer may have, in their own reality, vowed to avoid or aspired to become. The historic frame of the series and attention to detail in the carefully curated costumes and props (see Hamilton, 2012) also enables audiences to imagine what life was like for their parents or grandparents and to gain a sense of generational understanding in their lives (Mendelsohn, 2011: 8). Equally, the themes exploited in each episode across seven seasons, such as marginalisation, sexism, alcoholism, infidelity, work-life balance, lifestyles, consumerism, homophobia, inequity, manipulation, truth, deception, unequal power relations, success and failure, are all relatable for contemporary viewers. The patriarchal world of the ad agency on its surface portrays men as directing the work and in control of the office. In reality, the role of women within the advertising industry today may not have changed significantly given the continued persistence of the glass ceiling in the creative industries (McRobbie, 1998). Yet, the power relations in fictional terms are perhaps more complex as women in the workplace of Sterling Cooper, and in their domestic spaces, either as virtuous vessels or wanton predators (Hirschman and Stern, 1994), are seemingly in control of their appearance as much as they look after their own careers and relationships. The storylines in *Mad Men* are often universal to audiences searching to make sense of their commodified lives and their immersion in consumer culture (Weick, 1995), even in an entirely different era, such as the one we now inhabit in the early twenty-first century.

References

Arthurs, J., 2003. Sex and the city and consumer culture: remediating postfeminist drama. *Feminist Media Studies*, 3:1, pp.83–98.
Bell, E., 2008. *Management, work and organisations*. London: Palgrave Macmillan.
Boje, D. M., 1991. The Storytelling Organization: A Study of Story Performance in an Office- Supply Firm. *Administrative Science Quarterly*, 36:1 March, pp.106-126.
Boje, D. M., 1994. Organizational storytelling: the struggles of pre-modern, modern and postmodern organizational learning discourses. *Management Learning*, 25:3, pp.433–461.
Boozer, J., 2002. *Career movies: American business and the success mystique*. Austin: University of Texas Press.
Bourdieu, P., 1984. *Distinction a social critique of the judgement of taste*. Translated by R. Nice. London: Routledge and Kegan Paul.
Chandler, A. D., 1977. *The visible hand: the managerial revolution in American business*. Cambridge, MA: Harvard University Press.
Cook, G., 2001. *The discourse of advertising*. London: Routledge.
Creadick, A., 2006. Postwar sign, symbol and symptom: "the man in the grey flannel suit". In: E. H. Brown, C. Gudis and M. Moskowitz, eds. *Cultures of commerce: representation and American business culture 1877-1960*. Basingstoke: Palgrave Macmillan. pp.277–293.
Czarniawka, B. 1997. *Narrating the organization: dramas of institutional identity*. Chicago, IL: University of Chicago Press.
Czarniawka, B., 1999. *Writing management: organizational theory as literary genre*. Oxford: Oxford University Press.
Czarniawka, B., 2004. *Narratives in social science research*. London: Sage.
Czarniawka, B. and Rhodes, C., 2006. Strong plots: the relationship between popular culture and management theory and practice. In: P. Gagliardi and B. Czarniawka, eds. *Management education and humanities*. London: Edward Elgar. pp.195–218.
Deal, T. E. and Kennedy, A. A., 1982. *Corporate cultures: the rites and rituals of corporate life*. Harmondsworth, UK: Penguin Books.
Du-Gay, P., 1997. *Doing cultural studies: the story of the Sony Walkman. Volume 1: culture, media and identities series*. Milton Keynes: Open University Press.
Ewen, S., 1976. *Captains of consciousness: advertising sand social roots of consumer cultures*. New York: McGraw Hill.
Featherstone, M., 1991. *Consumer culture and postmodernism*. London: Sage.
Foucault, M., 1977. *Discipline and punish: the birth of the prison*. Translated by A. Sheridan. New York: Pantheon Books.

Friedan, B., 1963. *The Feminine Mystique*. New York: W.W. Norton and Company Inc.

Goffman, E., 1959. *The presentation of self in everyday life*. New York: Anchor Books.

Hall, S., 1973. *Encoding and decoding in the television discourse. Volume 7: Media studies occasional papers*. Birmingham: Centre for Cultural Studies, University of Birmingham Press. pp.507–517.

Hamilton, C., 2012. Seeing the world second hand: Mad Men and the Vintage Consumer. *Cultural Studies Review*, 18:2, pp.223–241.

Hassard, J. and Holliday, R., 1998. *Organizational representation: work and organizations in popular culture*. London: Sage.

Hirschman, E. C. and Stern, B. B., 1994. Women as commodities: prostitution as depicted in Blue Angel, Pretty Baby and Pretty Woman. In: C. T. Allen and D. R. Joen, eds. *NA - advances in consumer research*. Volume 21. Provo, UT: Association for Consumer Research. pp.576–581.

Hollander, A., 1993. *Seeing through clothes*. Berkeley, CA: University of California Press.

Marwick, A., 1998. *The sixties*. Oxford: Oxford University Press.

McRobbie, A., 1998. *British fashion design: rag trade or image industry?* London: Routledge.

Mendelsohn, D., 2011. The Mad Men account, *The New York Review*, 24 February–9 March. pp.4–8.

Morley, D. D. and Shockley-Zalabak, P., 1991. Setting the rules: an examination of organizational founders values. *Management Communication Quarterly*, 4, pp.422–429.

Nixon, S., 1997. Advertising executives as modern men: masculinity and the UK advertising industry in the 1980s. In: M. Nava, A. Blake, I. MacRury and B. Richards, eds. *Buy this book: studies in advertising and consumption*. London: Routledge. pp.103–119.

Ogilvy, D., 1963. *Confessions of an ad man*. London: Atheneum.

Ogilvy, D., 1983. *Ogilvy on advertising*. London: Vintage.

Perrow, C., 1991. A society of organisations. *Theory and Society*, 20:6, pp.725–762.

Peters, T. J. and Waterman, R. H., 1982. *In search of excellence: lessons from America's best run companies*. New York: Grand Central Publishing.

Schein, E. H., 1985. *Organizational culture and leadership*. San Francisco, CA: Jossey-Bass Publishing Inc.

Schein, E. H., 1990. Organizational culture. *American Psychologist*, 45:2, pp.109–119.

Schudson, M., 1984. *Advertising, the uneasy persuasion: its dubious impact on American society*. London: Routledge.

Shonfeld, K., 2000. *Walls have feelings: architecture, film and the city*. London: Routledge.

Sivulka, J., 1998. *Soap, sex and cigarettes: a cultural history of American advertising*. London: Wadsworth Publishing Co Inc.

Taussig, M., 1993. *Mimesis and alterity: a particular history of the senses*. London: Routledge.

Weick, K., 1995. *Sensemaking in organizations*. Thousand Oaks, CA: Sage.

Wenger, E., 1998. *Communities of practice: learning, meaning and identity.* Cambridge: Cambridge University Press.
Wernick, A., 1991. *Promotional culture.* London: Sage.
Wright Mills, C. 1951. *White collar: the American middle class.* Oxford: Oxford University Press.
Wright Mills, C. 1956. *The power elite.* Oxford: Oxford University Press.
Whyte, W. H., 1956. *The organization man.* New York: Simon & Schuster.
Yiannis, G., 2008. *Organizing words: a critical thesaurus for social and organizational studies.* Oxford: Oxford University Press.

Chapter 6

The Big Earn: A Study of Criminal Business Enterprises in Popular Culture

Carolyn Beasley

Abstract

From Tony Soprano's made men to Elmore Leonard's small-time scores to *Sons of Anarchy*'s corrupt cops, representations of characters engaged in criminal business saturate our screens and bookshelves. As well as revealing how the hidden world of cons and crims operates, these characters are often used to offer observation and social comment on how crime, commercialism and consumption interact in ways similar to 'legal' business. This chapter charts the history of these representations, explores the various character types, evaluates what makes them so popular and considers how they interact with the social and economic events of their era in a way that makes them valuable tools of critical social comment.

Keywords

criminal business, criminal entrepreneur, *Breaking Bad*, *The Sopranos*, *Weeds*, *The Wire*, *Sons of Anarchy*, *Boardwalk Empire*

Introduction

From E. W. Hornung's *Raffles: The Gentleman Thief* to HBO's series *The Sopranos*, the criminal as entrepreneur has long been a common representation in popular literary and screen culture. In addition to numerous appearances in best-selling fiction and film, this character type even has its own subgenre of crime novel, known variously as gangster fiction (Scaggs, 2005), criminal sagas (Knight, 1997) or deregulated fictions (Haut, 1999). This chapter considers how and why these fictions and media texts map the underbelly of urban life in ways sympathetic to criminals, crooked police and the contexts of their era, and places them in a typology that ranges from the sole trader, through to the entrepreneur, and to their various incarnations as organised crime rings and families.

Our culture's enthusiasm for stories about the fictional criminal businessperson and entrepreneur (Fields, 2004: 612) could be attributed to the dramatic and often charismatic way these characters offer observation and social comment on 'the relationship between crime, commercialism, and consumption' (Horsley, 2005: 184). This popularity should come as no surprise, given the public erosion of confidence in the ability of governmental and corporate institutions to navigate these relationships in a way that benefits the social, rather than individual, good. In a world where powerful organisations evade responsibility, in which the everyday citizen falls victim to widespread governmental and corporate corruption, and where an abstract legal system fails to offer remedy (Cawelti, 1979: 25; Nochimson, 2003: 13), the line between legal and illegal business activities is difficult to determine. As large portions of the population face losing their jobs, homes and identities to economic change and bad governmental financial management, many have little choice other than to create a sub-economy in order to ensure everyday financial survival (Haut, 1999: 30; Fields, 2004: 612) - as Rafael Alvarez suggests, '[…] if you deny an entire segment of society access to the big game, they will create a shadow game mirroring the establishment in every way but social legitimacy' (Alvarez, 2009: 265). Their skill set of financial expert, distribution manager or business strategist remains the same. However, they adopt occupations such as small-time gangster, professional thief or Mr Big rather than sharetrader, salesman or registered CEO.

Methodology

The stories and characters explored in this chapter are examples of how an unconventional but realistic application of business principles can make extremely engaging narratives of criminal activity. These texts are evidence that cultural and social changes can be successfully explored through the act of fictionalising and re-presenting (Moore, 2006). While the ability of fiction to make new connections between government policy, its effects and its possible endpoints should not need defending, it is worth noting that theoretical approaches such as Highmore's (2005) 'rhythm analysis' offer a useful frame through which the relationship of fiction to social analysis can be further legitimised. Highmore argues that cultural texts are not only worthy of analysis for their own sake, but are also analytic texts that can move beyond representation to critique and question. Creative texts, he argues, can interrogate just as effectively as academic texts, despite being located outside the traditional canons of 'theory and method' (Highmore, 2005: xiii).

Central to Highmore's approach is the idea that cultural texts are useful because they provide 'multiple accounts' of phenomena. This works particularly well in the case of entrepreneurism because, as outlined below, entrepreneurism has traditionally been considered a positive endeavour focusing on creativity and innovation (Jayasingthe et al., 2008). However, recent scholarship in the field has consistently begun to identify various alternative applications of entrepreneurism that challenge this notion of positive endeavour. For instance, there is increasing discussion on the negative or so-called 'dark side' of entrepreneurship. First popularised by de Vries in 1985, he and others after him (e.g. Williams, 2005) discussed this in the context of bad practice and hidden agendas (Gottschalk, 2010: 73). Fiction, with its ability to both model and remodel real-life drama, is particularly suited to communicating the many different types and experiences of entrepreneurship.

History

Interestingly, Simon suggests that images of criminality are a 'symbol of national pathologies' (2002: ix). If this is so, then perhaps the American public first diagnosed this ailment as a dominant aspect of American business culture as early as the Frontier era, when readers were both taken-with and taken-in by images of the morally corrupt but adventurous wild west confidence man (DeFino, 2004: 86). The small-time con man appeared in works such as *The Life and Adventures of Mr. Bampfylde-Moore Carew, Commonly Called the King of the Beggars* (Goadby et al., 1768). These men became notorious across American states for their scams, yet continued to prosper through an entwined mix of legal and illegal ventures.

Stories told from the point of view of the criminal were particularly common in the Depression era, as the embittered everyday citizen enjoyed hearing about those who rorted the system (Scaggs, 2005: 109; Haut, 1999). The public thrilled to a plethora of gangster films and complex characters such as Tommy Powers in the 1930s classic *The Public Enemy* (1931) and James Allen in *Scarface* (1932). The introduction of the Hayes Code in the 1930s flattened both 'good' and 'bad' characters into one-dimensional blandness and tightly censored depictions of violence, unintentionally making the real-life gangster characters appearing every day in the newspapers appear alluring and exciting (Nochimson, 2003: 7). The removal of the code coincided with the release of Mario Puzo's novel *The Godfather*. Its appearance in 1969 coincided with the political and social upheaval of the Vietnam War and offered a fictional space where bad guys upheld old-world values centred on family business. From this era emerged films like *Mean Streets* (1973) and *The Killing of a Chinese Bookie* (1976). The years of neo-liberal privatisation that followed from the 1980s to 2000 created a rash of fiction expressing discontent with both policy and its effects on everyday life (Scaggs, 2005: 109; Haut, 1999). Indeed, the Reagan–Bush years of the late 1980s to 1990s saw a particularly bright burst of these works as economic policies shifted towards selling public utilities and as government restrictions on commerce began to be stripped back (Haut, 1999: 124). These policies had a significant impact not just on citizen's pockets, but also on their imaginations. With this deregulation came the perception that many governing bodies were engaging in preferential tendering outcomes and in less than ethical and possibly illegal business practices. Haut suggests that in this era, the 'pandemic proportion' of crimes committed by those in public office, the police force and white-collar roles meant that public differentiation between criminals and individuals in power began to erode (1999: 135). This neo-liberal reform at both the national and state levels was also accompanied by fictional works, such as those by Lawrence Block, Elmore Leonard, Eugene Izzy and Australia's Garry Disher and Peter Temple, that explored this shift in trust through varying degrees of critique. The perceived moral ambiguity of the era made it easy for writers to move the traditional villain into the role of victim and so to position the villain as the centre of narratives in which he or she struggles to maintain an entrepreneurial economic and power base in the face of larger corruptions (Haut, 1999: 131).

The era from the late 1990s to early 2010 was also significant in the evolution of representations of the criminal businessperson. From 1998 onwards, a more visible, more popular and more enduring set of images of criminal economic activity have come to dominate our imaginations. This is the criminal hero of American cable channel television. Functioning across a range of subgenres and driven by a varying range of economic and personal motives, protagonists such as Tony Soprano, *Breaking Bad*'s Walter White (AMC, 2008–2013) and *Weeds'* Nancy Botwin (Showtime 2005–2012) emerged as a direct result of a new type of television production climate. This change in broadcast landscape began when HBO, a subscription network known mainly for rerunning Hollywood movies, tried an experiment of creating short-season, hour-long serial dramas featuring casts of morally challenged, unlikeable, but deeply human characters (Martin, 2013). Many of these characters, described by television writer Brett Martin as a 'gamut of criminals' (2013: 4), can be grouped with the protagonists from the novels mentioned above to form a typology of professional criminals who treat crime as a serious business.

The Sole Trader: Breaking Bad, Weeds, Burglars and Hitmen

The trials and tribulations of the sole trader, that is an individual in business who is self-employed (Morrison, 2011: 466), can be seen in the stories of ordinary men and women who enter into illegal economic exchange as an individual with a product or product line to sell. They tend to position their business as a step in a process or as a stage in the passage of a product from creation to distribution to point of sale. In light of Highmore's idea that fictional depictions can present multiple insights into the same phenomena, it is useful to examine two of the most popular representations of this type of criminal enterprise: *Breaking Bad*'s Walter White (AMC, 2008–2013) and *Weeds'* Nancy Botwin (SHO, 2005–2012). White, a high school chemistry teacher who discovers he has terminal cancer, uses his laboratory skills to manufacture methamphetamines as a way of supporting his pregnant wife, handicapped teenage son, and to pay the high medical bills that the state won't cover. As a sole trader who manufactures his own product with the help of a single employee, he suffers from the challenges typical of independent manufacturers: source material shortages, distributers trying to reduce his markup, impurities in his end product due to equipment breakdowns in the manufacturing process and shifting legislation that force him to alter where, when and how he creates his product.

This entry into criminality endears White to the reader because it demonstrates that he has evolved from passive victimhood to empowerment. He is originally belittled by disrespectful students, bullied by employers, emasculated by an assertive wife, mocked by family members, forced by the state's low payment of teachers into getting a job in a car wash that forces him to wash his students' cars and, finally, falls prey to an inoperable disease. Undertaking criminal business enables him to transform his behaviour and identity, and makes him unafraid to confront casual disrespect with aggression (Kovvali, 2013; Hudson, 2013).

This shift signals a realisation that a life lived in social appropriateness has not served him or his family well and that, in the face of death, he has little to lose. It, and the dramatic events that follow throughout the course of the series, also offers insight into the relationship between criminality, commerce and masculinity. Perhaps, it suggests that anyone is capable of turning their skill into a criminal enterprise if the stakes for survival are high enough. Men, the show constantly reiterates, feel the need to act to protect their families in any way they can. This need, however, seems attached to a sense of pride. Throughout the series, male characters frequently manipulate other men into acting criminally by questioning their manhood and role as providers (Kovvali, 2013). This raises the question of what really sits at the heart of this need: family or vanity (Hudson, 2013)? It is worth noting, too, that the other criminals in the series, from Jesse to the Neo-Nazis to the men in the Drug Cartel, are frequently exaggerated in their masculinity to the point of performance (Hudson, 2013). Yet, in the end, it is this anchorage to masculine ideals that worsen their dilemmas or cause their demise. Gustavo Fring, for instance, perishes after returning to torment an enemy about his complicit and unmanly relationship with the Drug Enforcement Agency, and Walter returns to the business after being reminded by Fring that a man should provide for his family selflessly (Kovvali, 2013). When Walter admits to his wife that he enjoyed his business, vengeance and violence, and that he did it for himself in order to feel alive, we understand that it is the rush of masculine power that he is really describing. Yet, in the very end, it is commerce that defeats masculinity when Walter's son thinks that the money that Walter has so determinedly and tragically earned for him is actually a gift from the rich friends whose charity Walter had long rejected (Kovvali, 2013). In the world of *Breaking Bad*, criminality as a masculine performance does not always pay off.

Similarly, *Weeds* presents the trials and tribulations of the sole trader forced into illegal commerce due to a change in personal circumstance. However, where *Breaking Bad* examines how the motivations of the criminal anti-hero are constructed and change, *Weeds* turns its lens on the moral and capitalist hypocrisy of the suburban world.

Nancy Botwin is a middle-class mother of two who is widowed when her husband suffers a heart attack while jogging through her manicured, utopian suburb of Agrestic, in Southern California (Lavoie, 2011). Now shaken out of her position of privilege as a homemaker, she searches for economic opportunities to support her family. She cannily realises that there is an opportunity to sell and distribute marijuana to the more conservative citizens of her town who are not comfortable buying from traditional street dealers and so begins to market her own brand known as 'MILF' (Mother I'd Like to Fuck). In the reverse of *Breaking Bad*'s production line, Botwin must source her product from the wrong side of town (whereas White sells his to the wrong side of town) and so is vulnerable to problems of supply (e.g. rival growers destroying her suppliers crops, quality dropping, prices rising). As a sole trader, she also faces product competition from a medical marijuana store. Realising she's lost her competitive advantage as the only 'safe' middle-class source of pot, she plays further on her identity as a suburban mother by opening a bakery stocked with pre-made Costco biscuits. The bakery acts as a front for larger movement of her product and allows smaller scale transactions through the sale of hash cookies. *Breaking Bad*'s Walter White only needs a few buyers because he does not initially distribute, whereas Botwin's position as the last step in the commercial cycle means that if she is to expand, she needs to find more buyers and hence needs more points of distribution. Soon she hires a workforce of salespeople and also begins, like White, to manufacture her own product.

Botwin's role as a criminal businesswoman is endearing to the viewer because she is positioned as a symbol of the dysfunctionality of the suburban dream (Lavoie, 2011), a dream she once epitomised. She has been empowered to engage in both commerce and leisure without needing to participate in the workforce and had been given status through her husband's income. Once these have been withdrawn due to the death of her husband, ironically through the middle-class leisure activity of jogging (Dyer, 1997), she cannot survive and has no officially sanctioned skills through which her family can be supported. Her most marketable quality is her adaptability, female attractiveness and network of middle-class friends. It is these that lead her to realise the hypocrisy of the apparently highly conservative community who generically regard drugs as a blight, yet eagerly consume them as a way of dealing with the boredom, pressure for perfection and ennui of affluence. Her movement into criminal commerce signals that she has seen the deceptive nature of the community and suburban dream as an opiate in itself and, by encouraging its dissatisfied citizens (who include a corrupt and sleazy town planner and oppressive, bullying housewives) to indulge their own illegal pastimes offers a form of controlled liberation. Botwin's movement into drug culture also exposes the inherent racism and 'othering' of non-white culture, as when drug cultivation, distribution and use is stigmatised as a black or racial commerce, it is associated with danger and moral decay (Lavoie, 2011). Yet when, in Agrestic, this commerce is co-opted for white pleasure and capitalist gain, it is regarded as harmless and benign. In this way, *Weeds* uses criminal business as a way to critique the supposedly morally upright 'ordinariness' of suburban life, the American dream and the passive comforts of capitalism.

Fiction, in comparison, tends to represent the criminal sole trader in the form of either the small-time burglar or the hitman. The typical sole trader whose business just happens to be burglary is most likely to be akin to Lawrence Block's Bernie Rhodenbarr[1] or Garry Disher's mysterious and self-contained Wyatt.[2] While admitting an addiction to the thrill of breaking and entering, Rhodenbarr is highly professional in his choice of burglary and chooses jobs that are not likely to be intensely investigated, such as small-scale thefts from cash-strapped people eager for insurance payouts. Wyatt is also cautious in his choice of victims, preferring to steal off other criminals who are themselves independent traders or at least unaffiliated with powerful crime organisations. Ever the typical sole traders, both Wyatt and Rhodenbarr provide a stand-alone service in the chain of supply and have a trusted distribution network that acts as a buffer between themselves and the end buyer. The product stolen is deliberately sourced for resale, and then passed onto another trader who delivers it to the final point of sale, with payment and markups accumulated each time the product changes hands. Fictional professional burglars who steal for financial gain are usually likeable protagonists despite their criminality because they limit their victims to those who treat others badly or have engaged in some form of corruption. However, it is their driving business sense that separates them from what are termed the 'gentleman' thieves of the past, such as E. W. Hornung's Arthur Raffles (1898–1909), Maurice Leblanc's Arsène Lupin (1905–1939) and Leslie Charteris' The Saint (1928–1963), who stole in order to correct a moral wrong and had little interest in financial gain.

The second most common fictional sole trader engaged in law-breaking activities is the contract killer. As their moniker suggests, they tend to hire out their services on a selective basis in exchange for a two-part set fee. In this way, murder is then an instrument of profit (Mandel, 1984: 103). Most, like the psychopathic Anton Chigurh in Cormac McCarthy's novel *No Country For Old Men* (2005), Lawrence Block's Keller in his *Hitman* series (2011) and the unnamed assassin in Frederick Forsyth's *The Day of the Jackal* (1971) are the criminal equivalent of the fly-in, fly-out worker, contracted for a single purpose and working for a range of employers in a sequence of jobs. Elmore Leonard's Armand Davis, for example, works for both the Mafia and his own choice of clients in *Killshot* (1989). As businessmen, their interactions with clients are generally minimal in order to preserve the effectiveness of the service, and their identity tends to be branded through the use of a cryptic pseudonym, such as Elmore Leonard's Armand Davis, known to his clients as 'Blackbird'. Unlike the criminal entrepreneur in the discussion to follow, they are singularly minded about fulfilling their contract, preferring to work on one job at a time rather than engaging in constant and long-term opportunity seeking (Gill, 2001: 280). This reflects the high cost of failure, which for the criminal whose sole trade is killing, can result in the death penalty or twenty years imprisonment.

The Entrepreneur: Boardwalk Empire, The Wire, Get Shorty

Entrepreneurship can be defined as being 'concerned with the discovery and exploitation of profitable opportunities' (Shane and Venkataraman, 2000: 217). The conditions for entrepreneurship are considered simple by some: 'the presence of lucrative opportunities and the presence of enterprising individuals' (Shane and Venkataraman, 2000: 218). The enterprising individual, according to Gottschalk, tends to have '[…] strong beliefs about a market opportunity and are willing to accept a high level of personal, professional or financial risk to pursue that opportunity' (2010: 70).

While much entrepreneurism is undoubtedly constructive, enterprising individuals may encounter lucrative opportunities that are on the wrong side of the law. If they choose to take up this opportunity, they are still entrepreneurial. Indeed, as Gill (2001), Klockars (1975) and Ruggiero (1998) argue, many criminals who undertake a full-time commitment to offending and who develop special skills in order to do so possess these conditions of entrepreneurship and so can be termed professional criminal entrepreneurs. They can even be distinguished from sole traders such as *Breaking Bad*'s Walter White or the protagonists in Lawrence Block's aforementioned series, on the basis that sole traders will frequently reject opportunities because they do not wish to step outside their risk-tested place in the supply process. The professional criminal entrepreneurs' desire to move forward into more profitable ventures, however, means that they will take up opportunities of greater risk.

The professional criminal entrepreneurs' approach to opportunity is a demonstration of this principle. Their commitment to offending tends to be framed as what Gill (2001: 280) terms a 'positive attitude' towards acts of crime; that is, they believe the crime can yield reliably lucrative and successful results through careful preparation, measured violence and the application of previously tested knowledge and techniques. Professional criminals tend not to be motivated by drug addictions, alcohol problems and gambling addictions and so do not usually face an immediate need for money. As a result, they do not seek or take advantage of sudden and unexpected opportunities to gain quick financial windfall. Hence, a positive attitude towards offending also means that they are highly selective about what opportunities they undertake. As these crimes are a career rather than a quick means to feed an addiction, they tend to engage in constant and long-term opportunity seeking; that is, they will have several crimes either underway or in planning at any one time (Gill, 2001: 280).

Positive offending in entrepreneurial ways is also represented to a more complex degree in the HBO series *Boardwalk Empire* (2010–2014). Set in 1920s New Jersey, it follows the manoeuvrings of Atlantic City treasurer Enoch 'Nucky' Thompson as he attempts to steer both the City and his own illegal profiteering through a new world of 'vicious thugs, emboldened by the promise of an easy dollar' (A Return to Normalcy). Thompson's criminal motivations fit within Gill's framework of attitudinal positivity towards offending: he holds no addictions, gambling debts or duress-led financial obligations, and is sparing in his commissioning of violence. His strategic negotiations through the politics of governance, racketeering, street gangs and organised crime can be attributed to a long apprenticeship under his predecessor and he is constantly searching for new financial opportunities, whether these be new markets for his illegal alcohol, new FBI officers to pay off or new ventures into which to invest. However, he lacks measured caution and will tend to seize an opportunity for quick financial gain due to greed rather than need. His pursuit of material pleasures comes to dominate his outlook and actions and eventually costs him much of the fortune and family he had treasured (Brace and Kingsbury, 2013). It is through this downfall that the series captures and critiques what

Horsley termed the interconnectedness of 'crime, commercialism and consumption' (2005: 184).

Boardwalk Empire also illustrates Gottschalk's point that 'criminal market is a meeting place for supply and demand' just as traditional markets are (2010: 68). A situation will be viewed as an opportunity if a high-demand item has limited supply. Typical items of this nature include drugs (as seen in *Boardwalk Empire*, *Breaking Bad* and *Weeds*), precious gems and bonds (Wyatt's thefts).

Nucky Thompson's ability to turn the problem of prohibition into a windfall is typical of the tendency of the entrepreneur to detect that a current or expected change in technology, a change in demand or a change in procedure will result in a gap in smooth functioning or current provision of supply. These 'competitive imperfections' (Gottschalk, 2010: 70) open the door to an alternate section of the market to that which the criminal has previously served, hence offering a new range of opportunities. These could be a change in banking laws, temporary breakdowns in security or, as in the case of the Mesic crime family in Garry Disher's *Cross Kill* (1994), lax management due to bad entrepreneurial choices. When a rogue Mesic brother returns from working overseas with casino-based mafia groups, he decides that his family should move ventures from car rackets to casinos and poker machines (Disher, 1994: 7). This turns the family members against each other and creates an opening for Wyatt to commit a robbery.

Criminal entrepreneurship is also highly distinguishable in fictions such as Peter Corris's Luke Dunlop series (1992–1994, for example *Set Up*, 1992), Elmore Leonard's small-time gangster worlds (for instance, *Get Shorty*, in which loan sharks and distributors of stolen goods work loosely under umbrella of the commission taking local made man, but are also given the freedom to undertake their own financial endeavours) and series like *The Wire* and *Shameless*.

In Corris's Luke Dunlop novels (1992–1994), both crooked police and criminals can operate as entrepreneurs by making careful evaluations of opportunity. Not only are the police on the take but also, by undergoing the same deceptions of identity as criminals, their personas even begin to overlap. In *Set Up* (1992), one-time corrupt cop Luke Dunlop undergoes a change of identity (sanctioned by a dubiously shady government agency), so that he can work as a protector in the Witness Protection Program. However, this throws him into what von Lampe calls the 'social microcosm of illegal entrepreneurs', a tapestry of 'co-offending, the social embeddedness of criminal networks, and the interaction between illegal and legal sphere of society' (2007: 132). Luke Dunlop's world is one in which savvy enterprising criminals and crooked cops call on the embeddedness of their criminal business interactions to testify against each other with the defiant intention of reducing their prison sentence or to avoid going to prison.

This could also be seen as an articulation of de Vries' (1985) notion of 'dark entrepreneurship', which is a proliferation of bad practice and hidden agenda. It is, for the criminal entrepreneur, effectively the end of business so is not a long-term strategic move, but serves as a 'get out of jail free' card when it becomes obvious that they have misjudged the risk probabilities of previous opportunities.

Whereas *Boardwalk Empire* presents characters of privilege maximising their opportunities for profit through corruption, *The Wire* (HBO, 2002–2008) and *Shameless* (Channel Four, 2004–2013) offer examples of desperate entrepreneurialism. In these series, marginalised citizens with no voice, limited opportunities and an entrenched belief that the civic world will offer them little need to make their own commerce to survive. While *The Wire* spans West Baltimore and *Shameless* is confined to a Manchester housing estate, the consistent message of the two series is that economic restructure and monied interests have devastated the industries and social frameworks that pumped life and dignity into their cities, leaving people with no choice but to earn their living wherever they can (Alvarez, 2009). The failure of social security income nets, return to work programs and health cover mean the already robust drug trade booms and becomes both an equal opportunity employer and a bountiful option for workers with an entrepreneurial spirit. The audience can't help but admire the resilience of the participants in this criminal commerce as they wirily dodge, adapt and innovate their way around the struggling and outdated forces of law enforcement.

The Organised Crime Ring and Crime Families: Sons of Anarchy and The Sopranos

Organised crime rings are also particularly entrepreneurial; their focus being 'continuing enterprise in a rational fashion, geared towards profit' (Gottschalk, 2010: 68). Marxist scholar Ernest Mandel perhaps puts it best when he argues that '[…] organised crime is capitalism freed from the bonds of penal law, but accepting most of the civil and certainly the commercial code' (1985: 103). The crime organisation approach towards opportunity is even more sophisticated than the single or small team professional criminal, as it tends to envelope a large range of individuals and activities in a number of crime sectors and markets (Levy, 2007) and often works as a syndicate.

Both SAMCRO (Sons of Anarchy Motorcycle Club, Redwood Original Charter) in the FX television series *Sons of Anarchy* (2008–2014) and the DiMeo/Soprano crime family empire under current boss Tony Soprano in the HBO series *The Sopranos* (1998–2007) function as examples of Gottschalk's notion of an entrepreneurial organised crime ring.

The Soprano family and the Sons of Anarchy motorcycle gang are umbrella structures constructed of small but highly regulated crime lines. The Sons of Anarchy central 'business' is maintaining control over the criminal activities in Charming, controlling the local police, gunrunning and wholesale drug distribution (Bellafante, 2008). These activities require them to extend their reach and to insert their trade into other sectors to maintain delicate relationships with other organised crime groups. The relationships between these groups and the Sons of Anarchy club shift from working as arms for larger organisations like the IRA, to supplying guns to a number of other motorcycles clubs whose territory is under threat, to mergers with other clubs (patch overs) to outright territory wars resulting in the death of members and erosion of profit. The Sopranos earn most of their income from protecting smaller traders, supplying and reselling stolen goods, fraud and money laundering scams and illegal gambling (DeFino, 2004).

The organisations also had legal outlets for their gains. The need to establish a legitimate place to invest profits has a long history. Investing illegal earnings into secure and legitimate businesses began in the United States when gangster money was channelled into the New York garment industry and then into money laundering, namely entertainment, gambling, construction and high-end hotel industries (Mandel, 1984: 97). Set against the era's growing corporate capitalism (Gardaphe, 2010), there was also gradual movement into second-tier areas such as banking, investment trusts and currency speculation (Mandel, 1984: 98). These also opened the door to another method of money flow: the trade in stolen or counterfeit stocks and shares (Mandel, 1984: 100). The movement into drugs by organised crime in the 1940s and 1950s saw a massive increase in profits and, by 1979, crime syndicates were estimated to be turning over around $62 billion a year (Charlier and Marcilly, 1980: 10). By 1982, the *Forbes* list of the richest 400 families included at least three crime families (Mandel, 1984: 98).

Both *Sons of Anarchy* and *The Sopranos* mirror this model. The Sons of Anarchy club invests in legal prostitution by partnering in a brothel, and runs a repair garage. As well as bringing in taxable income, these are also sites of money laundering. Tony Soprano's legal outlets are more complex. He has partnerships and shelf companies in hospitality, film and food distribution, full ownership of a legal adult entertainment venue and a garbage collection business. Thus, in both shows the organisations are criminally entrepreneurial and embedded in legitimate capitalist exchange. Murder is committed for the evasion of arrest and can, in rare circumstances, become a business decision intended to protect market share.

The organised crime narrative tends to 'paint a panoramic picture of society and its values' (Nochimson, 2003). There is an emphasis on the interconnectedness of social exchange as a vehicle for maintaining and developing commercial relationships, and it is this social exchange that is also a great cause of tension. The use of this type of criminal business organisation allows writers to explore not only this tension, but also the added difficulties of balancing filial and romantic connections, and the needs of the individual versus the collective good.

As suggested by the filial nature of their title, the Sons of Anarchy are a closed brotherhood who share a bond beyond commerce and motorcycles. While their public persona is as a recreational motorbike club, in reality they began as a group of mostly Vietnam War Veterans who dreamed of a communal way of post-Vietnam life that would allow them to exist outside the commercialism and consumer cannibalism of the modern western nation. As archetypal biker criminals, they hark back to the gangs of the wild west where outlaws fought as brothers and embraced the frontier as symbolic of freedom from authority. Business should be far from the minds of these easy riders as they live off their land in small-town America. The reality, however, is that they need money to survive. In response to this need for financial stability, they acquire an internal structure that is no different from most corporate organisations. They have a CEO (Clay) who makes hard decisions (Bellafrante, 2008), the salesman who glibly wheels and deals (Jax), the wise old-time employee who gives counsel (Bobby), the hard man who acts as enforcer (Tig) and the worker bee soldiers who carry out the menial tasks (Juice, Happy and the Prospects). In storylines often compared to *Hamlet* (Barsuglia, 2013) but typical of many corporations, shifting allegiances between younger and older members add tension and drama to the everyday manoeuvres and under-the-counter deals needed to earn a living.

So too *The Sopranos* explores the difficulties faced by the modern criminal organisation structured around both a real and a metaphoric family (Wynn, 2004; DeFino, 2004; Fields, 2004). The Soprano 'family' sprawls across continents and generations (DeFino, 2004). Its growth, unlike *Sons of Anarchy*, includes upwards mobility and it is this aspect that so defines *The Sopranos* against other organised crime narratives. The Sopranos represent middle-class suburbia (Fields, 2004). Their sprawling double-storey house has a pool, their children go to private schools and the parents drive SUVs. They, and their crime family, feel entitled to the social status and financial well-being that belongs to the middle classes (Fields, 2004). Tony ensures the income flows in both the families. With a middle-class existence, however, comes the bourgeois troubles of existential angst, seemingly causeless anxiety, despair over coming in at the end of an idealised Mafia past, moral ambiguity and the pressure of leading an old organisation in a new world (Wynn, 2004; DeFino, 2004; Fields, 2004). For a mob boss, the conflicts between the competitiveness of capitalism, and the emotional demands of family and individual need are untenable (Nochimson, 2003). Yet, it is exactly these challenges that make Tony Soprano an interesting study in criminal leadership and management technique.

One of the key aspects of Tony Soprano's strategy is that he believes his business is as legitimate as any other. In his eyes, there is no distinction between organised crime and corporate culture (DeFino, 2004). He moves with ease between illegal earns, 'fronts' and legitimate business deals, letting their elements overlap and blur. This type of flexibility is a sign of effective leadership (Schneider, 2004); his blending of opportunism and risk is handled with an absolutism that DeFino suggests could be drawn from Machiavelli's *The Prince* (2004: 84).

Survival in changing times requires rapid adaptation to new ways of earning capital and decisive movements to set these up. Tony gained the respect of his elders by a showy hold-up of a card game (DeFino, 2004), and it was this that led him to wrestle control of the business from his Uncle Junior. In the world of management success seminars, these examples prove that he is driven by clear strategic vision and a determination to act (Schneider, 2004). While the perpetually grumpy Junior wants to stick to the traditional drug money and union scams, Tony pushes the family into the twenty-first century with shares, stocks, defaulted loans, Internet investment frauds and real estate deals (DeFino, 2004). These capture the leadership qualities of being alert to opportunities, possessing a vision, having a plan and ensuring continuity (or knowing that the small score is just as useful as the big score) (Fisher, 2013; Martel, n.d.). Indeed, the fact that Tony sees a psychiatrist is evidence of his desire for forward movement, self-improvement and eagerness to be a better leader, particularly in terms of impulse control and anger management (DeFino, 2004: 83).

Conclusion

The entrepreneurial desire for profit through opportunity and through the acceptance of risk is captured in a range of criminal representations that present protagonists surviving financially in dedicated and often innovative approaches to making money. As they apply their skills to well-researched but risk-managed opportunities, they prove popular culture can help audiences understand motivations for crime, the pathology of the personalities that commit it and the workings of the business world.

It is of little surprise that these representations have proven so popular. The criminals of Bampfylde-Moore Carew, Elmore Leonard, Nucky Thompson and *The Wire* share an ethos of trying to get by in an increasingly corrupt and corporatised world. When Tony Soprano explains that his forebearers turned to crime because 'there was a time [...] when the Italian people didn't have a lot of options [...]' (1999, The Sopranos, 'College'), we understand that their motivations are just as relevant today. Whether they are scam artists or hitmen, they are victims of the economic obligations that hold them to others and to their society. So too the anxious consumption of the Soprano family and the characters in *Boardwalk Empire*, perched on the opposite edges of two global financial crises, remind the audience that while families need to be clothed and fed, there has been an erosion of the traditional values and continuity of industrial production that used to achieve this end. In the new, ever-shifting world of the modern Mafia boss, mothers hire hitmen to kill their sons and brothers, and their sons break the gangster code of silence by confiding in therapists.

If Ruth (1996) is correct to argue that criminal organisations can function as a reflection of our culture's ideals, the stripped back economic realism of the *Sons of Anarchy* heralds a shift in the manner, shape and nature of our expectations about consumption. Created as the financial rollback of America hit, it captures a world low on commodities but high on collective values. Yet, as Highmore's rhythm analysis suggests, there is no singular view of the criminal business world. Instead, there are multiple assertions of what type of business criminals undertake. So at the same time that the gloating excesses and political briberies of *Boardwalk Empire* present a 'criminally irresponsible capitalist ethos' (Horsley, 2005: 193), viewers can experience the socially accepted 'whiteness' of Nancy Botwin's drug smoking Agrestic and the explosive moral ambiguity of Walter White and Tony Soprano's fractured worlds, all through the comfortable and mediated veil of popular culture.

References

Abbott, P., 2004–2013. *Shameless*. Channel Four.

Alvarez, R., 2009. *The Wire: truth be told*. New York: Canongate.

Barsuglia, B., 2013. Sons of Anarchy: the Hamlet conclusion. *Influx Magazine*, [online] 12 November. Available at: http://influxmagazine.com/sons-of-anarchy-the-hamlet-conclusion/. Accessed 9 April 2015.

Bellafante, G., 2008. Sons of Anarchy: wild bunch on wheels, playing by its rules. *New York Times*, [online] 2 September. Available at http://www.nytimes.com/2008/09/03/arts/television/03sons.html?_r=0. Accessed 9 April 2015.

Block, L., 2011. *Hitman* (Vol. 1). London: Hachette.

Brace, P. and Kingsbury, M., 2013. How to be happy on the Boardwalk. In: R. Greene and R. Robison Greene, eds. *Boardwalk Empire and philosophy: bootleg this book*. Chicago: Open Court Books.

Cawelti, J., 1979. *Adventure, mystery, and romance: formula stories as arts and popular culture*. Chicago: University of Chicago Press.

Charlier, J. M. and Marcilly, J., 1980. *Le Syndicat du Crime*. Montréal: Presses de la Cité.

Chase, D., 1999–2007. *The Sopranos*. HBO.

Corris, P., 1992. *Set up*. Australia: Pan.

DeFino, D., 2004. The prince of New Jersey. *Journal of Popular Film and Television*, 32:2, pp.83–89.

de Vries, M. F. R. K., 1985. The dark side of entrepreneurship. *Harvard Business Review*, November–December, pp.160–167.

Disher, G., 1994. *Cross kill*. St Leonards: Allen and Unwin.

Dyer, R., 1997. *White*. New York: Routledge.

Fields, I. W., 2004. Family values and feudal codes: the social politics of America's twenty-first century gangster. *The Journal of Popular Culture*, 37:4, pp.611-633

Fisher, L. D., 2013. A wrong decision is better than indecision: eight leadership lessons from Tony Soprano. *Business Review Weekly*, [online] 21 June. Available at http://www.brw.com.au/p/leadership/wrong_decision_soprano_better_than_DAC3O BI5Vqe5iV499qK1gK. Accessed 9 April 2015.

Forsyth, F., 1971. *The day of the jackal*. New York: Viking.

Gardaphe, F. L., 2010. Mafia stories and the American gangster. In: C.R. Nickerson, ed. *The Cambridge companion to American crime fiction*. Cambridge: Cambridge University Press.

Gill, M., 2001. The craft of robbers of cash-in-transit vans: crime facilitators and entrepreneurial approach. *International Journal of the Sociology of Law*, 29, pp.227–291.

Gilligan, V., 2008–2013. *Breaking Bad*. AMC.

Goadby, R., Carew, B. M., Jones, T. and Fielding, H., 1768. *An apology for the life of Mr. Bampfylde-Moore Carew: commonly called the king of the beggars*. London: J. Buckland, C. Bathurst, and T. Davies.

Gottschalk, P., 2010. Criminal entrepreneurial behaviour. *Journal of International Business and Entrepreneurship Development*, 5:1, pp.63–76.

Haut, W., 1999. *Neon noir: contemporary American crime fiction*. London: Serpents Tail.

Heath, C. and Tversky, A., 1991. Preference and belief: ambiguity and competence in choice under uncertainty. *Journal of Risk and Uncertainty*, 4, pp.5–28.

Highmore, B., 2005. *Cityscapes: cultural readings in the material and symbolic city*. New York: Palgrave Macmillan.

Horsley, L., 2005. *Twentieth century crime fiction*. New York: Oxford University Press.

Hudson, L., 2013. Die like a man: the toxic masculinity of Breaking Bad. *Wired*, [online] 10 June. Available at: http://www.wired.com/2013/10/breaking-bad-toxic-masculinity/. Accessed 9 April 2015.

Jayasingthe, K., Thomas, D. and Wickramasinghe, D., 2008. Bounded emotionality in entrepreneurship: an alternative framework. *International Journal of Entrepreneurial Behaviour and Research*, 14:4, pp.242-258.

Klockars, C., 1975. *The professional fence*. London: Tavistock.

Knight, S., 1997. *Continent of mystery: a thematic history of Australian crime fiction*. Victoria: Melbourne University Press.

Kohan, J., 2005–2012. *Weeds*. Showtime.

Kovvali, S., 2013. Breaking Bad's big critique of the macho (and its problem with women). *The Atlantic*, [online] 1 October. Available at: http://www.theatlantic.com/entertainment/archive/2013/10/-em-breaking-bad-em-s-big-critique-of-the-macho-and-its-problem-with-women/280171/. Accessed 9 April 2015.

Lavoie, D., 2011. Smoking the other: marijuana and counterhegemony in weeds. *Substance Use & Misuse*, 46:7, pp.910–921.

Leonard, E., 1989. *Killshot*. New York: Harper Collins.

Leonard, E., 1990. *Get shorty*. New York: Harper Collins.

Levy, M., 2007. Organised crime and terrorism. In: M. Maguire, R. Morgan and R. Reiner, eds. *The Oxford handbook of criminology*. Oxford, UK: Oxford University Press.

Mandel, E., 1984. *Delightful murder: a social history of the crime story*. London: Pluto Press.

Martel, M., (n.d.). How to run your business like Tony Soprano...not get whacked. *Business*, [online] Available at http://www.evancarmichael.com/Business-Coach/7008/How-to-Run-Your-Business-Like-Tony-Sopranonot-get-whacked.html. Accessed 9 April 2015.

Martin, B., 2013. *Difficult men*. New York: Faber and Faber.

McCarthy, C., 2005. *No country for old men*. New York: Vintage.

Mean Streets, 1973. [Film] Directed by M. Scorsese. USA: Warner Brothers.

Moore, L. D., 2006. *Cracking the hard-boiled detective: A critical history from the 1920s to the present*. North Carolina: McFarland & Company.

Morrison, J., 2011. *The global business environment*. New York: Palgrave Macmillan.

Nochimson, M. P., 2003. 'Waddaya lookin' at? Re-reading the gangster genre through 'The Sopranos'. *Film Quarterly*, 56:2, pp.2–13.

Puzo, M., 1969. *The godfather*. New York: Putnum.
Ruggiero, V., 1998. *Organised and corporate crime in Europe*. Aldershot: Dartmouth.
Ruth, D., 1996. *Inventing the public enemy: the gangster in America culture, 1918-1934*. Chicago: University of Chicago Press.
Scaggs, J., 2005. *Crime fiction*. London: Routledge.
Scarface, 1932. [Film] Directed by H. Hawkes. USA: United Artists.
Schneider, A., 2004. *Tony Soprano on management*. Los Angeles: Berkley Trade.
Shane, S. and Venkataraman, S., 2000. The promise of entrepreneurship as a field of research. *Academy of Management Review*, 25:1, pp.217–226.
Simon, D., 1998–2007. *The Sopranos*. HBO.
Simon, D., 2002–2008. *The Wire*. HBO.
Simon, D. R., 2002. *Tony Soprano's America: the criminal side of the American dream*. Oxford: Westview.
Temple, P., 1996. *Bad debts*. London: Quercus.
The Killing of a Chinese Bookie, 1976. [Film] Directed by J. Cassavetes. USA: Faces Distribution.
The Public Enemy, 1931. [Film] Directed by W. Wellman. USA: Warner Brothers.
Ventakaraman, S., 1997. The distinctive domain of entrepreneurship research. *Advances in Entrepreneurship, Firm Emergence and Growth*, 3, pp.119-138.
von Lampe, K., 2007. Criminals are not alone. Some observations on the social microcosm of illegal entrepreneurs. In: P. van Duyne, C. Majevic, A. Dijck, M. von Lampe and J. Harvey, eds. *Crime business and crime money in Europe. The dirty linen of illegal enterprise*. Nilmegen, The Netherlands: Wolf Legal Publishers. pp.131–156.
Williams, C. C., 2005. The undeclared sector, self employment and public policy. *International Journal of Entrepreneurial Behaviour and Research*, 11:4. pp.244-257.
Winter, T., 2010–2014. *Boardwalk Empire*. HBO.
Wynn, N. A., 2004. Counselling the Mafia: 'The Sopranos'. *Journal of American Studies*, 38, pp.127–132.

Notes

1. First appearing in 1977, the Bernie Rhodenbarr collection of novels and short stories is one of best-selling American novelist Lawrence Block's many crime fiction series. Block's other well-known works include the Matthew Scudder set of novels about a New York Private Investigator and a series featuring a contract killer named Keller.
2. Australian novelist and children's writer Garry Disher is one of the Australia's most popular crime novelists. The first of his main series features professional urban thief Wyatt. The second follows police detectives Challis and Destry in procedural thrillers based in a seaside resort town.

Chapter 7

Brand IKEA in a Global Cultural Economy: A Case Study

Susie Khamis

Abstract

This chapter considers the global marketing of IKEA, the world's largest furniture and furnishings retailer, and an icon of contemporary global capitalism. Known primarily for its accessible, Swedish design, IKEA benefits from both the growing appeal of urban, apartment living, for which its design strengths are suited, as well as positive consumer perceptions of Swedish products. This chapter considers how IKEA sustains its brand image across increasingly diverse markets, particularly in regions that are culturally dissimilar to its main sales base – Western Europe. At stake is how, through marketing, IKEA articulates its brand identity to specific consumer groups, in ways that spotlight the brand's core values. Since IKEA does not adapt its product range for different markets, these more local initiatives are telling insights into how IKEA's consumers differ – even though IKEA's product range does not. This, in turn, highlights the degree to which global brands maintain their commercial dominance without necessarily bending to local conditions or preferences and tempers a tendency in consumer culture theory (CCT) to understate the extent to which brands successfully deal with consumer diversity.

Keywords

IKEA, branding, Swedish design, globalisation, marketing

Introduction

Since 1943 IKEA has grown into a multinational retail behemoth. With over 330 stores in 38 countries, IKEA is the world's largest furniture and furnishings retailer. Central to its marketing is the notion of accessible Swedish style, with innovative and functional design at low- to mid-range price points. These are achieved through various cost efficiencies – most famously, flat-packing and self-assembly. As IKEA expands beyond Western Europe and North America though, and particularly in Middle Eastern and BRICs markets (Brazil, Russia, India and China), its operations have been tested. As IKEA enters regions that are culturally distinctive and/or politically volatile, certain challenges emerge. This chapter considers IKEA's marketing strategies within this context of global expansion, takes stock of how the brand benefits from specific contemporary phenomena, and identifies branding risks therein. By virtue of its size, scope and popularity, IKEA warrants such analysis: in the fiscal year 2010, in the middle of the global financial crisis, IKEA's sales grew by 7.7 per cent to 23.1 billion euros, and net profit increased by 6.1 per cent to 2.7 billion euros; 80 per cent of these sales were in crisis-hit Europe (Euromonitor International, 2011: 4). Moreover, while IKEA continues to dominate the furniture sector in Europe, its expansion around the world points to a certain consonance between consumer groups in key global markets, and conveys dominant trends in contemporary popular marketing.

The challenge for IKEA is to address diverse markets in terms that are locally attractive, yet stay true to the brand's core identity. To this end, IKEA's marketing rests on two distinct features. First is shrewd appraisal and exploitation of several global trends. Specifically, and around the world, there is the growing number of people for whom the IKEA style has both aesthetic and pragmatic appeal, for reasons to be detailed shortly. Second though, and despite its presence in such geographically and culturally disparate markets, IKEA products are identical around the world; there is little variation in the IKEA range, or indeed the IKEA 'experience'. As such, IKEA appears an ostensibly global brand – standardised, predictable and bereft of local nuance. However, while several constants permeate the entire IKEA system, there is evidence of local inflection. This appears in IKEA's various promotional materials in different markets. While this does not disavowal the uniformity of the IKEA product – the range is fixed, from Sydney to Seoul, Bangkok to Brussels – it sheds light on how a global brand contrives local relevance. The brand's core identity does not bend (affordable and practical Swedish design), but the way IKEA frames and delivers this message does.

In its modest concessions to local interests, agendas or conditions, IKEA's marketing problematises one of the most salient aspects of consumer culture theory (CTT): the degree to which consumers are so often cast (and over-represented) as empowered, self-actualising agents, free to decode marketing messages and appropriate consumer goods in ways that are unpredictable, autonomous and inspired (Arnould and Thompson, 2005; Thompson, Arnould and Giesler, 2013: 155). As seminal as this 'cultural turn' in consumer research has been over the last twenty years (Fitchett, Patsiaouras and Davies, 2014: 501) the IKEA case study implies a 'catching up' on the part of big business, insofar as diversity and difference in the global cultural economy is absorbed into the marketing arsenal and reconfigured as a postmodern branding resource.

Origins and Expansion: From Sweden to the World

The name IKEA is based on the initials of the company's founder, Ingvar Kampred (born 1926), and those of the small farm village in Sweden where he grew up: Elmtaryd, Agunnaryd. Kampred displayed entrepreneurial skill from a young age, and rode his bicycle to houses in his village selling matches, fish, pencils and Christmas-tree decorations. In 1943, with a cash gift from his father, Kampred created IKEA. Initially selling small items like pens, picture frames and nylon stockings, Kampred was drawn to the work of mid-century design luminaries like Charles Eames, Arne Jacobsen and Russel Wright (Sculley, 2004: 16) – hence IKEA's move into furniture in 1948. Relying on manufacturers in forests close to his home, Kampred was able to keep the prices relatively low so that, by 1951, and in the brand's first catalogue, IKEA was selling just furniture. In 1953 Kampred opened the company's first showroom in Älmhult; in 1958 this became the site of the first store. At 6700 square feet, it was the largest furniture display in Scandinavia, and a hint of the 'big box' approach that would eventually characterise every IKEA store around the world.

According to Jonsson and Foss, the global expansion of IKEA is marked by three distinct phases (Jonsson and Foss, 2011: 1085–89). First was a period of 'explorative internationalisation' and 'trial & error' as various markets were tested between 1963 and the late 1970s. The second, between 1980 and the mid-1990s, was one of 'rigid replication', or 'exploitative internationalisation'. The third, since the mid-1990s, has been one of 'flexible replication'. This chapter is most concerned with this most recent phase. On the one hand, the 'flexibility' Jonsson and Foss identify acknowledges the pragmatics of multinational commerce, whereby staff in headquarters must liaise with counterparts and affiliates around the world and tiptoe around massive operational differences (legally, politically and so on). However, the 'flexibility' required at this logistical or bureaucratic level is a given, even in a post-GATT context. Less certain is 'flexibility' of product, or material adjustments for local preferences.

This inquiry surfaces when one considers IKEA's most recent forays into culturally distinctive regions. In terms of retail value, Western Europe remains IKEA's main region, and most of its sales (69 per cent) are there (Euromonitor International, 2011: 11). However, its expansion into the Middle East, Eastern Europe, China, India, North America and Latin America raises pertinent and pressing questions. Specifically: to what extent does IKEA integrate differences in local customs, climates and living arrangements into its design process? Put simply, for almost five decades, IKEA's international expansion has involved the repetition of a format; there is a degree of local responsiveness to different conditions, but this manifests in mostly marketing, operational and/or managerial terms. The hallmarks of the IKEA brand, and in particular the premium placed on Scandinavian design at accessible prices, remain. For this reason, IKEA seems impervious to the sorts of pressures placed on other global brands, whereby local responsiveness entails some manipulation or amendment to the actual product: IKEA's range actually varies little across diverse regions. On the one hand, this reflects the general market appeal of Scandinavian design, as well as specific global trends that IKEA benefits from; on the other, it underscores pressures to maximise economies of scale and maintain the price-point advantage for which IKEA is famous. In this way, IKEA tests both the cultural and commercial logics of 'glocalisation' (Robertson, 1995), the process whereby globally distributed commodities are adapted for local markets.

Scandinavian Design

Central to the IKEA brand is the value of Scandinavian design – a concept based on real consumer perceptions. Ana Roncha found consumers regard Nordic (Scandinavian) brands like Bang & Olufsen, Voss and Lego as symbolic of good design, functionality and superior quality. Focusing specifically on H&M, BoConcept and IKEA, she identified a long-term association between the Scandinavian region and particular connotations that have translated favourably in retail terms. Roncha dates this phenomenon from the 1950s to the 1970s, when Scandinavian design was distinguished at world fairs and expos by an aesthetic of purity, simplicity and democratic principles (Roncha, 2008: 23–25). In the early twenty-first century, this image has hardened and strengthened – Scandinavian design is widely seen as modern, ergonomic and innovative, with efficient use of natural, appropriate materials.

IKEA not only benefits from the favourable associations of Scandinavian design, but makes its Swedish origin a key part of its marketing. This surfaces at almost every point of contact between IKEA and its customers. It also informs the set of 100 core practices – what IKEA terms 'proven solutions' – to which every store must strictly adhere. For instance, the blue and yellow of the Swedish national flag are used for the IKEA brand. This is seen most clearly in shop signage (unchanged since the mid-1970s) and the store's shopping bags. The entire IKEA range of furniture and furnishings is designed in-house, and most often by Scandinavian designers, a point stressed by product names that are almost always in a Scandinavian language. These are showcased on a shop floor that must include four living-room styles: 'Scandinavian', 'Country', 'Modern' and 'Young Swedish'. In turn, traffic flow is orchestrated to encourage customers to view IKEA products in these idealised settings. All stores also have a restaurant with virtually the same menu of traditional Swedish food, most famously Swedish meatballs. On the basis of this alone, IKEA is now Sweden's second largest food exporter. So, and at almost every stage, the IKEA brand is overlaid with Swedish identity. One visitor to the 43,000-square metre IKEA store in Beijing even said: 'It makes you feel like you're abroad', while another, a 22 year-old student, added: 'I'm still living in a dorm, but I want my future home to look like this' (quoted in Euromonitor International, 2010: n.p.). In 2009, a theatre company in Hamburg even staged an opera in honour of IKEA called 'Wunder von Schweden' ('Miracle from Sweden'), a biography of the 'furniture messiah' – founder Ingvar Kampred – set to Swedish folk tunes. As it happens, Germany is IKEA's strongest market and accounts for 15 per cent of sales (*The Economist*, 2011: 67).

Global Presence

As the prevalence, salience and market dominance of IKEA beyond European markets grows, the brand is a symbolic icon of global commerce. In 2009 the business news agency Bloomberg introduced the 'IKEA Index'. Following the logic of the 'Big Mac Index', created by *The Economist* magazine in 1986, the 'IKEA Index' measures the purchasing power of consumers around the world (or at least those countries where IKEA is sold) by comparing what they pay for IKEA's Billy bookcase: specifically, the white, flat-packed model that is 80cm by 202cm. It is a staple of the IKEA range for 30 years, with over 41 million units sold; here the Billy bookcase becomes a barometer of local currency strengths and exchange rates (Sorensen, 2011: 44). If nothing else, this says more about the global presence of the IKEA brand than the design merits of the bookcase: as ubiquitous as the McDonald's Big Mac, it speaks to both the expansionary impulse of the IKEA brand, and the commercial logic of a generic product.

The fact that a similarly conceived 'Big Mac Index' preceded the 'IKEA Index' is telling. Few brands represent contemporary capitalism as emphatically as McDonalds, at least in terms of popular culture, or indeed academic literature. In his seminal work *The McDonaldization of Society* (1993), George Ritzer made a compelling case that McDonalds, as the archetypal global brand, embodies and enacts the dynamics of a thoroughly rationalised society. For Ritzer, a 'McDonaldized' society aims for streamlined management. It prioritises efficiency, calculability, predictability and control, but produces systems (from fast-food and fashion to education and health care) that are increasingly disconnected from human agency, endeavour and emotion. Ritzer highlights the irrationality of these 'rational' systems: in the quest for order, they override the individual. While Ritzer's thesis critiqued not just one brand but also a widespread drift towards a particular style of management, McDonald's remains a convenient point of reference. With worldwide recognition of its 'Golden Arches', McDonald's is one of several brands that seemingly enjoy global dominance, and have triumphed on the rational/irrational terms described by Ritzer: KFC, Starbucks, Coca-Cola and so on.

As the world's most dominant brand of furniture and furnishings, IKEA is as emblematic of a homogenised, pre-fabricated society as McDonald's. In David Fincher's *Fight Club* (1999), for example, the unnamed, disaffected protagonist, played by Edward Norton, walks through an apartment furnished almost entirely with IKEA items. The apartment, a facsimile of the IKEA catalogue, is the stylistic expression of his inner emptiness; the subtext is that the IKEA experience only succeeds in folding consumers into an unvarying, uninspiring identikit. At stake here then is the globalisation of this IKEA system – and what it reveals about both IKEA's operations and consumers around the world. What emerges is a brand that exhibits the cultural geometry of global corporatism: loyal to a narrow set of practices and products, but also affected by differences between various consumer markets. Not unlike other global brands then, IKEA has had to negotiate these differences.

Dealing with Difference

As IKEA expands into more markets, its negotiation of either atypical or idiosyncratic conditions surfaces on three levels: its dealings with managerial and/or operational differences; through an image of 'global eclecticism' that celebrates the cultural diversity of its 'IKEA Family'; and through marketing initiatives in specific countries, especially television commercials (TVCs). As it will be shown, these three factors are highly interrelated.

The first point to note is IKEA's engagement with boardroom bulwarks, whereby potentially problematic laws, technicalities or 'backdoor' practices are resolved. In June 2012, for instance, IKEA finally announced a 600 million-euro investment in India, after several years of frustrated attempts to deal with the nation's foreign investment laws. For IKEA, this investment rests on plans to open 25 of its stores and double the share of global supplies sourced to India to $1 billion. While this was due to some liberalisation of India's rules around direct foreign investment in retail, IKEA also pledged to honour an agreement that 30 per cent of its supplies would be sourced locally, but added that this would be difficult in the long term. Such legal manoeuvring is not just a matter of compliance but is also a function of public image. In 2010, the IKEA Group sacked two senior executives in Russia. Having campaigned against corruption and even frozen investments there at one point to protest against poor governance, IKEA was embarrassed to find these executives had ignored bribes that were paid by a subcontractor to secure electricity supplies for IKEA's stores in St Petersburg (Osipovich, 2010: 159–160). At the very least, IKEA's experiences in India and Russia speak to the lingering gaps in the rhetoric of free trade: 'open' markets are not uniform markets.

The literature and research around brand 'glocalisation' tends to focus less on these behind-the-scenes dealings than on how a brand presents to the buying public, and the extent to which it adapts or bends to different consumers.

To return to McDonald's, for example: notwithstanding Ritzer's devastating critique, there is also evidence that global brands cannot ignore cultural nuance around the world. Indeed, and not to overstate the dent this has made to its operations overall, it is worth noting differences in the McDonald's menu across the globe. There are, for instance, vegetarian burgers in India, kosher restaurants in Israel, grilled McLaks (salmon burgers) in Norway, sweet red-bean pies in Hong Kong and beer in Germany – and this is an abridged list. The point is, local dietary preferences and/or requirements are acknowledged and accommodated. While there is a business imperative here as much as a public relations one, it nonetheless sees cultural diversity converted into (modest) product diversity.

For IKEA, with furniture and décor its core products, forays into dissimilar cultural markets also offer opportunities to adapt. In terms of dress, it is possible that an IKEA customer that predominantly wears the hijab or burqua has different wardrobe requirements than one that wears mostly suits or jeans; in terms of climatic differences, it makes sense that consumers in some regions would have greater need for outdoor furniture than others. However, such differences are not factored into the IKEA design process at all. Rather, over the past decade, and as IKEA stores spread globally, the number of IKEA products has actually decreased to around 9500, mostly ready-to-assemble furniture pieces. It is IKEA policy that *every* store must carry the core product range (such as the Billy bookcase). Beyond that, local store managers can, at their discretion, select other pieces from the overall product range – which is very different to adapting the product range to local markets, since the actual product range remains unchanged.

Global Eclecticism

Ironically, and in place of product differentiation, IKEA projects an image of 'global eclecticism' – which is sustained more by emerging similarities around the world than differences. That is, and insofar as the IKEA brand complements a certain mindset and milieu, it is aided by contemporary global trends in housing and lifestyle. IKEA's specialty – fashionable, affordable, self-assembled pieces – is widely associated with urban, apartment living, and the people that gravitate towards this: students, young professionals and small-unit households (either singles or couples). Over the past decade, these groups have grown around the world, even in emerging and BRICs markets (Euromonitor International, 2008a: 1–9). In particular, there are a burgeoning number of consumers that live alone or with a partner, and a growing number that converge in urban centres – both of which opt for relatively small apartments rather than houses.

Both phenomena are fuelled by complex and long-term factors that exceed the scope of this chapter, but it will suffice to note two explanations. One is the growing acceptability of divorce, and the tendencies to either avoid or delay marriage (especially for women, which has implications for young children); the other is the growing appeal of and fashion for apartment city living, glamorised in international television hits such as *Seinfeld*, *Friends* and *Sex and the City*. These television exports (all from the United States, with New York settings) are not credited with this trend, but they capture the ostensible freedom and individualism of cosmopolitan life in an atomised society (Euromonitor International, 2008b).

This trend is most apparent in the United States, IKEA's second largest market. There, between 2000 and 2010, the nation's 366 metropolitan areas absorbed 92.4 per cent of all population growth, and 84 per cent of these chose to live in or close to a city of 50,000 people or more (Morrison, 2011: 32). Moreover, according to IKEA, these 'millennials' are often cost-conscious, style-conscious and environment-conscious. While *Fight Club* put a dystopian spin on this scene, it remains highly attractive, especially for young people. In the 2009 romantic-comedy film *500 Days of Summer* by Marc Webb, young lovers Tom and Summer (Joseph Gordon-Levitt and Zooey Deschanel, respectively) play a 'happy married couple' routine while shopping at IKEA. The routine is knowingly ironic – Summer is the flighty anti-wife – but the setting is not. IKEA suits this couple, aesthetically, pragmatically and (for Summer at least) philosophically.

The ascent of this ideal, particularly beyond Europe, works to IKEA's benefit. Much of its globally distributed promotional material pictures young, fashionable people in chic, fashionable apartments. This is seen most clearly in its two main print publications:

the annual IKEA catalogue (which accounts for 20 per cent of the annual marketing budget and is published in 27 languages) and 'IKEA Family Live' (hereafter referred to as 'Live'), the quarterly magazine for members of the 'IKEA Family' (the store's loyalty-card programme), which is printed in thirteen languages. The catalogue showcases the core product range, including any new additions, with prices, dimensions and styling suggestions. 'Live' is more akin to a conventional lifestyle magazine, and features interviews with IKEA consumers from around the world. They relay not only their tastes in furniture and décor, but also more personal details – such as their travels, relationships, hobbies and ambitions. The magazine presents an idealised collage of IKEA's international clientele, and thus contrives an image of global eclecticism: despite the variety of people spotlighted in 'Live', by virtue of its breadth the IKEA range suffices in meeting their décor needs.

In the Winter 2012 issue of 'Live', IKEA presents a highly attractive montage, with families in different regions, at different stages of life, creating beautiful homes in seemingly unique ways. They populate an idealised, postmodern world, of 'blended' families, fashionable philosophies and rakish style. Here, the IKEA tableau is inclusive and accommodating. Take Hanne for instance: she grew up in Norway, but now lives in Italy with her new partner and two sons. Describing her journey from 'house to home', she says:

> I find comfort in change – in being able to adapt and grow. The break-up of my marriage taught me this. I thought that the two of us would be here together forever. But over a lifetime you change, and that's normal. Where I am now is a good place. I run my own business, have gorgeous kids, a home we're always happy to come back to and a new man in my life.
>
> ('IKEA Family Live', 2012: 9)

There is also Frank and Olivia, who live in Berlin with their two-year old daughter Matilda. Of their 'journey', Frank says:

> It would be silly to say having a child doesn't change your life! But we didn't really give up anything for Matilda … We've realized that when you live in a grand old apartment like this, you can't be afraid to change it to fit your lifestyle and your personality. We both love changing things around, so who knows what this place will look like in a year's time!
>
> ('IKEA Family Live', 2012: 27)

In Tokyo, 'Live' finds Shin, Hal and Meg. Shin says:

> When we bought this place it was a typical Japanese three-bedroom apartment, with a very narrow entrance, small rooms and ceilings. I didn't like the idea of fitting our lives into an existing home, so we decided to create an empty box that we could fit with the things we love.
>
> ('IKEA Family Live', 2012: 49)

In 'Live' then, IKEA becomes a conduit for personal expression, signposting seminal lifestyle shifts – both individual and collective. Swedish couple Mikael and Mia is a case in point. Mia says:

> Mikael and I exchanged a thousand messages online before we actually met – we shared so many stories it was like we were old friends … When we decided to buy an apartment in Stockholm a year and a half later, we both knew we wanted somewhere old, somewhere with a story of its own. I think everything becomes more interesting when it ages. Even people.
>
> ('IKEA Family Live', 2012: 57)

In these vignettes, the IKEA brand does not so much ignore differences as celebrate them: the message appears that, for all the diversity, the IKEA range/system/experience meets consumers' needs. The premise is highly ambitious, even paradoxical: such is the brand's investment in 'Swedish design', a fixed product range is deemed sufficient for a growing clientele. As noted, several global trends bespeak a similarity of taste and need among key consumer demographics around the world. Insofar as key trends play to IKEA's strengths in décor and furniture (affordable and fashionable), IKEA's strategy makes sense. However, these similarities do not cancel out important cultural differences. In turn, IKEA is not immune from the fraught politics of micro-regions, nor is it oblivious to local sensitivities.

Prior to the opening of the first IKEA store in Israel in 2001, Israeli media was abuzz with news that IKEA had already opened stores in Kuwait, Saudi Arabia and the United Arab Emirates. Conservative Israeli commentators read IKEA's belated entry into Israel as proof that IKEA was implicitly anti-Israel – despite IKEA's public relations at the time boasting that the store in Netanya would be bigger than any other IKEA store in the Middle East. Despite the pre-launch anxiety, IKEA Israel was an immediate success (Ochs, 2011: 131–132). Moreover, while the IKEA furniture and décor products in Israel make no concession to Jewish festivities or rituals, there is one major difference. After a devastating fire at the store last year, IKEA Netanya reopened with an IKEA-first: a fully kosher kitchen for the IKEA restaurant. The Swedish meatballs are still on the menu – always at around $5 for the medium size, what IKEA calls 'part of the IKEA experience' (Mangla, 2008: 136) – but all food preparation is consistent with traditional kosher requirements. A decade after its launch, IKEA became Israel's leading furniture brand, with an 8 per cent share of value sales (Euromonitor International, 2012a).

Targeted Marketing: TVCs

For IKEA, pricing remains the most expedient way to unite seemingly disparate consumers. In most capitalist societies, fashionable products at relatively low prices are broadly attractive. This is IKEA's key proposition, hence its prominence in the brand's marketing, especially its TVCs around the world. These are the most obvious examples of brand differentiation, whereby IKEA frames marketing in terms consistent with specific cultural contexts. In 2010 for instance, IKEA Austria released a TVC that reflected the liberal sexual politics of Western Europe (and in the wake of a similarly inspired TVC for McDonald's France). It featured the passionate tryst of an attractive young couple in a chic, IKEA-styled apartment. Their secret rendezvous is halted though by the unexpected arrival of 'the boyfriend' – who shares the apartment with the amorous male (named Florian). As the woman hides in the kitchen cupboard, Florian enjoys wine with the unsuspecting cuckold and the voice-over says: 'Florian has things to hide. IKEA has solutions'. While this connects to a larger discourse of the lucrative 'gay dollar' (Miller, 2005: 15), here IKEA also pivots on a perceived affinity between its inclusive, egalitarian ethos, and the progressive politics of sexual freedom – an assumption that is commercially safe in the context of Austrian television. This can be contrasted with a TVC IKEA devised for Saudi Arabia in 2010. It sees two cars approach a traffic light, one with a middle-aged couple in traditional Islamic dress, the other with four young men in modern Western style clothing. The two drivers eye each other with barely concealed suspicion, but relax when they see the other's rooftop: both sport an identical IKEA couch – the 'Klippan' model. Here, IKEA papers over a potential clash in Saudi culture, between traditional mores and modern tendencies, with the unifying appeal of low-priced furniture. Clearly, the two TVCs, in Austria and Saudi Arabia, are not interchangeable, since they speak to very different worldviews. Like IKEA shoppers in Austria though, Saudis are attracted to the overall IKEA 'experience' (Euromonitor International, 2012b).

Despite these examples, there is a limit to just how much IKEA can acknowledge local custom without upsetting its brand identity. In the 2012 Saudi Arabian edition of the IKEA catalogue, women were completely airbrushed out of all imagery. In the traditional Islamic state, women rarely appear in advertisements, and almost never in anything other than modest Islamic dress (such as burqua or abaya). In this instance though, IKEA was widely criticised for the cultural compromise. According to Sweden's Equality minister, Nyamko Sabuni, IKEA was – despite its private company status – a cultural ambassador for Sweden, and as such was wrong to 'remove an important part of Sweden's image and an important part of its values in a country that more than any other needs to know about IKEA's principles and values' (quoted in Quinn, 2012: n.p.). In response, the IKEA Group, which had produced the catalogue for a Saudi franchisee, concurred: 'We are now reviewing our routines to safeguard a correct content presentation from a values point-of-view in the different versions of the IKEA catalogue worldwide' (Quinn, 2012: n.p.). For globally marketed brands, casting an address to consumers too broadly risks courting charges of hypocrisy, when the brand's 'content presentation' in one market undermines or ignores its 'content presentation' in another.

Conclusion

From Sweden to Saudi Arabia, the IKEA brand must meet the cultural diversity of patrons that span 38 countries. As IKEA's customer base diversifies then, so too have the service needs and expectations of these customers. To this end, IKEA has practical mechanisms to manage. It has, for instance, developed an automated customer service representative named Anna. Anna retrieves relevant information from the IKEA website, in response to specific online enquiries, and as Johnson and Selnes explain: 'Anna helps IKEA to manage an increasingly heterogeneous portfolio of customers in a cost-effective fashion that is consistent with its strategy' (Johnson and Selnes, 2005: 14). However, this acknowledgement of consumer diversity does not manifest in terms of product design: IKEA's product range has actually narrowed. Instead, IKEA wraps its core brand value – Swedish design at affordable prices – around various lifestyle settings. IKEA does not bend for local markets; rather, local markets find in IKEA the tools for fashionable, affordable living. This, in turn, plays to another strategy that IKEA has folded into the marketing in recent years: growing recognition of how consumers adapt IKEA products through their own stylistic twists. In 2009 for instance, to commemorate the 30th anniversary of the Billy bookcase, IKEA Germany invited Billy owners to submit pictures of their bookcases to a specially created website; IKEA created the final TVC from over 1000 pictures uploaded. Similarly, 'Live' magazine regularly shows how customers have personalised IKEA pieces. Quite explicitly then, the use of consumers' bricolage here becomes a form of 'unpaid labour' that contributes to IKEA's brand value: IKEA constructs a branded community that sustains and strengthens its image and appeal (Arvidsson, 2005: 247).

Growing emphasis on the versatility of the IKEA product, as something that can be upgraded through savvy appropriation, helps endear the brand to more consumer groups. Particularly in the United States, marketing has focused on how IKEA is not just for the young or thrifty, but also for older and more affluent consumers. In 2010, IKEA's tagline there became 'The Life Improvement Store', which launched a series of TVCs called 'Made by'. Each TVC showed people customising their homes with IKEA furniture and accessories, and ended with a line (like) 'Made by the Johnsons, Designed by IKEA' – with the focus on the family's personal touches (Vega, 2010: 6). Services were added (including a pick-up and delivery service, and extended warranties), ranges were extended (with 'premium' $500 rugs available as well as $5 ones) and user-generated photo sites like Share Space became popular ways US consumers showed how they use IKEA in their homes. In the United States, these initiatives have shifted perceptions that IKEA is not for 'grown-ups', with surveys indicating growing trust in the brand's quality (Zmuda, 2011: 14). Small adjustments in the home – such as a new vase or coffee table – are pitched as low-risk 'pick-me-ups'. This message was delivered with ironic aplomb in an award-winning TVC in 2002 for IKEA US, directed by Spike Jonze. In it, an old reading lamp is relegated to the curb for garbage collection, as its former owner is seen using her brand new IKEA replacement. The TVC ends with this piece to camera, in a Swedish accent: 'Many of you feel bad for this lamp. That is because you're crazy. It has no feelings. And the new one is much better'. Here, a new lamp transforms both the apartment and its owner – and IKEA trades (almost unfashionably) on this tenet of modernist faith (Sayeau, 2009: 494).

In terms of showcasing both the risks and rewards of global marketing, IKEA makes a compelling contribution to CCT: given CCT's over-identification with the self-directed, self-aware sovereign consumer, it would seem that a globally distributed product (like IKEA) would inspire more, not less, cultural differentiation, as diverse consumer groups author their own uses of the goods. Instead, IKEA advances an image of relevance and authenticity that transcends (and then flattens out) consumer difference. IKEA eschews the paternalistic overtone of twentieth-century marketing and champions the postmodern branding paradigm described by Douglas B. Holt, which 'is premised upon the idea that brands will be more valuable if they are offered not as cultural blueprints but as cultural resources, as useful ingredients to produce the self as one chooses' (Holt, 2002: 83). Certainly, early CCT research was vital to highlight the cultural dimensions of consumption (Askegaard and Linnet, 2011: 383), and seize some discursive recognition for what remains a marginal space in more business-oriented consumer research (Askegaard and Scott, 2013: 145). Nonetheless, case studies such as this one underscore the market's amazing capacity to deal with consumer resistance and opposition (not to mention diversity) in commercially successful ways (Cova, Maclaran and Bradshaw, 2013: 216).

The IKEA brand therefore offers enough latitude for myriad marketing imperatives, in ways that conflate economic efficiency with other interests and considerations. Even the brand's signature reliance on flat-packed furniture, for example, has been reconfigured as environmentally sensible: when the three-seat 'Ektorp' sofa was 'repacked' in 2010, IKEA boasted that not only had it doubled the amount of sofa that could be crammed into a given space, and lowered the purchase price, but that it had also significantly reduced the carbon-emissions required for its transport. For IKEA, then, the growing attractiveness of a particular lifestyle – urban-oriented, fashionable and increasingly atomised – becomes the optimum template for its own design strengths. Insofar as different markets require different modes of address, IKEA modifies the marketing approach – but not the core message: stylish products at affordable prices. In this way, IKEA's global presence is assured but – as the fallout from the Saudis' censored catalogue shows – not entirely unproblematic. As such, and while the catalogue remains the most famous aspect of IKEA's marketing, its smaller-scale initiatives in specific countries (especially TVCs) reveal its more nuanced and arguably more effective means by which consumer diversity is dealt with. This in turn relays the cultural logic of branding, as the TVCs convey the particularities of IKEA's target markets in ways that cannot be gleaned from any product differentiation – since the latter does not exist.

References

Arnould, E. J. and Thompson, C. J., 2005. Consumer culture theory (CCT): twenty years of research. *Journal of Consumer Research*, 31:4, pp.868-882.

Arvidsson, A., 2005. Brands: a critical perspective. *Journal of Consumer Culture*, 5:2, pp.235-258.

Askegaard, S. and Linnet, J. P., 2011. Towards an epistemology of consumer culture theory: phenomenology and the context of context. *Marketing Theory*, 11:4, pp.381-404.

Askegaard, S. and Scott, L., 2013. Consumer culture theory: the ironies of history. *Marketing Theory*, 13:2, pp.139-147.

Cova, B., Maclaran, P. and Bradshaw, A., 2013. Rethinking consumer culture theory from the postmodern to the communist horizon. *Marketing Theory*, 13:2, pp.213-225.

Euromonitor International, 2008a. *Single living: how atomisation – the rise of singles and one-person households – is affecting consumer purchasing habits.* [Strategy Briefing] Available at: www.warc.com. Accessed 10 June 2012.

Euromonitor International, 2008b. *From "taxi driver" to "sex and the city": urban living's chic makeover and its implications for consumer demand.* Available at: www.warc.com. Accessed 15 June 2012.

Euromonitor International, 2010. *Buying into the experience: why are savvy brands enriching the purchasing feeling for their consumers?* Available at: www.warc.com. Accessed 15 June 2012.

Euromonitor International, 2011. *Inter IKEA systems BV in retailing (world)*, June. Available at: www.warc.com. Accessed 12 June 2012.

Euromonitor International, 2012a. *Furniture and furnishings stores in Israel.* Available at: www.warc.com. Accessed 12 June 2012.

Euromonitor International, 2012b. *Furniture and furnishings stores in Saudi Arabia.* Available at: www.warc.com. Accessed 12 June 2012.

Fitchett, J. A., Patsiaouras, G. and Davies, A., 2014. Myth and ideology in consumer culture theory. *Marketing Theory*, 14:4, pp.495-506.

Holt, D. B., 2002. Why do brands cause trouble? A dialectical theory of consumer culture and branding. *Journal of Consumer Research*, 29, pp.70-90.

Johnson, M. D. and Selnes, F., 2005. Diversifying your customer portfolio. *MIT Sloan Management Review*, Spring, pp.11-14.

Jonsson, A. and Foss, N. J., 2011. International expansion through flexible replication: learning from the internationalization experience of IKEA. *Journal of International Business Studies*, 42, pp.1079-1102.

Mangla, I. S., 2008. An IKEA field guide. *Money*, 7:8, pp.136-137.

Miller, T., 2005. A metrosexual eye on queer guy. *GLQ: A Journal of Lesbian and Gay Studies*, 11:1, pp.112-117.

Morrison, M., 2011. Living for the city: what "urban boom" means for marketers. *Advertising Age*, 82:37, p.32.

Ochs, J., 2011. *Security and suspicion: an ethnography of everyday life in Israel*. Philadelphia: University of Pennsylvania Press.

Osipovich, A., 2010. Bed, bath & bribes. *Foreign Policy*, September-October, pp.159-160.

Quinn, B., 2012. Ikea apologises over removal of women from Saudi Arabia catalogue. *The Guardian*, [online] 2 October. Available at: http://www.guardian.co.uk/world/2012/oct/02/ikea-apologises-removing-women-saudi-arabia-catalogue. Accessed 3 January 2013.

Ritzer, G., 1993. *The McDonaldization of society: an investigation into the changing character of contemporary social life*. London: SAGE Publications

Robertson, R., 1995. Glocalization: time-space and homogeneity-heterogeneity. In: M. Featherstone, S. Lash and R. Robertson, eds. 1995. *Global modernities*. London: SAGE Publications, pp.25-44.

Roncha, A., 2008. Nordic brands towards a design-oriented concept. *Brand Management*, 16:1-2), pp.21-29.

Sayeau, M., 2009. IKEA modernism and the perils of innovation. *Modernism/modernity*, 16:3, pp.493-495.

Sculley, J., 2004. 'IKEA' *Time* [Style/Design Supplement], Summer, 163, pp.16-17.

Sorensen, C., 2011. Swedish for recession. *Maclean's*, 124:38, p.44.

The Economist, 2011. The secret of IKEA's success, 398:8722, pp.67-68.

Thompson, C. J., Arnould, E. and Giesler, M., 2013. Discursivity, difference and disruption: genealogical reflections on the consumer cultural theory heteroglossia. *Marketing Theory*, 13:2, pp.149-174.

Vega, T., 2010. A focus on families (and furniture), *New York Times*, 13 September. p.6.

Zmuda, N., 2011. For IKEA, it's time to overhaul perceptions. *Advertising Age*, 82:43, p.14.

Chapter 8

The 'Good' Corporation: The Uneasy Relationship Between Reputation and Responsibility

Robert Crocker

Abstract

Like modern branding, corporate PR was first professionalised in 1920s America, out of a need for credible positive narratives that could speak to the values, beliefs and expectations of ordinary Americans, and turn often large and previously rapacious conglomerates into corporate 'good citizens', with a positive role to play in building a 'better future'. Advertising, all forms of design and large staged events, like Expos and World Fairs, were marshalled to serve the ends of these campaigns. Widely adopted after World War II by leading European corporate giants, this style of corporate image-making has continued to shape the marketing and branding strategies of many large enterprises today.

The concept and metrics of corporate social and environmental responsibility were originally developed by leading consumer rights groups and environmental NGOs eager to hold this kind of corporate image-making to account. 'CSR' and 'sustainability reporting' have, in turn, become important vehicles for corporate marketing to present 'evidence' for a more credible 'cultural' narrative of corporate good citizenship. This chapter argues that 'sustainability reporting' has become an increasingly challenging field for many companies struggling to control the narrative of their own image, and can expose them to cynicism and anger when they seem to fail the standards set by their published commitments.

Keywords

corporate social responsibility (CSR), environmental reporting, ethics, branding, marketing, public relations (PR), sustainability

Introduction

Like modern advertising and marketing, public relations (PR) was first professionalised in 1920s America, out of a need for credible positive narratives that could speak to the values, beliefs and expectations of ordinary Americans and turn once rapacious conglomerates into corporate 'good citizens'. Advertising and design, including large staged events and elaborate stands at Expos and World Fairs, were marshalled to serve the ends of these campaigns, which presented a narrative of a new world of corporation-led social and technological improvements. Widely adopted after World War II (WWII) by leading European corporations, this style of image-making continues to shape the branding strategies of many large enterprises today.

This chapter argues that because PR early developed an ethical persona for the corporation, corporate social responsibility (CSR), along with environmental reporting, came to be seen as expected outcomes of responsible corporate management. However, the financial obligations of corporations to their shareholders created ambiguity about this assumed social and environmental responsibility. While the financial value attributed to corporate reputation has led to an assumption that CSR and environmental reporting are 'good for business', fear of reputation loss, rather than the profit motive, has driven more and more corporations to take up and value CSR and sustainability reporting. Greater sustainability and social responsibility are thus the results of a cultural change, a progressive ramp towards higher social and environmental standards. This has been led by rising consumer expectations and corporate anxieties to avoid the public shame of failing to live up to these expectations. This process of 'ethicalisation' is reinforced by the idealised narratives of corporate branding, which make conformity to consumers' ethical expectations seem a necessary attribute of corporate identity.

The Rise of the Consumer Citizen

> The milkman waters milk for me; there's garlic in my butter,
> But I'm only a consumer, and it does no good to mutter;
> I know that coal is going up and beef is getting higher,
> But I'm only a consumer, and I have no need of fire;
> While beefsteak is a luxury that wealth alone is needing,
> I'm only a consumer, and what need have I for feeding?
> My business is to pay the bill and keep in a good humor,
> And it really doesn't matter, since I'm only a consumer.
>
> The grocer sells me addled eggs; the tailor sells me shoddy,
> I'm only a consumer, and I am not anybody.
> The cobbler pegs me paper soles, the dairyman short-weights me,
> I'm only a consumer, and most everybody hates me.
> There's turnip in my pumpkin pie and ashes in my pepper,
> The world's my lazaretto, and I'm nothing but a leper;
> So lay me in my lonely grave and tread the turf down flatter.
> I'm only a consumer, and it really doesn't matter.
>
> (Waterman, 1911: 97)

Systems of mass manufacture, modern transportation and logistics, and large-scale department and chain store retail, became increasingly integrated in America and western Europe at the start of the twentieth century. Supported by more graphic forms of printed advertising and promotion, these new systems of provision framed, enabled and encouraged mass participation in the development of a 'consumer society' (Hilton, 2007; Smart, 2010). At this time the consumer's access to goods and services became a political and economic issue, because participation in an increasingly urbanised society depended upon the attainment of at least a 'living wage' with which to buy the necessities of life (Hilton, 2009; Trentmann, 2011). As Nixon Waterman's humorous poem from this period suggests, the word 'consumerism' was early tied to the image of the consumer as a perpetual victim of unscrupulous shopkeepers and tradesmen. In fact, the word 'consumerism' was first commonly used as a summary description of the consumer's political and economic interests. The interests of the consumer required a 'living wage', a decent standard of living and access to goods and services that were reasonably priced, unadulterated and not grossly misrepresented: thus consumerism was at first the ideology driving various campaigns for this social and economic goal (Hilton, 2009).

While it can be argued that the 'consumer citizen' had already emerged in late nineteenth-century Europe and America, the explicit use of this term, and the association of citizenship with consumption can be traced more directly to the first decades of the twentieth century in America, as this was the largest open and unified market in the world at the time. This market combined constitutional democracy, mass readership (and a little later mass commercial radio audiences), along with increasingly large industrial conglomerates, all of which led to the early 'professionalisation' of those assisting with the management, production, design, promotion and sale of mass-produced industrial goods and services (Laird, 1998; Marchand, 1998; McGovern, 2006). The emergence of the concept of the 'consumer citizen' was a direct result of these changes (Cohen, 2004: 112–120; McGovern, 2006; Schwarzkopf, 2011). For example, one advertising agent wrote of the extraordinary power of radio to shape consumer opinion across America in the early 1920s: 'In a democracy, public opinion is the uncrowned king. It is the advertising agency's business to write the speeches from the throne of that king' (cited in Schwarzkopf, 2011: 10; and see also McGovern 2006: 75). Whatever his or her political views, the consumer was now also the participant in a nationwide industrial democracy and subject to a constant stream of commercialised information and social and political opinion. Often, the aim of this propaganda was not only to persuade the consumer to purchase a particular corporate product but to support a related political position or social programme (Hilton, 2007; McGovern, 2006).

Driven by PR-mediated descriptions of themselves as 'good citizens', and creators and guarantors of a more prosperous and democratic technological future, many of the larger American conglomerates began to present themselves as a complete productive identity, serving the broader community or nation of consumers (Hoffman, 2007; Marchand, 1998). Design played a crucial role in this process, unifying the look and feel of these often very large and diverse companies, which were now also staffed with large numbers of professional managers, including, increasingly, PR and marketing experts (Laird, 1998; Meikle, 2010; Muratovski, 2013). The designers, working as corporate consultants, were first brought to the attention of corporate management by their advertising agents. They were then set to work to bring a visual unity to the company's products, and often also the company's buildings, interiors, uniforms, vehicles, logos and advertising materials, while the advertising agencies developed narratives around visual identity, in part to remedy the consumers' then negative perception of the corporations as rapacious and 'soul-less' monopolies (Marchand, 1998; Meikle, 2010). The intention of this was not only to make goods and services more visually appealing, to differentiate them from those of their rivals or to imbue them with a uniform identity, but also to link these with a story that revealed the corporation to be a moral entity – a 'good citizen' in its own dominant area of provision, actively working for the benefit of its customers, their region and nation (Marchand, 1998: 348–356; Hoffman, 2007). For example, in a series of story-rich illustrated advertisements from the 1920s, Bell Telephone attempted to counter negative public opinions of their monopoly status with a series of illustrated tableaux showing a local human face and dedication to service among their employees. Their corporate message was dramatised with their representatives struggling against a background of extraordinary odds, such as natural disasters, bad weather, social crises or other difficult, more personal circumstances, but nevertheless, acting out of devotion to *their* community as well as their corporation, triumphing in the end (Marchand, 1998: 52–87). Building on the legacy of a century of advertising, these PR-based strategies were surprisingly similar: the corporation, despite its gargantuan size and necessary distance from most of its customers, was a 'neighbour' or 'friend' of everyone on main street, and an active protector of ordinary Americans, sharing their values, familiar aspirations, moral life and human goals (Marchand, 1998: 354–363; McGovern, 2006: 96ff).

The promise of science and technology also played a central role in this positioning of the corporation as a 'good citizen', especially during the Depression years. For at a time of increasing social and economic tensions, the corporation offered a vision of a technologically liberated future of greater freedom, leisure, prosperity and mobility (Marchand, 1998; and see Brostermann, 1999). In the vast New York and Chicago Expos of the late 1930s and early 1940s, these visions of a sponsored sci-fi future for America were given a stylish theatrical reality (Appelbaum, 1977; Marchand, 1998). Each major corporate sponsor offered a futuristic tableau of a technologically enabled utopia of greater mobility, access to energy and a transformed, more hygienic, comfortable and leisured way of life. This imagined future always centred upon their carefully designed and branded products and services (Marchand, 1998: 302–311). Through the work of designers like Raymond Loewy and Norman Bel Geddes, the future was packaged in a special corporate narrative, including not only the designers' streamlined products but also their buildings, interior environments, films, clever mechanical moving scenery and eye-catching theatrical representations. For example, Bel Geddes' prescient 'Futurama' designed for General Motors for the 1939 New York World's Fair, dramatically brought to life his vision of a model city of the 1960s full of tower-blocks, cars and freeways, a vision clearly owing much to Le Corbusier's futuristic 'radiant city' (Marchand, 1998: 291ff.; Meikle, 2010). Bel Geddes, Loewy and the other 'industrial designers' (as they then labelled themselves) worked tirelessly and profitably on these projects, as expert consultants in a corporate world now full of other expert persuaders, including PR, advertising and marketing agencies (Meikle, 2010).

The Positioning of the Corporation as a Social Institution

The positioning of America's largest companies as 'good citizens' was not only the product of PR but also of managers' concerns about each corporation's public image and its reputation among its many and often very diverse employees. Many managers in the 1920s subscribed to various popular theories of social responsibility, often to counter the negative views generated by criticism by some politicians and the unions of these monopolistic behemoths (Banerjee, 2008; Hoffman, 2007). It was not always clear whether these early overtures to social responsibility were simply a response to the institutionalisation of the corporation in American public life, an astute cover for more ruthless profit-making activities, or the result of the personal, religious or ethical beliefs of particular corporate leaders (Banerjee, 2008). Nevertheless, the 1920s and 1930s were the golden age of promotional efforts for the recognition of the corporation as a 'good citizen'. What began in earnest as a greater concern for how the corporation was seen during the expansion of corporate power and influence during the 1920s, and was further intensified during the Depression years, was taken to a fever pitch of jingoistic social paternalism and reputation management in corporate advertising during WWII (Cohen, 2004; Ewen, 1996; Hoffman, 2007). The corporation, as a 'social institution' with duties to the nation and general public, as well as its own employees and shareholders, looked to the public relations and marketing experts to help shape its image both internally and externally, and to flesh out its story as a moral entity or 'good citizen' (Ewen, 1996; Hoffman, 2007). The internal dimension of this image-making can be seen in the large number of employee magazines produced by the corporations of the 1920s and 1930s, in the social services many developed to assist their employees and in the various charitable community programs that they sponsored, or which involved their staff (Hoffman, 2007).

In the years after the WWII, the sheer size of the leading American corporations, their effective monopoly status in the United States and their early venture into European markets meant that these businesses were well positioned to expand their activities more aggressively into these now more open overseas markets (de Grazia, 2005; Shroter, 2005). At this time most western European leaders were anxious to rebuild their nations on a more democratic, and nominally American plan, and so began the corporatisation of western Europe – often through the direct investment of American corporations in European branches or partnerships (Crowley, 2008; de Grazia, 2005; Shroter, 2005). Large European companies also copied American methods and approaches, which enabled them to directly benefit from America's financial commitment to western Europe's reconstruction in the so-called Marshall Plan, or 'European Recovery Plan' (1948–1952), a large-scale American funding package intended to encourage the political stability, industrial modernisation and trade reforms deemed necessary to protect 'free' Europe from Soviet influence (de Grazia, 2005). In this way the myth of the corporation as 'good citizen', and of the citizen defined by their participation in the emerging consumer society, became a global phenomenon, closely entwined with a wider western, anti-Soviet ideology, of freedom and self-determination. The corporations, as commercial representatives of the West, promised consumers an expanding array of choices, presented through technologically advanced consumer goods and services (Macdonald, 2004; Oldenziel and Zachmann, 2009). The 1950s car, with its chrome 'wings' and 'jukebox' dashboard, became a symbol of this democratic ideal, reflecting an ideology of individual freedom and social mobility closely associated with western anti-communist values (McCracken, 2005).

Since large manufacturers, whether American or native European, were the largest employers and paid their workers generously, thereby adding substantially to national tax revenues, western European governments after WWII actively encouraged partnership with such companies (Cohen, 2004: 129ff.; Sparke, 2012: 100–108). Examples of this include Philips in Holland, Morris in England and Fiat in Italy. These companies were seen to directly support and sponsor the new social order of the democratic West (Shroter, 2005; Sparke, 2012: 122–124.). Most western governments, intent on reconstruction, also subsidised or actively engaged in industrial and social redevelopment for projects such as road building, new housing, food production, healthcare and education. While the intention of this reconstruction effort was to counter the ideological threat posed by Communism, the strategy also helped release their citizens' disposable income for further consumption. This government-sponsored industrial and social reconstruction coupled with Keynesian economic policies following the war drove a 'long boom' of prosperity that seemed to promise a fairer, more equal, and more democratic future, and the larger corporations were seen as honoured partners in most western governments' efforts (Marling, 1994; Meikle, 1995). While democratic politics and economic theory were still driven by the ideal of granting a wider access to public as well as private goods, for the majority of consumers individual consumption became a path towards a new democratic and material understanding of well-being that seemed to contradict the collectivist, political understanding of consumption of the pre-war era (Hilton, 2007; Trentmann, 2011).

Product designers, architects, engineers and graphic designers all supported and profited from this expansion of mass consumption, its individualisation and the accompanying ideal of the democratic 'consumer citizen'. But they were also beholden to the 'marketing revolution' taking place within the larger corporations that organised and facilitated it (Dawson, 2005; Pavitt, 2008). This 'revolution' simply confirmed what had already commenced between the two wars in America: the placing of marketing and PR managers at the table of senior corporate management, who were then able to make production and design more responsive to their market-driven initiatives (Dawson, 2005).

Rising living standards had brought with them new consumer wants eagerly exploited by corporate marketing. They also brought to the fore new habits and increasingly wasteful practices, which were rapidly and widely adopted. For example, the widespread adoption of the car, the automatic washing machine and the fridge, led not only to changes in shopping behaviour and soon also to the arrival of the supermarket in Europe, but also to more and more packaged goods (Strasser, 1999), and to increasing energy and water use in the home (Shove, 2003). These changes were aided by the fact that now the resulting waste was made to 'disappear' from view through more efficient and centralised waste management systems and utilities (Strasser, 1998, 1999, 2003). New social practices in the home, around cleaning, washing and food preparation, led to higher standards and rising expectations, noticeably accelerating the cycle of purchase, use and disposal (Crocker, 2013; Meikle, 1995: 183ff.; Whiteley, 1987).

Obsolescence, whether merely visual or material, became the main trick product designers were asked to perform, whether they were styling vehicles or redesigning refrigerators, hair-dryers, gramophones or radios (Boradkar 2010: 180ff.; Slade, 2006). One of the founders of 'green design', Victor Papanek, expressed the frustration of many designers concerned with the increasing dependence of corporate design decisions on marketing, and its material and environmental consequences, in this famously excoriating judgment:

> Once they have succeeded in building new dissatisfactions into people's lives, they are then prepared to find a temporary solution. Having constructed a Frankenstein, they are eager to design its bride.
>
> (Papanek, 1984 [1972]: 215)

This 'throwaway' approach to design seemed justified by the Cold War faith in a more democratic and prosperous utopian future, which was to be implemented through continuous economic growth – an individualistic consumerist fantasy of an ever more exciting array of new technological products and services. But these were at heart 'remedial' products and services, that is, they were intended to *remedy* what was in fact not really a problem in the first place (Marling, 1994; Meikle, 1995; Oldenziel and Zachmann, 2009). A good example of such a remedial product described by Strasser was the 'In-Sink-Erator', a plumbed-in device to grind up kitchen scraps and put them directly into the domestic sewage system. This was widely promoted in the United States during the 1950s and 1960s, despite its likely role in increasing water pollution (Strasser, 1998). In this continuous expansion of consumerism, even good and useful products were soon replaced by 'better' but more short-lived, more 'advanced' versions of the same, which in return resulted in increased material flows, increased pollution and waste (Crowley, 2008; Slade, 2006; Strasser, 1998).

The social imagery of endless increases in production and consumption (with all resulting waste swept out of sight) became a visual narrative explaining and justifying a new democratic, open, but thoroughly western consumerist world order (Marcus, 1998). It implied rising standards of prosperity, to be had by all, at least within the family of western democratic nations. This ideological consumer democracy was presented to the world as an enticement to join the West against their Soviet opponents, through a new generation of international Expos sponsored by the American government during the 1950s and 1960s, presented in partnership with America's leading corporations (Macdonald, 2004). These large-scale travelling exhibitions, involving many of America's leading corporations and designers, served two main functions: to propagandise the advantages of the 'free' democratic West over its Soviet counterpart, and to demonstrate the pragmatic superiority of American science and technology, often developed for notably accessible, homely purposes, in the kitchens and bathrooms of the 'model homes' (and kitchens) on show. The corporations presented themselves as essential partners in converting this advanced science and technology to everyday peaceful, domestic uses, for the benefit of every 'citizen-consumer' (Masey and Morgan, 2008).

Environmentalism, Design and the Moralised Corporation

Fifty years of corporate marketing, advertising and PR had created a myth that each corporation was both a 'social institution' of sorts, and an ethical 'person', defined and reflected in a unifying identity expressed in the branding of its products and services. This appeared in an oft-repeated narrative, a logo and a strict design grammar, covering everything from lettering to colours, shapes and printed visual materials. In many ways this became a visual and material version of the influential legal nicety that the corporation was in fact a 'person', whose overriding purpose was to improve and benefit the daily life of its many citizen-customers (Hoffman, 2007; Marchand, 1998). In this way the corporation became, in its public image at least, a human organisation with a broad social role, and certain ethical, social and even political aims and responsibilities (Holzer, 2010). Nevertheless, there were tensions apparent in this carefully managed image-making. Part of the problem here was political: just as some leading US corporations had fought the American government's 'New Deal' in the 1930s by publicising their engagement in social programmes to make the government's efforts at social amelioration seem less necessary, so the larger corporations of the 1950s and 1960s had promoted the idea that only self-regulation was necessary when it came to all business, big or small (Banerjee, 2008; Beder, 2002; Schor, 2010). The image of the corporation as a 'social institution' was essential to this push for freedom from government oversight. In some organisations, indeed, this ethical image-making, where the social value of the corporation was a central assumption, took on all the missionary trappings of an evangelical Christian organisation, an association long present within conservative American business culture (Lindsay, 2007: 180ff.; McGovern, 2006: 263).

Deeply engaged in this corporate image-making, modern design by the late 1950s had largely become, as Fry says, a 'directive practice' whose goal was the generation, expansion and acceleration of mass consumption (Fry, 2009: 29–39). Fixing any imagined 'problems' the marketing department could devise, the remedial products that resulted rapidly populated the home and workspace. Dominant products such as the car, the TV or the computer acted like gravitational 'suns', drawing many smaller 'planets' of dependent products and services into their powerful orbits (Manzini, 2002). The resulting product-system dependence created by the market dominance of key corporations, in turn, shaped consumer behaviour and expectations. For example, buying a TV involved purchasing a window onto a whole new world of advertised products and services, many of them dependent on driving to a new supermarket or shopping centre, and bringing home large numbers of packaged goods (Marling, 1994). Many of these changes also involved concealed or *distanced* environmental impacts that were carefully hidden by the hyperbole of corporate advertising (Princen, 2002b). However, by the mid-1960s this ambitious, increasingly global, attempt to persuade consumers of the corporations' ethical reputation and necessary role in improving and indeed underpinning the everyday life of the 'free' West was encountering some serious obstacles (Marwick, 1998).

Firstly, there was a growing chorus of public concern about the environmental and social impacts of a wide range of 'high-tech' corporate products or services, from pesticides and chemicals to cars (Beder, 2002; Andrews, 2006: 201ff.). The image of many corporations had been closely associated with breakthroughs in new technologies and innovations that were supposed to benefit all. By the early 1960s this benefit was seen to have some dangerous environmental consequences, of the kind exposed in Rachel Carson's *Silent Spring* (1962) (see Lytle, 2007). A new 'ecological' consciousness gathered strength throughout the 1970s, deepening as each new and seemingly more dramatic environmental crisis occurred. The underlying problematic of unrestrained economic growth was eloquently summarised in *The Limits to Growth* (Meadows et al., 1972), a book commissioned by the Club of Rome that subjected the combined effects of growth in consumption, population, resource use, waste and pollution to systematic scrutiny for the first time (Thiele, 2011: 23–28; Meadows, Randers and Meadows, 2004). Designers also became increasingly aware of their seemingly complicit role in this unfolding crisis (Papanek, [1972] 1984). Younger designers flocked to presentations by pioneering critics of industrial practice such as Buckminster Fuller (Lopez, 2014; Turner, 2006), with some starting their own 'alternative' design studios. In Italy, for example, the home of a large and very successful design industry, young radical designers engaged in a series of public 'confrontations', experiments, exhibitions and written protests, all widely reported in the design and popular press, calling into question the consumerism and corporate profits supporting Italy's successful post-war export boom, with a large exhibition of their work travelling to New York at the end of the decade (Ambasz, 1972; Branzi, 1984: 96ff.; Sparke, 1988). In Britain, and also in America, a number of designers began experimenting in 'ecological' design, self-consciously calling into question the direction of the profession and its profitable subservience to the corporate mainstream (Anker, 2010; and see Weder, 2009).

Secondly, the 1970s also produced a series of ecological disasters on American soil that seemed to vindicate the arguments of the pioneers of ecological thinking. For example, the 'Love Canal' disaster of 1977–1979, in Niagara, New York, resulted when land including a former factory's waste chemicals dump was bought and built on by the city council, with many residents and children affected. It resulted in a series of high-profile reports detailing alarming rates of birth defects, chemical burns, cancers and abnormalities among residents, along with grass and trees turning black from exposure to leaking chemicals from the dump beneath (Gibbs, 2010). Similarly, the Three Mile Island disaster of 1979 was another high-profile example of high technology 'gone wrong', exposing a notable lack of public oversight and corporate responsibility (Andrews, 2006: 185). In this instance a nuclear plant in Pennsylvania suffered the first stage of a cooling system meltdown, the first stage of a Chernobyl-type disaster, graphically revealing to the public the dangers of allegedly safe, 'peaceful' applications of nuclear technology (Walker, 2004). Love Canal and Three Mile Island appeared after a decade of high-profile political debates about corporate and government environmental responsibility, and the potential dangers of toxic chemicals like dioxins (Love Canal) and plutonium (Three Mile Island) (see Andrews, 2006: 227ff.). This perhaps explains the relatively bipartisan support Republican President Nixon enjoyed when he established the federal Environmental Protection Authority in 1970 (Andrews, 2006: 229–237).

Thirdly, while hundreds of thousands of American jobs had once depended on the activities of General Motors, Ford, Westinghouse, General Electric, Bell, etc., this no longer seemed to be so clearly the case, especially during the economically more turbulent mid-1970s. During the 1940s and 1950s there had been broad popular support for the corporation as a keystone employer, often dominating a particular city or town. Purchasing this or that product or service appeared to result in keeping another person, possibly a neighbour, in a job – a circular economic process that promised greater prosperity for all, and one enthusiastically supported by many politicians (Cohen, 2004: 114ff; Marling, 1994). The belief in the corporation's ability to provide a stable and well-paid 'job for life' underpinned the widespread belief in this so-called 'economic consumerism', and corporate in-house magazines were full of images of this kind of corporate 'community building' (Cohen, 2004). But the increasing economic problems of the early 1970s, and in particular the international oil crisis of 1974, when the oil-producing nations in OPEC decided to unilaterally raise their prices, ushered in a period of instability and stagflation. These conditions led to cost-cutting and lay-offs in many industries, and undermined the once seemingly dependable relationship between corporate employer and consumer-employee (Lytle, 2006; Schor, 2005).

Finally, and most dramatically, the Vietnam War rapidly undermined the public's acceptance of the ideal of the corporate 'good citizen' in both America and Europe. A number of high-profile American corporations, such as Westinghouse and Du Pont, had been heavily involved in arms manufacture or in the supply to the American government of such new horrors as napalm (Beder, 2002; Marwick, 1998). Before the military involvement in this distant war, Americans and Europeans might have been forgiven for believing that many corporations indeed might be the good citizens they claimed to be (Cohen, 2004; Lytle, 2006). For Europeans in particular, following America's leading role in the liberation of Europe at the end of WWII, the United States was seen in a positive light (de Grazia, 2005; Marwick, 1998). However, now ordinary Americans and Europeans could witness the horrors of real war on TV, and even atrocities carried out by American troops and their allies, which led to a profound questioning of the US alliance, and of the corporate 'military-industrial complex' that seemed to profit most directly from it (Eisenhower, 1961, in Griffin, 1992). The visible role of the corporations in the war seemed to directly contradict the narratives on which the corporation as good citizen had been built. The Vietnam War also lent credence to the critique of the corporate and government 'establishment' in 1960s 'counter culture'. Through pop music especially, this more openly negative view of American government and corporate culture was carried like a virus around the world (Lytle, 2006; Marwick, 1998).

Corporate Social Responsibility, Sunk Costs and the Re-Moralised Corporation

Pressure from more restrictive environmental and social standards (for example, the US National Environment Policy Act, 1969, and the US Clean Air Act, 1970 [Andrews, 2006: 228ff.]), along with the higher costs of a well-paid workforce, once the boast of many corporations in the 1930s and 1940s, became in their turn important incentives to shift manufacturing offshore (Schor, 2005). It became easier and more profitable to sign up to the required legislative obligations now legally binding in America, while 'dirty' and cheaper manufacturing, mining or assembly work could take place where there were few rules, and where the resulting damage to people or environment could not be seen by the producer's own customers (Dauvergne, 2010: 3–17; Princen, 2002a; Schor, 2005).

While globalisation from the 1980s onwards became a 'get out of jail' card for many large manufacturers, who slashed their workforces and opened new low-cost plants in Asia, economic survival often came at a further externalisation of environmental and social costs (Dauvergne, 2010; Princen, 2002a; Schor, 2005). However, NGOs and activists were soon able to gain access to many of these offshore plants, document some of the environmental and social issues associated with them and publicise the results (Beder, 2002). Naomi Klein's *No Logo* (1999) is a classic example of this kind of forensic investigation, its appendices filled with data on the slave-like pay and conditions provided in these distant factories (Schor, 2010; Princen, 2002a). Unable to so easily escape the scrutiny of this 'bad news' from afar, which could in turn have a serious impact on the profitability of the company, many corporations responded to this new PR threat by issuing their own environmental and ethical report cards.

Most corporations in the 1980s and 1990s had to face an inherent contradiction, and one reflected in business school debates around 'reputation management' ever since (Mitnick and Mahon, 2007). On the one hand, their economic power and political influence had dramatically expanded with growing global consumption and affluence, and this gave them increasing social and cultural leverage. On the other hand, their legal standing, and financial duty to their shareholders, required them to pursue profits wherever possible, at least within the law. This resulted in a somewhat two-faced institution, described by neoclassical economists like Milton Friedman as having more limited, predominantly financial priorities to shareholders, and by management consultants like Peter Drucker in radically different, more explicitly social terms, with moral obligations to all 'stakeholders', including their workers and the environment affected by their activities. For these, the corporation was not just an economic institution but also a social one, and a critical one at that (Moura-Leite and Padgett, 2011; Yani-de-Soriano and Slater, 2009).

While at first it appears that from the late-1970s the neoclassical view of the corporation edged out the older and more socially inclusive one, this is somewhat misleading. For the earlier more consciously ethical and social model of corporate strategic responsibilities led to the evolution of a performance-based model of CSR, which assumes that the socially and environmentally responsible management is necessarily in the interest of the corporation, because this improves the reputation of the company (Hoffman, 2007; Moura-Leite and Padgett, 2011). And there is always considerable evidence to support this view, much of it by negation. For example, in one of the world's worst industrial disasters, at Bhopal in India in December 1984, an exploding tank released around 40 tons of toxic fumes used in the manufacture of pesticides, killing at least 2,500 outright and seriously injuring another 10,000 (Andrews, 2006: 273). The damage to the reputation of the plant's owner, Union Carbide, was widely understood and reported on, resulting in further legislative controls on companies in the United States and, in the end, in the eventual sale of both the plant and the company itself. Over time poisoning up to half a million of Bhopal's inhabitants, the city has been the site of a struggle between local activists, the city's government and the original American owners of the company for compensation ever since. This major chemical spill disaster revealed in forensic detail how a major environmental catastrophe could rapidly erode a company's public reputation, with its then CEO pursued unsuccessfully for mass murder by the activists through the Indian courts (Fortun, 2001; Kurzman, 1987).

This helps explain why CSR and sustainability reporting since the 1990s has increasingly been centralised and integrated into PR within many corporations, with CEOs generally taking a close interest in its results. It also explains why since the 1980s more and more Fortune 500 companies now issue CSR reports, with those, paradoxically, most likely to be associated with environmental damage, more likely to invest in CSR reporting.

For CSR, along with environmental reporting, is all about presenting the 'good news' of what the company is doing to its social and environmental stakeholders, and perhaps also tentatively pointing out where the company could do better. But as students of CSR will note, like marketing, this can skate over serious operational issues and create a legacy of disbelief that is often difficult to rectify (Moura-Leite and Padgett, 2011; Raufflet and Mills, 2009; Ethical Corporation, 2013). Competitive demands for higher results more quickly can increase the risk these companies operate under, and this can lead to spectacular failures, as in the Deepwater Horizon disaster for BP in Florida (Balmer, 2010).

However BP's performance is categorised, which one researcher described as 'total brand collapse' (Balmer, 2010), a central issue here is that certain types of business involve extraordinary environmental risks. These can be seen as negative 'sunk costs', which are prior commitments, sometimes of many years' standing, to activities that are neither environmentally nor socially beneficial (Cunha and Caldiararo, 2009; and see Kelly, 2004). Such environmentally questionable 'sunk costs' underpin many industries, especially in extraction, but also in manufacturing, communication and transportation. For example, many years of designing petrol-based combustion engines for cars, or building large national road systems for the benefit of these cars, cannot be reversed or changed easily because of the same sunk costs (Soron, 2009). Rather like a series of Russian dolls, a series of legal and financial obligations binds corporations to profit-making first, making substantial but not directly profitable social and environmental commitments a much lower priority. Nevertheless, most corporations driven by their obligations to shareholders attempt to try, if only to avoid the shame of exposure for failing to do so (Arvidsson, 2010).

For example, in response to mounting public concerns about 'conflict metals' such as the Coltan used in most mobile phones, Apple recently announced its attempts to map the sources of the rare metals used by its suppliers, and improve these (Monbiot, 2013; and see Wilhelm, Yankov and Magee, 2011). This background attempt to make more ethical sense of the complexities of global supply chains shamefully entangled in West African civil wars and child labour issues suggests that Apple's management have become determined to avoid a repeat of the kind of 'shame' they were exposed to by a well-publicised spate of suicides among workers in their Chinese manufacturing plant (Monbiot, 2013).

Because of its global reach and excellent brand reputation, Apple, like most similar transnational corporations, is stuck on a ramp of ethicalisation, with the sunk-cost effect of ethically problematic global supply chains and toxic materials at its murky bottom, and the widely admired totem of its brand image at its top (Laufer, 2003; Vos, 2009). In Apple's case, as in many smaller, more agile and creative companies, a more active design involvement, and an attempt to analyse the dependent social and material relationships behind its products, has become a means of initiating some progress towards greater social responsibility and sustainability (Monbiot, 2013). However, the main problem Apple, like so many others, faces is the central ambiguity of the corporation as a social institution: bound by the law itself to maximise profits for its shareholders first, the costs of its social and environmental activities, even if they are secondary, must be justified in terms of reputation and eventual profit, of avoiding the dangers of any potentially loss-making 'shame' (Arvidsson, 2010).

Apple's attempt to analyse the material and social relationships within its supply chains is in many respects analogous to the techniques involved in lifecycle assessment commonly used in sustainable design (Vezzoli and Manzini, 2010). It has the potential in companies of Apple's size to have significant and positive impacts on the global environment and the social sustainability of developing nations. In fact, Dauvergne and Lister (2012) suggest that activists should not wait for individual governments to implement constraining legislation and should work more directly with transnational corporations instead. Since the economic weight of a Walmart, an IKEA or an Apple is so great, improved conditions along their supply chains and within their products could have a more immediate impact on the environment than the slower, often more politically conflicted path of legislative reform (Dauvergne and Lister, 2012). Another possible spur to change, trialled by the little Dutch charitable start-up, Fair Phone, is to model for larger corporations just how production should occur, in an ethical, rather than in a brutal neoclassical, economic world (Fair Phone, 2013). This assumes that it is possible to make a product that, if not designed for disassembly should at least be internally upgradeable, have replaceable batteries, should be unbreakable and be made from as much recycled material as possible (Fair Phone, 2013). Given the publicity generated by this small start-up, many of Apple's customers may look to the giant to make similar improvements.

The sunk-cost effect, in this case, is the provisioning system under which Apple operates. This is conditioned to a great extent by the telecoms, or service providers, who link Apple's iPhone and iPad to short-term Internet or phone service agreements that help generate a global over-consumption of mobile phones (Crocker, 2012). Within a year or so of purchase, these products are made to seem obsolete – in part because new phones or tablets are offered as incentives to customers to purchase new service contracts, and in part because manufacturers like Apple introduce new minor technological improvements into their products every six months or so to increase the 'incentivisation' required by their largest customers, the service providers (Crocker, 2012; Park, 2010).

Designers have responded to this now increasingly typical dilemma in manufacturing – where demand is accelerating and supplies diminishing, by re-examining and experimenting with product-service systems (for example, where a product is leased to the customer and then repurposed for reuse after the period of the service agreement) (Vezzoli, 2013); and by modularisation (where component parts can be more easily reused or replaced) (Vezzoli and Manzini, 2010). Both these approaches aim to reduce and conserve resource use, and extend, where possible, the consumer's too brief relationship with the product (Park, 2010). Free Phone's entry into mobile phone manufacture may not be successful, but it represents a 'demonstration product' that giants like Apple might envy, since it jumps ahead of the pack where it often counts most, in reputational and environmental terms (Free Phone, 2013).

It is useful to recall at this point Norbert Elias's understanding of 'shame avoidance', not only as it might be applied to corporations anxious about losing their environmental or social reputation, but also as it can be applied to consumers (Elias, 1969; Binkley, 2009). The ramp of 'ethicalisation' puts pressure on both parties to become good, or at least better, citizens. Purchasing a more ethical brand becomes a path to shame avoidance for many consumers, and reduces the risks involved in the emotive business of choosing certain products or services over otherwise similar ones (Arvidsson, 2010; Binkley, 2009). Elias's theory suggests that there is a ratchet effect at work here, a two-way dialogue motivated by shame avoidance and initiated by producers attempting to reduce or negate any 'ethical exposure' by reporting on their own performance and announcing annual improvements in environmental and social areas (Pearse, 2012). This reporting, a direct descendant of the PR used in the 1930s, aims to argue that the corporation is still a 'good citizen', or at least not as bad as its competitors (Raufflet and Mills, 2009). Despite negative public perceptions of 'green-washing', it buys time for the corporation affected by such sunk-cost effects, and creates a time and space for analysis and reflection on potential reforms, often in very unpromising domains, where the sunk costs might be the most difficult to change (Pearse, 2012).

Conclusion

As this suggests, CSR and sustainability reporting are not just the inevitable outcome of particular decisions in responsible management, but the result of a much longer, historical process of dialogue, or even open conflict, between the narrower self-interest of the corporations, often based on their financial and legal obligations to shareholders, and the interests of their customers and other stakeholders, including the environment in which they operate, their workers and the broader global society. The long and winding road to CSR and sustainability reporting described above is to a great extent conditioned by the conflicting interests of corporations and consumers, of sellers and buyers. The idealised image-making activities developed by corporate designers, advertisers, marketers and PR agents over time tend to raise consumers' ethical and material expectations of the corporation's products, value and intentions. The projected 'perfection' of the corporate image associated with the brand and its narrative can generate assumptions among consumers that the product itself, if not perfect, is at least among the best in the field, and is produced or manufactured in an ethical, sustainable and responsible manner.

Consumers rightly assume a consistency between the ideas and values promoted in the media and the company and its products, and the practices they follow in bringing these products to market. Greater sustainability and CSR are best characterised as a 'ramp' between these rising ethical consumer expectations and the ideal represented by the corporate brand and its products. Reputational anxieties, often brought to public attention by the activities of environmentalists or other activists, are important indicators of the existence of this 'ramp' and its upward pressure. Paradoxically, branding itself with its idealised imagery puts increasing pressure on the corporation to not only appear to be *good*, but to demonstrate this good citizenship in every activity they engage in, from the treatment of distant workers back down the supply chain, to the use of materials, their products' recyclability and the packaging they use. The *good* corporation, as a social and environmental actor, is a work in progress that needs to be more directly engaged with, by regulators, shareholders and ordinary citizens (Ethical Corporation, 2013).

References

Ambasz, E., 1972. *Italy: the new domestic landscape: achievements and problems of Italian design*. New York: Museum of Modern Art.

Andrews, R. N. L., 2006. *Managing the environment, managing ourselves: a history of American Environmental Policy.* 2nd ed. New Haven, CT: Yale University Press.

Anker, P., 2010. *From Bauhaus to Eco House: a history of ecological design*. Baton Rouge, LA: Louisiana State University Press.

Appelbaum, S., 1977. *The New York World's Fair, 1939/1940 in 155 photographs by Richard Wurtz and others.* New York: Dover.

Arvidsson, A., 2010. Speaking out: the ethical economy: new forms of value in the information age? *Organization*, 17, pp.637–644.

Balmer, J. M. T., 2010. The BP deepwater horizon debacle and corporate brand exuberance. *Journal of Brand Management*, 18:2, pp.97–104.

Banerjee, S. B., 2008. *Corporate social responsibility: the good, the bad and the ugly*. Cheltenham, UK: Edgar Elgar.

Beder, S., 2002. *Global spin: the corporate assault on the environment*. Rev. ed. Totnes, Devon: Green Books.

Binkley, S., 2009. The civilized brand: shifting shame thresholds and the dissemination of consumer lifestyles. *European Journal of Cultural Studies*, 12, pp.21–38.

Boradkar, P., 2010. *Designing things: a critical introduction to the culture of objects*. Oxford: Berg.

Branzi, A., 1984. *The hot house: Italian new wave design*. London: Thames and Hudson.

Brosterman, N., 1999. *Out of time: designs for the twentieth-century future*. New York: Abrams.

Carson, R., 1962. *Silent spring*. New York: Houghton Mifflin.

Cohen, L., 2004. *A consumers' republic: the politics of mass consumption in postwar America*. New York: Vintage Books

Crocker, R., 2012. Getting to zero waste in the new mobile communications paradigm: a social and cultural perspective. In: S. Lehmann and R. Crocker, eds. *Designing for zero waste: consumption, technologies and the built environment*. London: Earthscan. pp.115–130.

Crocker, R., 2013. From access to excess: consumerism, 'compulsory consumption' and behaviour change. In: R. Crocker and S. Lehmann, eds. *Motivating change: sustainable design and behaviour in the built environment.* London: Routledge, pp.11–32.

Crowley, D., 2008. Europe reconstructed, Europe divided. In: D. Crowley and J. Pavitt, eds. *Cold War Modern: design, 1945-1970.* London: Victoria and Albert Museum. pp.43–65.

Cunha, M. and Caldieraro, F., 2009. Sunk-cost effects on purely behavioral investments. *Cognitive Science*, 33, pp.105–113.

Dauvergne, P., 2010. *The shadows of consumption: consequences for the global environment.* Cambridge, MA: MIT Press.

Dauvergne, P. and Lister, J., 2012. Big brand sustainability: governance prospects and environmental limits. *Global Environmental Change*, 22:1, pp.36–45.

Dawson, M., 2005, *The Consumer Trap: Big Business Marketing in American Life.*Chicago: University of Illinois Press.

De Grazia, V., 2005. *Irresistible empire: America's advance through twentieth-century Europe.* Cambridge, MA: Harvard University Press.

Elias, N., 2000 [1969]. *The civilizing process: sociogenetic and psychogenetic investigations.* Rev. ed. Oxford: Blackwell.

Ethical Corporation, 2013. *Ethical Corporation.* Available at http://www.ethicalcorp.com. Accessed 5 September 2013.

Ewen, S., 1996. *PR! A social history of spin.* New York: Basic Books.

FairPhone, 2013. *Fairphone.* Available at http://www.fairphone.com. Accessed 5 September 2013.

Fortun, K., 2001. *Advocacy after Bhopal: environmentalism, disaster, new global orders.* Chicago, IL: Chicago University Press.

Fry, T., 2009. *Design futuring: sustainability, ethics and new practice.* Oxford: Berg.

Gibbs, L. M., 2010. *Love canal and the birth of the environmental health movement.* Rev. ed. Washington, DC: Island Press.

Griffin, C., 1992. New light on Eisenhower's farewell address. *Presidential Studies Quarterly*, 22, Summer, pp.469–479.

Hilton, M., 2007. Consumers and the state since the Second World War. *Annals of the American Academy of Political and Social Sciences*, 611, pp.66–81.

Hilton, M., 2009. *Prosperity for all: consumer activism in an era of globalization.* Ithaca, NY: Cornell University Press.

Hoffman, R. C., 2007. Corporate social responsibility in the 1920s: an institutional perspective. *Journal of Management History*, 31:1, pp.55–73.

Holzer, B., 2010. *Moralizing the corporation: transnational activism and corporate accountability.* Cheltenham: Edgar Elgar.

Kelly, T., 2004. Sunk costs, rationality and acting for the sake of the past. *Nous*, 38:1, pp.60–85.

Klein, N., 1999. *No logo: taking aim at the brand bullies.* New York: Alfred Knopf.

Kurzman, D., 1987. *A Killing Wind: Inside Union Carbide and the Bhopal Catastrophe.* New York: McGraw Hill.

Laird, P. W., 1998. *Advertising progress: American business and the rise of consumer marketing.* Baltimore, MD: Johns Hopkins University Press.

Laufer, W. S., 2003. Social accountability and corporate greenwashing. *Journal of Business Ethics*, 43, pp.253–261.

Lindsay, D. M., 2007. *Faith in the halls of power: how evangelicals joined the American elite.* New York: Oxford University Press.

Lopez, L. P., 2014. *R. Buckminster Fuller: World Man.* Princeton, NJ: Princeton University Press.

Luger, S., 2000. *Corporate power, American democracy and the automobile industry.* Cambridge: Cambridge University Press.

Lytle, M. H., 2006. *America's uncivil wars: the sixties era, from Elvis to the fall of Nixon.* New York: Oxford University Press.

Lytle, M. H., 2007. *The gentle subversive: Rachel Carson, silent spring, and the rise of the environmental movement.* Oxford: Oxford University Press.

Macdonald, G., 2004. Selling the American dream: MOMA, industrial design and post-war France. *Journal of Design History*, 17:4, pp.397–412.

Manzini, E., 2002. Context-based wellbeing and the concept of regenerative solution: A conceptual framework for scenario building and sustainable solutions development. *Journal of Sustainable Product Design*, 2, pp.141-148.

Marchand, R., 1998. *Creating the corporate soul: the rise of public relations and corporate imagery in American big business.* Berkeley, CA: University of California Press.

Marcus, G. H., 1998. *Design in the fifties: when everyone went modern.* Munich: Prestel.

Marling, K. A., 1994. *As seen on TV: the visual culture of everyday life in the 1950s.* Cambridge, MA: Harvard University Press.

Marwick, A., 1998. *The sixties: cultural revolution in Britain, France, Italy and the United States, c.1958-1974.* Oxford: Oxford University Press.

Masey, J. and Morgan, C. L., 2008. *Cold War confrontations: US exhibitions and their role in the cultural Cold War.* Baden, Switzerland: Lars Muller.

McCracken, G., 2005. When cars could fly: Raymond Loewy, John Kenneth Galbraith and the 1954 Buick'. In: G. McCracken, ed. *Culture and consumption II: markets, meaning and brand management.* Bloomington, IA: Indiana University Press. pp.53–90.

McGovern, C. F., 2006. *Sold American: consumption and citizenship, 1890-1945.* Chapel Hill, NC: University of North Carolina Press.

Meadows, D. H., Meadows, D. L., Randers, J. and Behrens, W. W., 1972. *The limits to growth: a report for the Club of Rome's Project on the predicament of mankind.* New York: Potomac Books.

Meadows, D. H., Randers, J. and Meadows, D. L., 2004. *Limits to growth: the 30-year update.* White River Junction, VT: Chelsea Green.

Meikle, J., 1995. *American plastic: a cultural history.* New Brunswick, NJ: Rutgers University Press.

Meikle, J., 2010. *Twentieth century limited: industrial design in America, 1925-1939*. 3rd ed. Philadelphia, PA: Temple University Press.

Mitnick, B. M. and Mahon, J., 2007. The concept of reputational bliss. *Journal of Business Ethics*, 72:4, pp.323–333.

Monbiot, G., 2013. My search for a smartphone that is not soaked in blood. *Guardian*, [online] 11 March. Available at: http://www.guardian.co.uk/commentisfree/2013/mar/11/search-smartphone-soaked-blood. Accessed 20 March 2013.

Moura-Leite, R. C. and Padgett, R. C., 2011. Historical background of corporate social responsibility. *Social Responsibility Journal*, 7:4, pp.528–539.

Muratovski, G., 2013. Advertising, public relations and social marketing: shaping behaviour towards sustainable consumption. In: R. Crocker and S. Lehmann, eds. *Motivating change: sustainable design and behaviour in the built environment*. London: Routledge. pp.178–197.

Oldenziel, R. and Zachmann, K. eds., 2009. *Cold War kitchen: Americanization, technology and European users*. Cambridge, MA: MIT Press.

Papanek, V., [1972]1984. *Design for the real world: human ecology and social change*. 2nd rev. ed. London: Thames and Hudson.

Park, M., 2010. Defying obsolescence. In: T. Cooper, ed. *Longer lasting products: alternatives to the throwaway society*. Farnham, Surrey: Gower. pp.77–106.

Pavitt, J., 2008, Design and the Democratic Ideal. In: D. Crowley and J. Pavitt, eds. *Cold War Modern: 1945-1970*. London: Victoria and Albert Museum. pp.73-93.

Pearse, G., 2012. *Greenwash: big brands and carbon scams*. Melbourne: Black Inc.

Princen, T., 2002a. Consumption and its externalities: where consumption meets ecology. In: T. Princen, M. F. Maniates and K. Conca, eds. *Confronting consumption*. Cambridge, MA: MIT Press. pp.23–42.

Princen, T., 2002b. Distancing: consumption and the severing of feedback. In: T. Princen, M. F. Maniates and K. Conca, eds. *Confronting consumption*. Cambridge, MA: MIT Press. pp.103–131.

Raufflet, E. and Mills, A. J. eds., 2009. *The dark side: critical cases on the downside of business*. Sheffield: Greenleaf.

Schor, J. S., 2005. Prices and quantities: unsustainable consumption and the global economy. *Ecological Economics*, 55:3, pp.309–320.

Schor, J. S., 2010. Combating consumerism and capitalism: a decade of 'no logo'. *Women's Studies Quarterly*, 38:3/4, pp.299–301.

Schwarzkopf, S., 2011. The consumer as 'voter', 'judge', and 'jury': historical origins and political consequences of a marketing myth. *Journal of Macromarketing*, 31:8, pp.8–18.

Schroter, H. G., 2005. *Americanization of the European Economy: A Compact Survey of American Economic Influence in Europe since the 1880s*. Dordrecht, Netherlands: Springer.

Shove, E., 2003, *Comfort, Cleanliness and Convenience: the social organization of normality*. Oxford: Berg.

Slade, G., 2006. *Made to break: technology and obsolescence in America.* Cambridge, MA: Harvard University Press.
Smart, B., 2010. *Consumer Society: Critical Issues and Environmental Consequences.* London: Sage.
Sparke, P., 1988. *Italian design: 1780 to the present.* London: Thames and Hudson.
Sparke, P., 2012. *An introduction to design and culture.* 3rd ed. London: Routledge.
Strasser, S., 1998. 'The convenience is out of this world!': the garbage disposer and American consumer culture. In: S. Strasser, C. McGovern and M. Judt, eds. *Getting and spending: European and American consumer societies in the twentieth century.* Cambridge: Cambridge University Press. pp.263–280.
Strasser, S., 1999. *Waste and want: a social history of trash.* New York: Henry Holt.
Strasser, S., 2003. The alien past: consumer culture in historical perspective. *Journal of Consumer Policy*, 26:4, pp.375–393.
Thiele, L. P., 2011. *Indra's net and the Midas touch: living sustainably in a connected world.* Cambridge, MA: MIT Press.
Trentmann, F., 2011. Consumers as citizens: tensions and synergies. In: K. M. Ekstrom and K. Glans, eds. *Beyond the consumption bubble.* London: Routledge. pp.99–111.
Turner, F., 2006. *From Counterculture to Cyberculture: Stewart Brand, the Whole Earth Network, and the Rise of Digital Utopianism.* Chicago: University of Chicago Press.
Vezzoli, C., 2013. System design for sustainability: the challenge of behaviour change. In: R. Crocker and S. Lehmann, eds. *Motivating change: sustainable design and behaviour in the built environment.* London: Routledge. pp.276–290.
Vezzoli, C. and Manzini, E., 2010. *Design for environmental sustainability.* London: Springer.
Vos, J., 2009. Actions speak louder than words: greenwashing in corporate America. *Notre Dame Journal of Law, Ethics and Public Policy*, 23, pp.673–697.
Walker, J. S., 2004. *Three mile island: a nuclear crisis in historical perspective.* Berkeley, CA: University of California Press.
Waterman, N., 1911. Cheer to the consumer. In: M. P. Wilder, ed. *The wit and humor of America.* 10 vols. New York: Funk and Wagnell. 4, p.97.
Weder, J., 2009. Little big mag. Radical magazines and architectural criticism. *Border Crossings*, 28:1, pp.70–74.
Whiteley, N., 1987. Toward a throw-away culture. Consumerism, 'style obsolescence' and cultural theory in the 1950s and 1960s. *Oxford Art Journal*, 10:2, pp.3–27.
Whysall, P., 1997. Interwar retail internationalization: boots under American ownership. *International Review of Retail, Distribution and Consumer Research*, 7:2, pp.157–169.
Wilhelm, W., Yankov, A. and Magee, P., 2011. Mobile phone consumption behaviour and the need for sustainability innovations. *Journal of Strategic Innovation and Sustainability*, 7:2, pp.20–40.
Yani-de-Soriano, M. and Slater, S., 2009. Revising Drucker's theory. *Journal of Management History*, 15, pp.452–466.

Chapter 9

Acceleration in Consumerism, Technology and Sustainability

Robert Crocker

Abstract

The networked computer has progressively colonised, transformed and accelerated older established technological systems in transportation, communication and manufacture over the last 30 years. In today's global economy, the increasing mobility of people, goods and information enabled by this technology has led to an acceleration and expansion of consumerism, giving rise to what has been termed appropriately, 'hyper-consumption'. Reflecting upon Rosa's concept of 'social acceleration' (2003), and the important contribution of a computer-enabled blending of the material and virtual evident in recent technologies and scientific advances, this chapter argues that, despite appearances to the contrary, there seems little in the way of good news for resource-use reduction and sustainability. Rather than attaining a progressive 'dematerialisation' that was once predicted to slow or replace the 'box economy', the material economy is being expanded and accelerated by the virtual economy. Using the 3D printer as a case study, it becomes apparent that this supposedly 'cleaner' and more democratic technology cannot 'solve' our existing ecological problems, and may in fact make these worse. For the 3D printer, despite optimistic talk of this 'disruptive' technology, will predictably become one more source of a growing army of cheap 'stuff' in the home, in its turn adding to resource depletion, overconsumption and waste. Rejecting the equally optimistic notion that greater sustainability can be achieved through the democratisation and localisation enabled by this innovation, the chapter concludes by arguing that industrial 'unsustainability' is not so easily undone. Rather, it is systemic and grounded in today's hyper-consumption, whose psychosocial or cultural basis cannot be substantially changed by material innovation alone.

Keywords

consumerism, Internet, consumer practices, technological acceleration, dematerialisation, waste, 3D printing

Introduction: Computerisation, Dematerialisation and Hyper-Consumption

In about 1997 when mobile phones were beginning to be used more widely in Australia, I had a defining experience. I was in a busy public toilet and in the next cubicle a phone suddenly rang. The stranger in this cubicle immediately answered and then proceeded to talk as though he was at his desk in his office. I remember feeling shocked and very surprised, not because there were any terrible secrets revealed by the ensuing conversation, but by the fact that this stranger had felt obliged to answer his mobile phone in this most private of public places. Since this time, like many others, I have become used to the frequent interruptions to conversation, work or other activities accompanying the use of this device (Ling, 2004: 140–143). The impulse to connect, to text or to check a mobile phone in the presence of others, and even in the most intimate or public, even risky, dangerous situations, seems irresistible (Turkle, 2008).

The 'connected presence' of the mobile phone links individuals in a network that is distinct from the community, place and time in which each is situated (Ling, 2008: 180–183). It brings distant individuals together in a sort of 'co-presence' and simultaneously creates a distance between the individual caller and their immediate social and material environment (Turkle, 2008; Campbell and Park, 2008). From the person sitting next to someone texting or talking, the co-presence with another looks like an absence, an 'absent presence' (Gergen, 2002: 227–229). This absence can have serious consequences, as police, medical and emergency services now attest (e.g. Alosco et al., 2012).

From a historical perspective, this 'absent presence' is not as new as it seems. Rather, the distraction of the mobile phone seems the latest moment in a series of modern technologies of communication that disrupts proximate human-to-human and human-to-place relationship (Urry, 2002; Gergen, 2002). While Turkle describes the link between humans and the new communication technologies in terms of a 'tethering' of the self (2008), it is also possible to consider it an 'untethering' of the self, to what or whom is proximate to the self (Urry, 2002; Borgmann, 2010). Eroding or replacing slower, often more collaborative and proximate focal activities with faster, more individually based activities seems to be a part of technological modernisation. This has shaped new distanced and hybrid forms of individual-to-individual and individual-to-world relationships quite distinct from what had once been established ways of experiencing the world and each other (Fortunati, 2002; Urry, 2002; Verbeek, 2005).

It is also apparent that each of these socially transformative technological innovations has been accompanied by exaggerated predictions of future benefits, some more fanciful and utopian than others (Chapman, 2004). This draws upon a deeper mythological set of particularly western beliefs, which Leo Marx and David Nye term 'the technological sublime': through the lens of this myth, technology is seen to transform the world into a better place (Marx, 1964; Nye, 1996, 2000). In its everyday form, technology is supposed to 'change everything', invariably for the better (Mosco, 1999: 5–8; Borgmann, 2010). Experts and spruikers are always ready to predict a wonderful future of Jetson-like greater leisure, mobility, comfort, sociality and pleasure that each technological innovation would bring (Mosco, 1999). The Internet, for example, was thought to transform human communication, information retrieval and many aspects of daily life, implying a future of greater prosperity, equality, democracy and more leisure, with less need to consume so many physical 'atom-based' objects (Negroponte, 1995; Mosco, 1999). This belief in the ameliorating power of technology has also helped make a succession of monopolistic corporations stage-managing these innovations seem both natural and inevitable (Wu, 2010; Naughton, 2014). A good example is the 'cult' that developed around the Apple Mac, where the ideal of a better future enabled by the Mac became closely entwined with the image of Steve Jobs and the belief that the Mac would somehow change everything for the better (Stein, 2002; Belk and Tumbat, 2002).

One reoccurring theme in the literature relating to computerisation has been the idea that some form of 'dematerialisation' is the inevitable result of technological advance (Negropointe, 1995). Meaning many things, computer-enabled dematerialisation is understood to somehow fix the environmental problems associated with many forms of industrial production (Carolan, 2004). Dematerialisation is also understood in terms of industrial efficiency, which will somehow 'dematerialise' production and energy consumption, something that with more reason can be verified in many areas, but is much harder to predict at a larger, global scale (Ausubel and Waggoner, 2008). Dematerialisation is thus a somewhat ambiguous term, since it is used to refer simultaneously to efficiency gains, miniaturisation and even the virtualisation occurring in many areas, from online shopping to music and film downloading (Negropointe, 1995; Mosco, 1999).

While it is certainly possible to show some real examples of progressive dematerialisation due to greater technological efficiencies and its benefits in specific instances, unfortunately, there is rarely any discernable global environmental gain resulting from this (Carolan, 2004; Herring, 2006). This is because the gains identified are most usually offset by an increase in related or neighbouring consumption (Magaudda, 2011). This failure of dematerialisation to do what it is supposed to do is worth considering in more depth. There are three paradoxes that have been associated with consumption. Each, in their way, adds to the expansive, self-reinforcing and accelerating nature of modern consumption, termed by Lipovetsky 'hyper-consumption' (2011). Unfortunately, these paradoxes are rarely considered by those interested in 'ecological modernisation' whose laudable goal is a reduction in material flows through various technological improvements to production (Carolan, 2004).

Firstly, there is the Jevons paradox. British economist, William Stanley Jevons, predicted many years ago that efficiency gains would increase the consumption of a service or system, if the price were sufficiently lowered, since greater productive efficiencies tend to generate more demand and thus more consumption (Alcott, 2005; Herring, 2006). Although Jevons' original calculations were based on a gas supply system, his insights are often referenced in discussions of the 'rebound effect' in other areas. For example, in the 2000s the Dutch government attempted to reduce domestic electricity consumption by giving away energy-efficient light bulbs and phasing out incandescent ones. In this case, the lower cost of running the new lights resulted in a dramatic increase in demand (Verbeek and Slob, 2006: 3–12).

Secondly, there is what might be termed the paradox of the democratisation of luxury, which results from luxury's role as a continually evolving lodestar for everyday consumption choices (Berg, 2005; Berry, 1994). Once something has been recognised as a luxury and has become more accessible, it eventually attains the status of becoming a fashionable item, and then a 'must have' for middle-class people (Berg, 2005). Over time, the luxury's now standard status lowers its value in the consumer's eyes and becomes a necessity (Crocker, 2013). For example, the plumbed-in bathroom was originally a luxury but has now become a standard feature in all modern homes (Shove, 2003). As a result of this paradox, much business activity is now devoted to either creating a luxury or to promoting an existing luxury in order to generate more demand (Frank, 1999).

Thirdly, there is the paradox of 'rematerialisation', which occurs when and where the impact of dematerialisation in consumption seems inevitable or most assured, such as in the provision of music online. The phenomenon of the paperless office is suggestive of this paradox. People now print more, seemingly in a desire to rematerialise (or store securely) what is already accessible in digital form (York, 2006). This rematerialisation is also evident in digital music; listening has generated a plethora of objects that consumers believe will improve, enrich or give music some symbolic expression (Magaudda, 2011). There may be many reasons why rematerialisation becomes attractive, from fear of loss of data (as in paper printing) to a dislike for reading on-screen print, to a desire to somehow symbolise or give visual or material form to what is most valued (Magaudda, 2011). But the consequences are unambiguous: the effects of the dematerialisation documented are undermined or cancelled out by a closely related rematerialisation.

These three paradoxes are present in some form or another in today's global computer-enabled hyper-consumption. The networked computer, the smartphone and tablet also draw attention to these paradoxes because of their striking efficiency and virtualisation gains. They themselves, their peripherals and accessories are objects of consumption made rapidly redundant by their consistently rapid advances. In the process, a rapid turnover of these products is created, spawning a vast river of plastic and toxic chemical trash (Slade, 2006; Crocker, 2012). As older household appliances and machines are in turn computerised and linked together in the 'Internet of things', a reduction in lifespan and durability of many household objects becomes inevitable (Park, 2010). Therefore, dematerialisation, facilitated by computerisation, has stimulated an expanded and accelerated consumption with increasingly serious environmental consequences (Crocker, 2012a, 2012b).

Computerisation's increasing integration with older technologies has also driven increases in volumes of consumption and product obsolescence globally, and with this has dramatically increased pollution and waste (Slade, 2006; Park, 2010). By strategically realigning manufacturing, transport and retail, computerisation has progressively lowered the time and cost barriers that once prevented consumers buying 'more for less', and more, more often (Lipovetsky, 2011; Conca, 2002; Schor, 2003). Computerisation has also reduced the lifespan of many products, since functionality now depends on soon-to-be-redundant parts. The handmade watch, for example, once had a 'lifetime' of use, but this was reduced in the 1980s to a maximum of five to ten years through digitisation (Glasmeier, 1991). Today lower prices and abundant supplies have led to the accessorisation of watches, and their proliferation as fashion items. Many people now have up to half a dozen stored in their bedroom, a time-telling type of branded and stylish jewellery that is expected to 'go with' their outfit or activity. Low-priced goods like these, many with similarly computerised or digital parts, are now standard in many domains. The excess resource use and the environmental consequences of this shift to the digital are largely hidden or distanced from their end-users, becoming 'somebody else's problem' (Crocker, 2012a; Princen, 2002; Clapp, 2002).

The cultural juggernaut of the networked computer has thus played a central role in a broader expansion and acceleration of consumption from the 1980s, as its enabler, virtual platform and facilitator, giving rise to the present global hyper-consumption (Lipovetsky, 2011). Blending or combining in new ways virtual information with material goods or systems, the networked computer's greater speed, efficiency and functional ability has generated larger varieties and larger volumes of goods and services, but often with dramatically shorter lifespans (Park, 2010). Whatever gains have been made through greater efficiency and virtualisation, these have been offset by an increase in the overall volume and variety of goods and services for consumption (Dauvergne, 2010; Brennan, 2003).

The role of computerisation in this expansion and acceleration of production and consumption is now taken for granted. It can be seen especially in the history of transportation where a computer-enabled mobilisation is one of the keys to globalisation. Even shipping containers, a relatively new but simple idea, have taken a central role in global transportation largely through the coordinating powers of computer-controlled logistics (George, 2013; Urry, 2014). Similarly, airline travel expanded dramatically once it became coordinated and controlled by computers. It is now the largest service industry in the world. One million people are flying each day and around two billion tickets are sold annually (Cohen, 2011; Urry, 2010: 93–94). What had once been a luxury has now become a necessity (Urry, 2010, 2014). Thus, the computer's integrative capabilities have slowly colonised and replaced the older mechanical control and communication systems of the early jets, just as they have in ships, trains and now cars and trucks. This has resulted in the extraordinary technical choreography of contemporary globalisation, involving the complex logistics of moving vast numbers of goods, people and information across the world every day (Urry, 2014; Elliott and Urry, 2010). Without the networked computer, relatively cheap jet travel would be impossible (Owen, 2014). Even a slight redesign in seating requires complex computer-based mathematical analysis to determine its impact on aircraft weight and fuel demands (Owen, 2014).

Social Acceleration and Hyper-Consumption

One of the great difficulties in understanding this global speeding up or intensification of social and technological processes is that it seems to be closely aligned to the processes and consequences of modernity itself (Smart, 2010). Continuously primed by the multiple effects of the networked computer, this acceleration is also simultaneously transforming both subjective and objective sides of human experience (Urry, 2008). Of the various recent attempts to describe this engine of global change, Hartmut Rosa's notion of 'social acceleration' has been especially influential (Rosa, 2003, 2010; Rosa and Scheuerman, 2008; Rosa and Trejo-Mathis, 2013). Rosa's thesis emphasises a continuous feedback loop between three kinds of self-reinforcing acceleration: the technological acceleration already discussed, an accompanying acceleration of 'social change' including greater mobility and a generalised subjective sense of change, which he refers to as the 'acceleration of the pace of life' (Rosa, 2003: 8–10).

While Rosa believes that the 'logic of capitalism' connects continuous and destabilising economic growth with acceleration, through the need to continually increase production (growth) as well as productivity, he concedes, as others have, that this economic motor seems insufficient to explain many aspects of 'social acceleration' (Rosa, 2003: 13). It is at this point in his argument that he introduces a 'cultural motor', which he believes is indispensible to any effective theory of social change (Rosa, 2003: 13). Rosa explains this cultural motor in classic sociological terms as a social and personal *eudaemonistic* impulse towards a 'better life' (from the Greek: *eudaemonia*, or 'human welfare', 'happiness'). This motivation towards what Borgmann refers to in his famous study of technology as the human pursuit of 'the good life' (1984) has become increasingly entangled with consumption. This results in contemporary 'consumerism': a 'way of life and state of mind' dependent on various activities associated with consumption (Smart, 2010: 8–10). Consumerism is thus the pursuit of happiness or the 'good life' through material, commoditised means (Campbell, 1987, 2004).

One of the more interesting aspects of Rosa's thesis is that social acceleration also becomes more visible in apparently oppositional or countervailing moments of 'desynchronisation'. This refers to ways of doing things that negatively interact with one or more forms of acceleration (Rosa, 2003: 3–6). Often manifesting in an apparent resistance to particular forms of acceleration, this can be found especially in the failure of older forms of government, aspects of culture or some varieties of religion to accept or keep up with the pace of continuous change. In capitalism, as Rosa notes after Marx, to stand still is to fall behind. Desynchronisation in modern life is also revealed in our common use of the language of change, of 'fast' and 'slow', especially in such clichés as political or economic demands for greater 'efficiency'. So right-wing commentators can resist and blame the speed of social change and romanticise the past. But they can also blame the Left's preference for organised social services as somehow 'slowing down' the inevitable economic progress determined by the market (Vieira, 2011). Not dissimilar types of 'political desynchronisation' have been found in the Victorian and Edwardian eras, in response to periods of intense socio-technological change (Vieira, 2011). In fact, as Rosa observes, examples of desynchronisation, like those of acceleration, seem to be present with the coming of modernity itself (Vieira, 2011; Rosa, 2003: 3–6).

In terms of our experience of an accelerating 'pace of life', Rosa draws attention to the 'contraction of the present' that occurs in a state of acceleration, a state that forces us to live and think within more confined, short-term time scales (Rosa, 2003: 7; after Lübbe, 2008). Today's contraction of the present can be seen particularly in contemporary consumerism. The presence of networked computers, smartphones and tablets generates an endless series of choices and decisions for consumers to make (Tomlinson, 2007). Consumer choice responds to an imagined future of enjoyment or ownership, and the acceleration and expansion of possible choices entails a 'speeding up' of decision making, and of all processes associated with consumption (Lipovetsky, 2011; Campbell, 2004). This continuous distraction and often diversionary forms of engagement in various forms of consumption through new communications technology destroys what Manzini refers to as 'contemplative time', that is, the time that was once unallocated or free, our own to think, relax and daydream in (Manzini, 2002). So by the 'contraction of the present', Rosa draws attention to not only results from a seemingly 'closer' past and future, but also from an imagined future thrust upon us through the promise of a 'better life' (Rosa, 2003; Borgmann, 2010).

As this suggests, one way of looking at Rosa's social acceleration is through the lens of today's hyper-consumption. Always on and online, the virtual stores and libraries of contemporary hyper-consumption never close (Taylor, 2014). Whether what is consumed is free (as in a news item or Facebook notification) or priced (as in buying books or music from Amazon), online choice is often intimately tied to some form of transaction, even if this is not apparent (Turow, 2011; Taylor, 2014). This is because the presence of the consumer in the virtual space contributes to traffic, which is priced and reused by others to better target consumers (Turow, 2011; Taylor, 2014). The corporate gatekeepers of the online world have been likened to feudal lords for whom digital consumers 'work' like 'digital sharecroppers' providing the content they need to attract consumers, a form of work for which they alone, like the lords of old, are handsomely paid (Taylor, 2014: 17; Naughton, 2014).

While the links between computerisation, social acceleration and hyper-consumption can be seen in many domains, there are two global trends involved in this self-reinforcing interrelationship. Firstly, most Internet-dependent technological systems are now tasked, directly or indirectly, with accelerating the experience of the consumption of content, and not necessarily of paid-for objects or services (Taylor, 2014). This might be based upon downloading images, video clips, information, ideas or more formal media products, for free to the consumer, but priced in the background by those who target the consumer as web traffic. This content consumption is tracked and sold on by the keepers of the Internet, rather like the owners of a mall who also sell the numbers of visitors to the shops they attract (Taylor, 2014: Ch.1; Turow, 2011).

Secondly, with the advent of so many new handheld Internet-ready technologies, consumption is no longer restricted to material goods or experiences, and to certain times and places, as it once was. Instead, it now spans both the virtual and real in a new self-replicating and self-reinforcing hybrid, or 'liquid' state of accelerated material-virtual consumption, which is always available (Baumann, 2000). The store and the till are now in our consumer's pocket. In this state, the virtual and real are interwoven, an evident consequence of computerisation in many fields, from the Internet of things to interaction between bricks and clicks in retail, and the optimally accelerated world of big finance (Tomlinson, 2007). The hybridity of virtual image and real object and their interactive interdependence dramatically expand and accelerate consumer opportunities. Flitting from page to page, from site to site, the wandering surfer can now research, find, locate and download or purchase an object or experience in minutes, a fore-shortening of learning processes with profound consequences for our brains and senses (Carr, 2010).

This hyper-consumption has had a cumulative impact on the speeding up of the experience of life itself (Rosa, 2003; Baumann, 2000). As Rosa's analysis suggests, the hypermobility and instantaneity of the hybrid interactivity enabled by the global-networked computer has eroded and fragmented the individual's sense of place and continuity, and their once more assured connection with the environment. Thus, the 'contraction of the present' also involves an erosion of a sense of time and place (Rosa, 2003).

Dematerialisation and ReMaterialisation in 3D Printing

As the above suggests, dematerialisation, as well as rematerialisation, is part of the hybrid, accelerated character of contemporary global consumerism. Whether this is exchanging photos, videos, music or links online, what is in a dematerialised form can be turned into a real object or physical experience, often within a short space of time. Online dating or messaging can result in real meetings and relationships, exchanging information about exotic travel destinations can result in real travel, downloading music can result in purchasing new equipment (Magaudda, 2013). As a result, nothing in contemporary consumption trends suggests a long-term trend in the dematerialisation of real-world consumption, even if efficiency gains in background production systems can be discerned and described in these terms (Ausubel and Waggoner, 2008).

One of the most interesting examples of the dematerialisation–rematerialisation equation involved in social acceleration is 3D printing or 'rapid prototyping' as it is sometimes called (Berman, 2012; Campbell and Ivanova, 2013). I first encountered this in a factory demonstration in Italy in 1997. The manufacturer made a range of stainless steel goods and, in the factory's design studio, I was shown a CAD-CAM-engineered drawing of what was to be a stainless steel door handle. In a few seconds, a 3D version of the on-screen drawing emerged. Since this early and pioneering period of rapid prototyping,

3D printing has become more sophisticated and much cheaper. As an additive form of desktop manufacturing, it has spread from the design studio to the factory floor and also to the private home, with take-home models now selling for under $1000 US (De Roeck et al., 2012; Garrett, 2014).

Three-dimensional printing's use in manufacturing is often not remarked on. It is now widely used in the manufacturing of parts of cars, trains, planes and thousands of home appliances, and in the production of shoes and small objects like jewellery (Wittbrodt et al., 2013; Mertz, 2013). It is also used widely where exact, complex modelling and shaping is required, as in the production of medical prosthetics. NASA and the American military are experimenting with the technology, since one of the most notable early discoveries of hobbyist inventors and artists was the machine's capacity for self-replication (Campbell and Ivanova, 2013). This promises to overcome the logistical problems of getting supplies or replacement parts into dangerous or distant places such as a battlefield or a space station (Campbell and Ivanova, 2013). Several construction companies have also adapted this new 'additive manufacturing' technology, scaling it up to make large parts and even whole buildings of cement and construction waste. Researchers are also experimenting with printing aeroplane wings, space stations, large structures and even human organs and food (Miranov et al., 2003; Campbell and Ivanova, 2013). This is indeed a 'disruptive' technology (Berman, 2012).

As in the history of many breakthrough technologies, designer-maker enthusiasts, journalists and business entrepreneurs echo the kind of speculative technophilia once common in the first years of technologies such as the personal computer and the Internet (Wu, 2010; Mosco, 1999). These early adopters explain that 3D printing will be as transformative as the computer once was, freeing designers and manufacturers of former time constraints and reducing the shop-floor skills required (Petrie, 2013; Guth, 2007; De Roeck et al., 2012). More controversially, they also claim that it will lead to a re-localisation or de-globalising of industrial production, and bring production and consumption into some kind of new balance or realignment, and in the one place (Birtchnell and Urry, 2013; Potstada and Zybura, 2014). It is also even implied that this will result in a more ethical, sustainable world (Ricca-Smith, 2011).

Three-dimensional printing reduces the costs of complex one-off or small batch manufacturing, and has already given rise to a wave of mass customisation or personalisation in areas such as shoe production, where consumers can design and order their own styles and colours from a limited range of alternatives online (Berman, 2012). It is also claimed, with some truth, that because it is an 'additive' technology, there is essentially no waste in production, and therefore it must ultimately benefit the environment, a logical inference that is, more experienced users argue, also seriously flawed (Campbell and Ivanova, 2013). Like the publishing trade, where printing on demand is now common, 3D printing may eliminate many of the problems that seem to go with large-scale manufacturing, such as the storage of parts, of inventory and the use of large quantities of toxic chemicals (Berman, 2012). But, as in many areas of mass production, greater efficiencies and lower costs, once passed on to the consumer, invariably increase both production and consumption. This leads to increased resource depletion, energy use, pollution and waste (Dauvergne, 2011).

Even leaving aside 3D printing enthusiasts' more misleading predictions, the specialised results of 3D printing are still noteworthy. It has democratised design and manufacture for smaller or specialised users and has sped up the design and production of complex and difficult tasks (Birtchnell and Urry, 2013). It has also created an extraordinarily flexible means of one-off or small batch production (Campbell and Ivanova, 2013). It is widely used by inventors and designers wanting to experiment or bring to market products that might have been uneconomic through traditional and less flexible manufacturing (Strickland, 2013; Shapeways, 2014). But whether it can replace the mass-manufacture of common objects remains to be seen.

Expressing an important trend, Shapeways.com is one of the leading 3D printing services business supplying its users with online design software and instructions, and visual examples, to design and build their own products. Once complete, they can then sell their products through the Shapeways.com website to others (Shapeways, 2014; Strickland, 2013). Some designers have built small profitable businesses designing, remotely manufacturing and then selling objects from silver jewellery to plastic toys (Shapeways, 2014). These online print-shops cut out the middle men (manufacturers, distributors and retailers) and can democratise creative activities as well as substantially reduce costs. The designer is charged a small fee and once designed, it can be reproduced in any number, from one to several thousand (Garrett, 2014). The hobbyist consumer can also realise the objects in three dimensions that before, perhaps, he or she could only realise in two dimensions, such as a favourite game character or avatar (Guth, 2005).

Three-dimensional printing typifies the speed and hybridity of hyper-consumption. Instantly downloadable, the design files for any printable object may be globally transferable and readable. They might be just 'code' but can become something physical, and quickly physical. This hybridity and speed inevitably raises concerns about the social and material consequences of 3D printing (Johnson, 2013). Socially damaging objects can now be made in the secrecy of one's own home or workshop from a simple downloadable file, for example guns, knives, weapons and in one recent case, a child sex toy (Desai and Magliocca, 2014). Like many other new technologies, 3D printing is open to abuse, and its democratisation makes it available to criminals, scammers, terrorists and fraudsters, pornographers and gun enthusiasts (Desai and Magliocca, 2014).

On Pirate Bay, a file-sharing site, a new category of downloadable pirated files has been created: 'physibles' – 'data objects that are able (and feasible) to become physical' through the use of 3D printing (Wikipedia in Zimmer, 2013: 253). In a famous example of this new hybrid, a gun enthusiast (Cody Wilson) uploaded a 'physible' for a plastic gun (Jensen-Haxell, 2012; Johnson, 2013). Originally uploaded to Thingiverse, and after removed by the site's administrators, Wilson reloaded the file to his own site, Defcad.org. Over two days of availability, more than 100,000 copies were downloaded before Wilson was ordered to take down his files by the State Department (Zimmer, 2013: 253). In a nation where gun massacres such as Columbine and Sandy Hook *increase* gun sales, Wilson became a libertarian hero. His pro-gun philosophy was reported in *Wired* magazine and on prime-time television while authorities scrambled to reinforce legal prohibitions against this type of unlicensed manufacture, and potential export, of weapons (Johnson, 2013).

Conclusion: More of the Same?

Embodying the virtual-real hybridity and instantaneity described above, 3D printing will predictably become a major issue for those concerned with sustainability, waste management and the reduction of material flows and energy consumption. Typifying the Jevons paradox on an accelerated global scale – that greater efficiency of a commodity, in meeting the needs of consumers, will increase its consumption (Alcott, 2012) – 3D printing typifies a central problem in hyper-consumption (Slade, 2006). A 'physible' can empower and encourage a universal interactive form of consumption through DIY production (Petrie, 2013). In this process, the 'dream' of a consumer, the mental image of what he or she most desires, however damaging or dangerous to others or the environment, can be made real in seconds, at a low cost in the privacy of their home. Despite the objections and more optimistic arguments of technophiles, this explosion of DIY design, making and consuming will predictably have serious environmental consequences, and may also, as the case of Cody Wilson suggests, have serious legal and social consequences (Zimmer, 2013).

Two recent 'sci-fi' future scenario-building explorations of 3D printing, one from the point of view of business and entrepreneurship (Potstada and Zybura, 2014) and one from sociology (Birtchnell and Urry, 2013), both speculated on what life would be like if home-based and industry 3D printing became as common as the personal computer. Potstada and Zybura (2014) were more interested in the process of sci-fi scenario building as a predictive tool for business imagining, suggesting a world in 2030 where even complex objects like mobile phones were printed according to the consumer's wants. The environmental implications of this expansion of consumer sovereignty are not addressed in their paper. However, Birtchnell and Urry (2013) were a bit more direct in looking into this issue. They imagined a similarly futuristic world where 3D printing was increasingly integrated into the home and also into the manufacture of ordinary products, with local workshops making an increasing range of domestic goods, more accessibly and much faster. These the consumer could order online, a further development of the mass customisation referred to above. While the potentially revolutionary benefits of adoption of the machine were noted by both, Birtchnell and Urry alone looked into a more dystopian future, where the product would likely generate more waste, as users were tempted to make and remake favoured items that had not quite turned out as expected (Birtchnell and Urry, 2013: 32).

As both scenarios suggest, without careful regulatory intervention 3D printing will not result in a 'waste-less' world, or even a world of dramatically reduced emissions, since like many of its technological predecessors it will further reduce the costs of manufacture. This may simply add to existing waste and pollution problems (Birtchnell and Urry, 2013). Reminiscent of the problem of the 'paperless office', the 3D printer will probably result in more waste, even if it reduces industrial pollution and waste elsewhere. The Jevons' paradox will also apply: as 3D printing increases, so will its environmental consequences, and these may add to, and not necessarily replace, those we already have (Park, 2010). It also is predictable that, rather like desktop printing of paper, desktop manufacturing will result in a similarly exponential increase in 'throughput' of the required materials, some of which might be toxic and harmful to human health in their raw form (Birtchnell and Urry, 2013). Indeed, there is already a growing literature among health specialists on the respiratory problems of those who work too closely with 3D printers – from the fine airborne particles resulting from the process (Drizo and Pegna, 2006).

As with the production of designer drugs in secret laboratories, also notable gifts of the networked computer, we can expect both the best and the worst from this new disruptive technology. But we can also expect an increasing social acceleration, and one that will not result in less consumption and energy use, but over time, relatively more, even if the 3D printer succeeds in massively reducing the environmental costs of traditional manufacture and transportation. In the foreseeable future, the 3D printer may not replace larger mass-producing factories, but supplement their output, with more targeted and potentially more interesting creations. Designers, business people and consumers need to understand that every new increment of technological innovation cannot alone determine a greener world. This will require a more active and considered human agency, and a more fundamental change in the way we not only make, but also use and discard our possessions.

Three-dimensional printing's greatest gift may be its ability to enable more marginalised and 'under-served' groups to develop online their own technological solutions, free of many of the governing tyrannies of globalisation (Wittbrodt et al., 2013; Pearce et al., 2010). For while re-localisation and de-globalisation may not be the inevitable and universal determined result of 3D printing's spread, the democratisation of this technology can bring once impossibly sophisticated or expensive solutions into the reach of much poorer, marginalised communities, for example making their own irrigation pumps, cooking stoves and even wind turbine systems for generating electricity (Pearce et al., 2010). It is in these small-scale, mostly low-tech, community-driven 'co-design' projects that this new 'disruptive' technology may come into its own and result in many of its promises being fulfilled (Pearce et al., 2010). But it is this kind of reimagining of our social and economic system around such promising technologies that is often most resisted by the corporate economic and political status quo.

References

Alcott, B., 2005. Jevons' paradox. *Ecological Economics*, 54, pp.9–21.

Alosco, M. L., Spitznagel, M. B., Hall Fischer, K., Miller, L. A., Pillai, V., Hughes, J. and Gunstad, J., 2012. Both texting and eating are associated with impaired simulated driving performance. *Traffic Injury Prevention*, 13:5, pp.468–475.

Ausubel, J. H. and Waggoner, P. E., 2008. Dematerialization: variety, caution, and persistence. *Proceedings of the National Academy of Sciences*, 105:35, pp.12774–79.

Baechler, C. and DeVuono, M., 2013. Distributed recycling of waste polymer into RepRap feedstock. *Rapid Prototyping Journal*, 19:2, pp.118–125.

Baumann, Z., 2000. *Liquid modernity*. Cambridge: Polity Press.

Belk, R. and Tumbat, G., 2005. The cult of the Macintosh. *Consumption Markets and Culture*, 8:3, pp.205–217.

Berg, M., 2005. *Luxury and Pleasure in Eighteenth Century England*. Oxford: Oxford University Press.

Berman, B., 2012. 3-D printing: the new Industrial Revolution. *Business Horizons*, 55, pp.155–162.

Berry, C., 1994. *The idea of luxury: a conceptual and historical investigation*. Cambridge: Cambridge University Press.

Birtchnell, T. and Urry, J., 2013. 3D, SF and the future. *Futures*, 50, pp.25–34.

Borgmann, A., 1984. *Technology and the character of contemporary life*. Chicago, IL: Chicago University Press.

Borgmann, A., 2010. Reality and technology. *Cambridge Journal of Economics*, 34, pp.27–35.

Campbell, C., 1987. *The romantic ethic and the spirit of modern consumerism*. Oxford: Blackwell.

Campbell, C., 2004. I shop therefore I know that I am: the metaphysical basis of modern consumerism. In: K. M. Ekstrom and H. Brembeck, eds. *Elusive consumption*. Oxford: Berg. pp.27–44.

Campbell, S. M. and Park, Y. J., 2008. The social implications of mobile telephony: the rise of personal communication society. *Sociology Compass*, 2:2, pp.371–387.

Campbell, T. A. and Ivanova, O. S., 2013. Additive manufacturing as a disruptive technology: implications of three-dimensional printing. *Technology and Innovation*, 15, pp.67–79.

Carolan, M. S., 2004. Ecological modernization theory: what about consumption? *Society & Natural Resources*, 17:3, pp.247–260.

Carr, N., 2010. *The shallows: how the internet is changing the way we read, think and remember*. London: Atlantic Books.

Chapman, G., 2004. Shaping technology for the 'good life': the technological imperative versus the social imperative. In: D. Schuler and P. Day, eds. *Shaping the network society*. Cambridge, MA: MIT Press. pp.43–65.

Clapp, J., 2002. The distancing of waste: overconsumption in a global economy. In: T. Princen, M. Maniates and K. Conca, eds. *Confronting consumption.* Cambridge, MA: MIT Press. Ch.7.

Cohen, S., 2011. Binge flying: behavioural addiction and climate change. *Annals of Tourism Research,* 38:3, pp.1070–89.

Conca, K., 2002. Consumption and environment in a global economy. In: T. Princen, M. Maniates and K. Conca, eds. *Confronting consumption.* Cambridge, MA: MIT Press. Ch.6.

Crocker, R., 2012a. 'Somebody Else's Problem': Consumer Culture, Waste and Behaviour Change: the Case of Walking. In S. Lehmann and R. Crocker, eds., *Designing for Zero Waste: Consumption, Technologies and the Built Environment.* London: Earthscan/ Routledge): Chapter 1: 11-34.

Crocker, R., 2012b. Getting to Zero Waste in the new mobile communications paradigm: a social and cultural perspective'. In S. Lehmann and R. Crocker, eds., *Designing for Zero Waste: Consumption, Technologies and the Built Environment.* London: Earthscan/ Routledge: Chapter 6: 115-130.

Crocker, R., 2013. From Access to Excess: Consumerism, 'Compulsory Consumption' and Behaviour Change. In R. Crocker and S. Lehmann (eds), *Motivating Change: Sustainable Design and Behaviour in the Built Environment.* London: Routledge: Chapter 1: 11-32.

Dauvergne, P., 2010. *The shadows of consumption: consequences for the global environment.* Cambridge, MA: MIT Press.

De Roeck, D., Slegers, K., Criel, J., Godon, M., Caleys, L., Kilpi, K. and Jacobs, A., 2012. I would DiYSE for it! A manifesto for do-it-yourself internet-of-things creation. *Human-computer interaction proceedings of the 7th Nordic Conference Nordi-CHI'12.* Copenhagen, 12–17 October. pp.170–179.

Desai, D. R. and Magliocca, G. N., 2014. Patents, meet napster: 3D printing and the digitization of things. *Georgetown Law Journal,* 103, pp.1691-1841 Available at: http://papers.ssrn.com/sol3/papers.cfm?abstract_id=2338067##. Accessed 24 May 2014.

Drizo, A. and Pegna, J., 2006. Environmental impacts of rapid prototyping: an overview of research to date. *Rapid Prototyping Journal,* 12:2, pp.64–71.

Druckman, A. and Jackson, T., 2010. The bare necessities: how much household carbon do we really need? *Ecological Economics,* 69, pp.1794–1804.

Elliott, A. and Urry, J., 2010. *Mobile lives.* London: Routledge.

Fortunati, L., 2002. The mobile phone: towards new categories and social relations. *Information, Media and Society,* 5:4, pp.513–528.

Frank, R. H., 1999. *Luxury fever: why money fails to satisfy in an era of excess.* New York: The Free Press.

Garrett, B., 2014. 3D printing: new economic paradigms and strategic shifts. *Global Policy,* 5:1, pp.70–75.

George, R., 2013. *Deep sea and foreign going: inside shipping, the invisible industry that brings you 90% of everything.* London: Portobello.

Gergen, K., 2002. Cell phone technology and the challenge of absent presence. In: J. E. Katz and M. Aakhus, eds. *Perpetual contact: mobile communication, private talk and public performance.* Cambridge: Cambridge University Press. Ch.14.

Glasmeier, A., 1991. Technological discontinuities and flexible production networks: the case of Switzerland and the world watch industry. *Research Policy*, 20:5, pp.469–485.

Guth, R. A., 2007. How 3-D printing figures to turn web worlds real. *Wall Street Journal*, [Online] 12 December, p.B1. Available at: http://online.wsj.com/news/articles/SB119742129566522283. Accessed 24 May 24 2014.

Herring, H., 2006. Energy efficiency – a critical view. *Energy*, 31, pp.10–20.

Jensen-Haxell, P., 2012. 3D printers, obsolete firearm supply controls, and the right to build self-defense weapons. *Golden Gate University Law Review*, 42, pp.447–496.

Johnson, J. L., 2013. Print, lock and load: 3-D printers, creation of guns, and the potential threat to Fourth Amendment Rights. *University of Illinois Journal of Law, Technology and Policy*, 2, pp.337–361.

Ling, R., 2004. *The mobile connection: the cell phone's impact on society.* San Francisco, CA: Morgan Kaufman.

Ling, R., 2008. *New tech, new ties: how mobile communication is reshaping social cohesion.* Cambridge, MA: MIT Press.

Lipovetsky, G., 2011. The hyperconsumption society. In: K. M. Ekström and B. Glans, eds. *Beyond the consumption bubble.* London: Routledge. pp.25–36.

Lübbe, H., 2008. The contraction of the present. Translated by J. Ingram. In: H. Rosa and W. E. Scheuerman, eds. *High-speed society: social acceleration, power, and modernity.* Philadelphia, PA: Pennsylvania State University Press. pp.159–178.

Magaudda, P., 2011. When materiality 'bites back': digital music consumption practices in the age of dematerialization. *Journal of Consumer Culture*, 11:1, pp.15–36.

Manzini, E., 2002. Context-based wellbeing and the concept of the regenerative solution: a conceptual framework for scenario building and sustainable solutions development. *Journal of Sustainable Product Design*, 2, pp.141–148.

Marx, L., 1964. *The machine in the garden: technology and the pastoral ideal in America.* Oxford: Oxford University Press.

Mertz, L., 2013. New World of 3-D printing offers 'completely new way of thinking': Q&A with author, engineer and 3-D printing expert Hod Lipson. *IEEE Pulse*, 4:6, pp.12–14.

Miranov, V., Boland, T., Trusk, T., Forgacs, G. and Markwald, R. R., 2003. Organ printing: computer-aided jet-based 3D tissue engineering. *Trends in Biotechnology*, 21:4, pp.157–161.

Mosco, V., 1999. Cyber-monopoly: a web of techno-myths. *Science as Culture*, 8:1, pp.5–22.

Naughton, J., 2014. We're all being mined for data – but who are the real winners? *The Observer*, [online] 8 June 2014. Available at: http://www.theguardian.com/technology/2014/jun/08/big-data-mined-real-winners-nsa-gchq-surveillance. Accessed 10 June 2014.

Negroponte, N., 1995. *Being digital.* London: Hodder and Stroughton.

Nye, D. E., 2003. Technology, nature and American origin stories. *Environmental History,* 8, pp.8–24.

Owen, D., 2014. Game of thrones: how airlines woo the one per cent. *The New Yorker,* [online] 21 April. Available at: http://www.newyorker.com/reporting/2014/04/21/140421fa_fact_owen?currentPage=all. Accessed 10 June 2014.

Park, M., 2010. Defying obsolescence, in T. Cooper, ed., *Longer Lasting Products: Alternatives to the Throwaway Society.* Farnham, Surrey: Gower: Chapter 4: 77-105.

Pearce, J. M., Blair, C. M., Laciak, K. J., Andrews, R., Nosrat, A. and Zelenika-Zovko, I., 2010. 3-D printing of open source appropriate technologies for self-directed sustainable development. *Journal of Sustainable Development,* 3:4, pp.17–29.

Petrie, C., 2013. The age of DIY. *IEEE Internet Computing,* 17:6, pp.93–94.

Potstada, M. and Zybura, J., 2014. The role of context in science fiction prototyping: the digital industrial revolution. *Technological Forecasting and Social Change,* 84, pp.101–114.

Princen, T., 2002. Distancing: consumption and the severing of feedback. In: T. Princen, M. Maniates and K. Conca, eds. *Confronting consumption.* Cambridge, MA: MIT Press. Ch.5.

Ricca-Smith, C., 2011. Could 3D printing end our throwaway culture? *The Guardian,* [Online] 18 November 2011. Available at: http://www.theguardian.com/technology/2011/nov/17/3d-printing-throwaway-culture. Accessed 24 May 2014.

Rosa, H., 2003. Social acceleration: ethical and political consequences of a desynchronized high-speed society. *Constellations,* 10:1, pp.3–33.

Rosa, H., 2010. Full speed burnout: from the pleasures of the motorcycle to the bleakness of the treadmill: the dual face of social acceleration. *International Journal of Motorcycle Studies,* 6:1. Available at: http://ijms.nova.edu/Spring2010/IJMS_Artcl.Rosa.html. Accessed 24 May 2014.

Rosa, H. and Scheuerman, W. E. eds., 2008. *High-speed society: social acceleration, power, and modernity.* Philadelphia, PA: Pennsylvania State University Press.

Rosa, H. and Trejo-Mathis, J., 2013. *Social acceleration: a new theory of modernity.* New York: Columbia University Press.

Schor, J. S., 2005. Prices and Quantities: Unsustainable Consumption and the Global Economy. *Ecological Economics,* 55:3, pp.309-320.

Shapeways, 2014. *Shapeways.com,* [online] Available at: http://www.shapeways.com/. Accessed 10 June 2014.

Shove, E., 2003. *Comfort, cleanliness and convenience: the social organization of normality.* Oxford: Berg.

Slade, G., 2006. *Made to break: technology and obsolescence in America.* Cambridge, MA: Harvard University Press.

Smart, B., 2010. *Consumer society: critical issues and environmental consequences.* London: Sage.

Stein, S., 2002. The '1984' Macintosh ad: cinematic icons and constitutive rhetoric in the launch of a new machine. *Quarterly Journal of Speech*, 88:2, pp.169–192.

Strickland, E., 2013. Shapeways: bringing 3-D printing to the masses. *IEEE Spectrum*, 50:11, p.22.

Taylor, A., 2014. *The People's Platform: Taking Back Power and Culture in the Digital Age*. New York: Metropolitan Books.

Tomlinson, J., 2007. *The culture of speed: the coming of immediacy*. London: Sage.

Turkle, S., 2008. Always-on/always-on-you: the tethered self. In: J. E. Katz, ed. *Handbook of mobile communication studies*. Cambridge, MA: MIT Press. pp.121–137.

Turow, J. 2011. *The Daily You: How the new advertising industry is defining your identity and your worth*. New Haven, CT: Yale University Press.

Urry, J., 2002. Mobility and proximity. *Sociology*, 36:2, pp.255–274.

Urry, J., 2008. Speeding up and slowing down. In: H. Rosa and W. E. Scheuerman, eds. *High-speed society: social acceleration, power, and modernity*. Philadelphia, PA: Pennsylvania State University Press. pp.179–198.

Urry, J., 2010. Sociology and climate change. *The Sociological Review*, 57:2, pp.84–100.

Urry, J., 2014. *Offshoring*. Cambridge: Polity Press.

Verbeek, P.-P., 2005. *What things do: philosophical reflections on technology, agency and design*. Philadelphia, PA: Pennsylvania State Press.

Verbeek, P.-P. and Slob, A. F. L. eds., 2006. *User behaviour and technology development: shaping sustainable relations between consumers and technology*. London: Springer.

Vieira, R. A., 2011. Connecting the new political history with recent theories of temporal acceleration: speed, politics, and the cultural imagination of *fin-de-siècle* Britain. *History and Theory*, 50, pp.373–389.

Wittbrodt, B. T., Glover, A. G., Laureto, J., Anzalone, G. C., Pppliger, D., Irwin, J. L. and Pearce, J. M., 2013. Life-cycle economic analysis of distributed manufacturing with open-source 3-D printers. *Mechatronics*, 23, pp.713–726.

Wu, T., 2010. *The master switch: the rise and fall of information empires*. New York: Vintage Books.

York, R., 2006. Ecological paradoxes: William Stanley Jevons and the paperless office. *Human Ecology Review*, 13:2, pp.143–147.

Zimmer, S., 2014. The right to print arms: the effect on civil liberties of government restrictions on computer-aided design files shared on the Internet. *Internet, Information and Communications Technology Law*, 22:3, pp.251–263.

Notes on Contributors

Gjoko Muratovski, Tongji University / Auckland University of Technology

Gjoko Muratovski has over twenty years of multidisciplinary design and branding experience that spans from Asia and Australia to Europe and the United States. Over the years, he has worked with a range of businesses, organisations, universities and government institutions. Currently he is a Senior Manager of the School of Art & Design and Head of the Communication Design Department at the Auckland University of Technology; Guest Associate Professor at Tongji University; and Editor-in-Chief of the *Journal of Design, Business & Society*.

Kathleen Connellan, University of South Australia

Kathleen Connellan is a Senior Lecturer in Design History and Theory in the School of Art, Architecture and Design at the University of South Australia. She has researched and published on issues of marginalisation in disability, race, gender and culture with a particular focus upon the symbolic attributes of the colour white in the design of space, products and messages. Her most recent work concentrates upon well-being and designing for a therapeutic milieu. She has had numerous leadership roles in design research over the past decades where her concern has always been to link an understanding of art, architecture and design with ethical issues in visual representation and human involvement.

Lloyd Carpenter, University of Canterbury

Lloyd Carpenter is a 50-year-old scholar of Ngati Toa Rangatira, English, Cornish and Highland Scots descent. He has worked in sales, the insurance industry, in secondary education as a teacher of Mathematics and Economics, was a Salvation Army officer and recently completed a Ph.D. examining aspects of the Central Otago gold rush, New

Zealand. He is a lecturer in Early New Zealand History and Maori Studies at Lincoln University and publishes widely on Australasian gold rushes, landscape theory, wine history and early colonial gastronomy.

Anne Peirson-Smith, City University of Hong Kong

Anne Peirson-Smith is an Assistant Professor in the Department of English, City University of Hong Kong. She has a professional background in advertising, branding and public relations and is the co-author of the book, *Public Relations in Asia Pacific: Communicating Effectively Across Cultures* (2010).

Carolyn Beasley, Swinburne University of Technology

Carolyn Beasley writes widely on crime fiction. She taught in Australian prisons for five years and has published about the *Underbelly* literary and television franchise, as well as numerous works on the nature of criminal fictions. She is Program Director of Writing at Swinburne University of Technology, Melbourne.

Susie Khamis, University of Technology Sydney

Susie Khamis is a Senior Lecturer in the School of Communication at the University of Technology Sydney. She has developed a research profile in the areas of branding, food cultures, media representation and fashion media, and is the founding editor of *Locale: The Australasian-Pacific Journal of Regional Food Studies*. She currently teaches in the field of Public Communication.

Robert Crocker, University of South Australia

Robert Crocker is a Senior Lecturer in Design History and Theory in the School of Art, Architecture and Design at the University of South Australia. With an Oxford doctorate in Modern History, he became interested in sustainability twenty years ago through his community work on pedestrian rights and safety, and this led him to help develop the University's interdisciplinary Master of Sustainable Design programme.